W9-BDL-568

Police in Trouble

POLICE IN TROUBLE

Our Frightening Crisis
in
Law Enforcement

by
JAMES F. AHERN

Foreword by John V. Lindsay

HAWTHORN BOOKS, INC.
Publishers
New York

To my family and to my friends
in the closed fraternity

Foreword

No quality is rarer in public life than a sense of uncompromised outrage. Jim Ahern has that sense—not a wishful idealism, but a concrete and particular wrath at things that are not as they should be. In this remarkable book he has shown us what it really means to be a tough cop.

As police chief of New Haven from 1968 to 1970, Ahern had to deal with the enduring crises of law enforcement: the treacherous link between narcotics, organized crime, and politics; the scandalous disrepair of our courts and prisons; the gap between rhetoric and reality in the administration of the criminal law. Ahern confronted another, more immediate crisis as well: the massive demonstrations and public anxiety surrounding the arrest and trial of seven Black Panthers for the May, 1969, murder of Alex Rackley. With a national rally scheduled for New Haven on May 1, 1970, federal and state law-enforcement officials not merely feared the prospect of uncontrolled bloodshed but by their actions increased its likelihood.

Ahern's handling of both these challenges can serve as a national model. He firmly shut the door to political interference in the selection and promotion of police officers while keeping the police force properly subject to civilian guidance on matters of policy. He revamped the training program to emphasize the day-by-day imperatives of human relations as well as the techniques for handling a crisis. When the crisis came, the New Haven police responded in a disciplined and professional way to a situation fraught with hazard. May Day in New Haven could have been a day of tragedy. Ahern's courage and judgment helped make sure it wasn't.

These accomplishments aside, however, *Police in Trouble* is not really a success story. Most of the book is about failure—not Ahern's failure, but society's. America has told its policemen to do an impossible job and then harshly berated them for their imperfect success. We have truly handcuffed our police—not, as some say, by court decisions on civil liberties or by reform strengthening civilian control, but by starvation budgets, antiquated police training, nonoperating procedures, political manipulation, and public hypocrisy.

We expect police to enforce laws on gambling and morals which millions of citizens daily, and without compunction, disobey. We waste our police on the tasks of sweeping up drunks from sidewalks, while the pusher openly displays his wares to twelve-year-olds. We expect police to reduce the crime rate, while we let our prisons become institutions of higher criminal education. We expect police to dismantle organized crime, when its influence begins not at the neighborhood precinct house but at the old party clubhouse.

As these pages make clear, modernizing and revamping police forces is but one step in the process of improving criminal justice. Real progress depends on changing other institutions as well: sweeping from the books the laws that breed corruption, training the men in prisons for something other than a promotion in crime, clearing court calendars for the real work of administering justice rather than the make-work of whiplash claims and uncontested divorces. No single book offers a better understanding of the agenda of reform than *Police in Trouble*.

John V. Lindsay

Acknowledgments

Special thanks are due to Alexander Sidar, III, Thomas W. Brunner, and Stephen B. Shiffrin for their research assistance. Also to Louise Fitzsimmons, Shelley List, John Heaphy, now special assistant to New York Police Commissioner Patrick Murphy, Leonard Slater, Leonard M. Ross, Associate Professor of Law at the Columbia Law School, and to all the others who read the proofs, go the author's appreciation for tough but constructive criticism. The author gratefully acknowledges permission to quote from *Varieties of Police Behavior: The Management of Law and Order in Eight Communities,* by James Q. Wilson, copyright © 1968 by the President and Fellows of Harvard College, and from *The Mayor's Game: Richard C. Lee and the Politics of Change,* copyright © 1967 by Allan R. Talbot and published by Harper & Row. Special gratitude also goes to the countless policemen whose labor and experience are the material on which this book is based.

J. F. A.

Contents

1

The Closed Fraternity

IF YOU STAND on East Rock in New Haven, Connecticut, and look down, you can see any American city.

You can see oil tanks and railroad yards, buildings of steel and glass and tile and stone, clustered around the green patch of a downtown park, and the roofs of factories, warehouses, and gas stations. You can see highways banking and curving with high-speed traffic, branching onto exit ramps and turning onto asphalt, smooth at first, then rutted and patched. You can see the enclave of a university with courtyards and Gothic architecture.

You can see the old sections, where ethnic populations have supplanted one another again and again: areas that were once Irish, now Italian; areas that were once Italian, now black. You can see complexes of low housing projects, the vertical ghettos of urban renewal, and the suburbs of middle-class WASPs and Jews, fading away at the city's edges to shopping centers, junk yards, and countryside.

1

POLICE IN TROUBLE

What you cannot see is the constant dynamic of people moving on this wide and intricate map. You cannot see them stirred to fruitful and creative action. Nor can you see them abrasive, angry, demanding, destructive.

You cannot see the lines of conflict where neighborhoods merge. You cannot see people furtively looking behind them as they walk on the streets or locking their car doors when they drive through certain neighborhoods or keeping in closed, protective groups. You cannot see young people gathering on street corners or in coffee houses or junkies waiting for connections.

You cannot see people fighting in their homes. You cannot see drunken brawls. You cannot see muggings and murders.

You cannot see the police.

Perhaps you can make out the building that is police headquarters without seeing what is inside. Perhaps you can see a squad car or hear a siren. But the car will disappear, and the sound will die away. So people see the police: noiseless, anonymous, and distant.

You cannot see small police successes. You cannot see police failure. Even if you have been inside the station house—even if you have ridden in a squad car—there are countless things invisible to you, countless subtle pressures that act on police from day to day, year in and year out, to shape what they do and determine who they are.

No one outside the policeman's closed fraternity knows the cop. Shrewdness and mistrust separate him from the people in the houses his speeding car passes. He does not mix with them. They do not seek him out. Yet national problems and local problems all focus on him in the end. The cop in the squad car who is underqualified or undereducated or undertrained, who is subject to all the warping influences that society brings to bear on him, is the basic unit of police service. He is the person who interacts with the public, and he is the person who personifies police service.

Who are these people—the policemen? What are their lives really

2

The Closed Fraternity

like, and how are they changed from the day they first put on a uniform or from the day they first enter a police academy?

A national overview of the state of police service today means nothing without an understanding of these people, upon whose individual integrity and capability the entire system ultimately depends.

The day the new recruit steps through the doors of a police academy, he leaves society behind to enter a "profession" that does more than give him a job; it defines who he is. For all the years that he remains, closed into the sphere of its rituals and its absurdities in the town where he began, until he takes the ransom money of his pension and retires, he will be a cop.

Few if any jobs claim a man so completely, and there are few other jobs whose moments of glamour have held more fascination for the public. The moments of glamour *are there*. At times they rival the perfections of fiction. Yet the public that buys murder mysteries in bookstores and watches cop shows on television is ignorant of what a policeman's job really is and of what kind of person it makes him.

In recent years platitudes about the policeman's role have changed. He used to be a cops-and-robbers caricature. Now he is a psychologist, a social worker, a doctor, a lawyer, and a part-time judo expert who occasionally arrests criminals as a sideline.

It is true that in failing to provide people with so many basic services, our society has forced the policeman to perform many of them by default. But to maintain seriously that they are valid police functions is to approve of the removal of more and more of society's responsibilities onto the shoulders of a group that cannot meet even the special challenges of its own profession. It is to say that there is no law-enforcement function and that social workers should be sent to combat syndicated crime.

The policeman is by necessity a generalist. He must briefly and superficially play a number of roles. But unless he is trained and educated to respond as a generalist—as a diagnostician, in effect—

3

he may attempt to be a number of things he is not; and he will be frustrated.

The policeman today is not a frustrated psychologist or lawyer. He is a frustrated policeman. It is only because he has no support in his role as a policeman that he is sometimes tempted to try to solve problems that should not be his. The fact that he may be so tempted (or so forced) does not mean that he has any power to act meaningfully on the social and personal problems that confront him, any more than he is free to discharge the primary obligations of his profession. Life within the closed fraternity is a great deal more petty and a great deal less meaningful than that.

The young man who walks into the police academy has already lost some of his original naïveté about the "profession" he is entering. In some cities he is likely to have paid $500 for his appointment. He is even more likely to have had to approach a few "outstanding members of the community"—often rather narrowly defined as ward aldermen, or the equivalent, of the political machine in power—to support his application to the force.

Why has he come to them in the first place? What has made him want to become a cop?

While I was chief of the New Haven Police Department incoming rookies were asked to write short essays telling why they had become policemen. Their answers reflected that they had already learned one lesson about police work—that there was no need to stand out, to reflect, or to tell the truth. The essays were all the same. To a man, they had become cops to help people, to render obedient service to society, and to uphold the laws of the land. It sounded as if they had become policemen simply to be "good people." Only a few acknowledged that as cops they would have to deal largely with "bad people," that they would have to arrest thieves, narcotics pushers, and belligerent drunks who didn't want to be arrested and who would not feel that they had been helped or served by those who had arrested them.

Some said they believed police work to be honorable, reliable,

4

and steady. A few admitted the attraction of a secure pension at the end of twenty-five years of service. But none admitted that they wanted exciting jobs. None admitted that they wanted action and were willing to take certain risks to get it. None admitted that they were eager to pit themselves against people who had committed criminal offenses and had challenged society to deal with them if it could. But this is why most of them became cops.

There are good societal reasons for not admitting these motivations, especially today. Psychologists and sociologists have pointed out that police work attracts authoritarian personalities who seek legal license to subjugate others and who often in the process become aggressive and even brutal. This is true. But it is not true, even in view of the dismally low selection standards of police departments, that a majority or even a sizable minority of policemen are people of this type.

Nonetheless, policemen are sensitive to these criticisms and will go to opposite extremes in characterizing themselves to deny them. In doing this, however, they tend to obscure the qualities that make a cop especially fitted for police work: psychological balance, a capability to comprehend delicate human situations, alertness, energy, curiosity, and ambition. The defensive posturings of police also obscure an important truth about them—that policemen often take excessive pleasure in helping people who are genuinely in need.

In some departments, particularly in large ones, there will always be a few recruits with cynical motives for becoming policemen— usually with the specific intention of becoming rich through graft. Even in New Haven, a city that has never offered spectacular opportunities for graft, recruits occasionally enter with this intention.

For some cities, such as New York, cops who enter in search of graft can be a major problem. Ten years ago New York made a great effort to recruit policemen from outside the state, assuming that a widened recruitment base would increase the quality of their recruits and reduce the number coming into the department looking for payoffs. Ironically, many people willing to relocate in New

POLICE IN TROUBLE

York City were those who were drawn specifically by the promise of graft.

The average trainee entering a police academy, while he may have little patience with "school" as he has known it, is anxious to learn about his new job. He has a vague idea what it will be like. But as soon as he takes his seat in a dim auditorium and begins to listen to the machinelike voice of a lecturer reciting the various degrees of murder, he turns his mind off. He makes marks in his notebook, he remembers brief outlines and facts until he is tested on them, and he passes.

The recruit may already know that he will not decide what charges will be brought against homicide defendants. He has undoubtedly learned that homicides are rare, that they are among the most readily solved of crimes, and that they are handled not by patrolmen but by detectives. As the hours drone on, although he may have an abstract interest in the techniques of investigating homicide, he knows that by the time he is in a position to use them years will have passed, and the details, if they have any relation to reality, will be forgotten.

What the recruit often feels more intensely than anything is the need to know himself. The training at the academy teaches him the elementary techniques of first aid, and it gives him a set of rules that keeps him safe and limits his personal liability. But it does not give him answers to his questions about himself. It does not even start.

As he sits listening to empty words, waiting to get out onto the street, he envisions bloody accidents, women giving birth, and children drowning. He is like a soldier wondering how he will react in battle. Will he move the accident victim when he should not? Will he fail to move him when he should? Will he get the mother to the hospital too late? Or will he crash his car trying to get her there when the delivery is hours away? In its emphasis his formal training actually reinforces his belief that these problems will be among the

6

most important that he has to face. It will be some time before he realizes that such crises soon become disturbingly routine.

The vacuousness of the training program forces the recruit to rely heavily on the support and approval of his peers. Only they can help him gain the self-confidence he knows he will need in the years ahead. Although they know no more than he does, he finds himself joining with them in deriding the program, in joking and trading rumors and stories. In this way he represses the real questions that disturb him. When he does, he is comforted by what he has been told by his political sponsor or by older members of the department: that all he need do to complete the training program is keep quiet, refrain from making a fool out of himself by asking questions of the lecturers, and pass the required tests. Eventually he finds himself nodding off to sleep in the lectures, but even if he is caught, it does not matter. He finds that people are not washed out of police academies. In New Haven—a department with a good reputation—only one person was dropped out of the police training program in the quarter century preceding 1968. Recruits in most cities virtually have to commit crimes, and often serious ones, to be kicked out of police training programs. Once he senses this, the trainee also knows that he can allow the training program to fly by overhead and that it will get where it is going without him as long as he does not bother it.

After he has completed his training, the police recruit raises his right hand, takes an oath, and is invested with the rights and privileges of the police profession. To the new cop, this usually means no more than "I've made it."

Until a few years ago, the rookie cop's first assignment was sure to be a walking beat, and in many cities this is still true. Most policemen who are working today started off as walking men. But except in certain situations in heavily congested or problem areas, the walking cop is an anachronism.

Most people believe in an archetypal cop on the beat whose intimate knowledge of his neighborhood makes him wise, tolerant, humane, and somewhat fatherly. But whatever truth lies in this notion comes from the fact that the walking cop is phenomenally bored and needs to find diversions that have nothing to do with police work.

In recent years many police departments have come under public pressure to increase their use of walking men. It might make sense for communities to pay men in uniforms to wander around, idly passing the time of day with shopkeepers and wearing out shoe leather, if there were not many vital police functions that simply cannot be performed while time and manpower are being wasted in this fashion.

The walking cop usually alternates hours standing on a corner and walking a predetermined and precisely timed route. While he stands on his corner, departmental regulations are likely to dictate to him which particular square of concrete he will occupy. He must usually be as close to the curb as is practical, the idea being that in this position he is more visible to the public than he would be leaning against a building. During this hour, if he walks down the street to exercise his legs, to look in a store window, or to talk to a friend, he must make up an excuse for the sergeant, whose sole job it is to check on his position.

Anyone with a moderate degree of intelligence and the slightest bit of energy will go insane standing on the same street corner for an hour at a time. Occasional passers-by who ask the cop for directions offer him little stimulation. Once a week there may be an auto accident nearby, or a store owner may complain of shoplifting, or the cop may come upon someone peddling merchandise without a license. But these things happen so seldom that the cop must seek diversion, and the first effect of his new job is usually to make the rookie into an incorrigible liar.

He wanders down the street to see a friend. He ducks into a movie for a while. He sits down in an alley and reads a book. He goes for a cup of coffee. When the sergeant finds him off his corner, he must have an excuse. He went to help a lady who was locked out

8

of her car. He took a lost child home. He thought he saw a wanted person. If he is not told by veterans before he goes out on a beat for the first time, the rookie soon learns from experience to stick to his story, no matter how absurd it may be, no matter how much evidence his supervisor may have that he is lying. This is usually good advice, as sergeants have spent years themselves playing the same games and, if they like a particular recruit, may admire his steadfast lies or ingenious stories.

During the hour when the cop is not standing on his corner, he is walking the city streets. He has a number of appointments with trees and telephone poles. On these are located Gamewell boxes—standard fire-alarm boxes—the back of which the policeman must open with a key. Inside there is a lever, and, rather like a trained monkey, he pulls it down and closes the box. The cop has probably been told that his box pulls are recorded on tapes at the station and are for his own protection. But he disabuses himself of this notion when he learns that the tapes are not read until hours after he makes them, or perhaps not until the next day. Should he miss a pull, however, the rookie soon learns the real purpose of the Gamewell box. He is summoned to the office of the ranking officer who reads the tapes, who demands that he explain any deviations from his beat pattern. If he does not have an airtight excuse the first time, he does thereafter, and the disciplinary function of the Gamewell box goes the way of the bogus safety function.

The walking beat is stultifying on the day and swing shifts; it is impossible on the midnight shift. Here the policeman is strictly a night watchman. When he is not standing on his corner, he is trudging up and down streets trying doors and checking windows to make sure they are all locked. It is here that the cop's job has the least resemblance to police work, and consequently it is here that his ingenuity is put to the strictest test. He prepares to meet the challenge with a number of standard tricks. He collects the driver's license and car registration numbers of all his friends. If he is caught off his beat or if he misses a box pull, these come in handy for phony reports.

9

POLICE IN TROUBLE

"1:00 A.M. Stopped blue Chevrolet, 1966, Conn. lic. #BMT-3244, acting suspiciously near State and Elm. On questioning, operator, Ronald Jones, op. lic. #GT3956–948, informed me he was taking his girl friend home. Same stated he had just left Lincoln Theater when his car began to heat up. Advised him to go to nearest garage."

But tricks like this can be used only so often, and the cop whose sole job is to stand on a vacant corner for an hour and to patrol equally vacant streets for another needs hundreds of such excuses. He may smash a few bottles on the street a block from his corner so he can later tell his sergeant he heard breaking glass. If he is really desperate, he may kick a shop door until he sets off a burglar alarm and tell his sergeant he interrupted an attempt at breaking and entering. An entire book could be written on the excuses cops give for being where they are not supposed to be.

But if they aren't where they are supposed to be, where are they? On the midnight shift they are probably asleep. The rookie cop, after he has been a walking man on the midnight shift once, learns that the first thing to do upon being assigned to a new beat is to find a "hole"—a place into which he can disappear in the middle of the night and sleep in safety and comfort. A hole can be anything from a back room in a store to which a cop has a key, to an all-night theater. The favorite of a friend of mine was the lounge of Trumbull College at Yale. The campus police would let him in when they closed it late at night, and he would stretch out and read or sleep for hours on its sofa, secure in the knowledge that a sergeant would never be able to find him.

Some holes are not as good as others. Another New Haven cop decided that the coils of hoses in a fire-department truck made an appealing mattress. The firemen did not know he was there, and one night he woke up to find himself being carried miles off his beat on the way to a fire.

The rookie soon finds that although there are a few beats on which the most experienced policeman can find no holes, usually he can manage to spend the most boring hours of every night asleep.

10

This does not make him happy; it only makes him less unhappy. He has not become a cop to sleep. He sleeps because he is not allowed to be a cop.

But the rookie will find that he cannot spend the whole of his midnight shift sleeping, and he soon realizes that there are minor fringe benefits to working the early-morning hours which, although they point to the absurdity of his position, help to pass the time. The midnight shift is a great time to play practical jokes and to get revenge for petty irritations and grudges.

Suppose one day a policeman tickets a number of cars illegally parked in front of a store. He is halfway down the block when the store owner comes running after him with a fistful of tickets, demanding that he take them back. The store owner is vituperative, indignant, and harangues the officer for twenty minutes. But the cop refuses to take the tickets back.

The next morning the cop learns that the store owner has a friend who is a police lieutenant. He is informed that it is departmental policy not to ticket cars in front of this particular store, and a familiar-looking fistful of tickets is returned to him. That night—or a few nights later, if the cop wants to be subtle—he takes an old key and breaks it off in the store's lock.

Or perhaps the store is a luncheonette. The cop waits for a bakery truck to leave several dozen hard rolls on its front step early in the morning. When the truck is gone, he picks up the boxes and trots a block down to a coffee shop that has just had its delivery of doughnuts from the same bakery. Minutes later, he trots back, carrying different boxes.

One of the advantages of wearing a blue uniform is that the policeman is never suspected in such cases. He is free to shake his head in wonder as a locksmith extracts broken keys from locks or to commiserate with a luncheonette owner and suggest how ham sandwiches can be made out of jelly doughnuts.

At times policemen will do completely facetious things out of sheer boredom. On the whole, they have a friendly resentment for

11

firemen, who, while they are working, get to do something meaning-ful and relatively unambiguous and, while they are not working, have the undisputed right to long periods of sleeping in comfortable beds or card-playing or reading. Often a bored cop will ring a fire alarm at four in the morning just to get the firemen out of bed. One New Haven cop once told me how he pulled the same alarm box at the same location for so many nights in a row that the firemen knew he was doing it but couldn't seem to catch him. One night, however, they responded so rapidly that he had no time to escape by his usual route and was forced to dive into a hedge close to the alarm box. From there, he watched the boots of firemen inches away as they reset the alarm and searched for him in bewilderment. Finally they left, and he was never caught.

A rookie's slight pangs of guilt about deceiving his supervisor fade rapidly. If he has worked for a private business, he is used to supervisors who, on the whole, are there to help him. But since the police sergeant who supervises walking men has very little to help his men *do*, the only possible measure of his efficiency is the amount of disciplinary action he takes. The sergeant who is am-bitious finds that the more red ink he uses, the "better" he is. For-tunately for the walking cops, the sergeant's pattern of checking on them is often as regimented as their own beat plans. When I was promoted to sergeant after many years away from the walking beat, I was, as is the custom, put out to supervise walking men for a time. I spent one night huffing and puffing up and down city blocks, meeting cops standing on corners like tin soldiers and rubbing the sleep out of their eyes, and became convinced I was accomplishing nothing.

Although on the whole the policeman's sleeping and practical joking is no more than a rational reaction to the situation he is placed in, at times—those rare early-morning hours when something really happens and another patrolman or a citizen needs help—sleeping on the job can be dangerous. But ironically, even this dan-ger is in a way compensated for. The walking cop who follows a rigid pattern is completely ineffective as a crime deterrent because any criminal planning a burglary can easily avoid him. It is a well-known adage in police departments that the only time a cop on a walking beat is likely to make "a good pinch" is when he is sleeping or loafing—in short, when he is somewhere he is not supposed to be.

Whether or not he is assigned to a walking beat immediately, the rookie cop is soon introduced to the petty corruptions that may, because they are so easy and so widely accepted, eventually make more serious corruption possible. The cop learns, or is told, which candy and drugstores he can drop into for free cigarettes and which lunch counters and restaurants will feed him free meals. As time goes on, he finds that restaurant owners may invite him to bring his family in for free meals when he is off duty. Although many people who feed cops for free, or who buy them drinks, do so because they feel that cops do a difficult and thankless job for small rewards, most of them also expect that if they require police service, they will get prompt and sympathetic action. Or if the restaurants happen to be fronts for bookie joints or other illegal operations, they may expect prompt and sympathetic inaction.

If a young cop is "straight" and idealistic when he joins the department, and if he at first sees the danger in these petty corruptions, his idealism soon vanishes, and he is likely to go from accepting free cigarettes and meals to accepting $10 a week from store owners for keeping an extra close watch on their property. The "straight arrow" who will not go along with these practices is ridiculed by older cops and by his peers, and he soon finds himself ostracized from what is rapidly becoming the only society left to him. He is asked whether he is "too good" for the others. He is told that there is nothing wrong with these practices, that they are accepted by everyone. He comes to see them as part of the way the world works. He is reminded that people in higher positions in government or society make many times what he ever will out of practices that are far more suspect.

The peer-group pressure on the rookie in this situation is enor-

13

mous, and when he finds out that his peer group is everything, he adapts, usually quite comfortably, to what he considers to be "honest graft." He begins to make a distinction between "legitimate gifts," which are understood to be fringe benefits of his job, and "dishonest graft," money taken directly from hard-core criminals.

Even if he accepts the police department as he finds it, it is generally a good two years before the rookie is trusted by the older members of the force, before they will talk openly in front of him about the realities of the police department or the city. A number of changes must take place in the rookie's situation that bind him completely to the closed fraternity before he is entitled to know its inner workings.

Before joining the police force, the policeman has probably had a circle of friends with whom he has been more or less close for years. As soon as he joins the force, it begins to shrink. The cop's strange hours make him difficult to reach. But more important, his identity as a police officer makes him a social liability, even when he is off duty. Wherever he goes he is recognized by bartenders, bookies, newspaper sellers, and waitresses, who want to talk shop with him. And even if these people are not around, others who realize that he is a policeman stop him to harangue him about the inadequacies of police service. In this way the cop's "professional" situation is similar to that of the doctor, who cannot go out without hearing about half a dozen appendectomies, but it is hardly as enviable.

So the cop tends to socialize with other cops. When he gets off duty on the swing shift, there is little to do but go drinking and few people to do it with but other cops. He finds himself going bowling with them, going fishing, helping them paint their houses or fix their cars. His family gets to know their families, and a kind of mutual protection society develops which turns out to be the only group in which the policeman is automatically entitled to respect.

This shrinking of his circle of friends, which usually continues until only one or two very close friends are left, invariably makes

The Closed Fraternity

the policeman dull. His life becomes routine. And even as it does, the pettinesses of police politics become more real.

The cop learns to leave his book of parking-ticket stubs in his locker for several days before turning it in for processing, to give superior officers time to go through them and remove stubs of tickets to be fixed.

In literally every city, the cop learns that he must not make extra work for people. This means that he must do nothing on his own initiative. It means that he must not make "unnecessary" arrests, which inconvenience everyone from the desk sergeant to the man in charge of the lockup. In some cities policemen who make arrests on their own initiative—without a citizen complaint—are merely grumbled at. In others, they may have to pay off the desk sergeant for every "unauthorized" arrest they make. Whatever the system, personal initiative is discouraged. The rookie cop soon finds that, except in cases involving people against whom the department has an animosity, it is best to avoid arrest at all costs.

When the foot patrolman *does* work, he typically performs the most distasteful and, on the whole, the least exciting of the "order maintenance" * jobs that have fallen to police departments over the years. He gives out parking tickets and directs traffic. When he is not doing these things he is dealing with drunks, derelicts, addicts, prostitutes, and people who create visible disturbances. In situations of order maintenance, as Wilson points out, the cop finds that his power of arrest is only one among many techniques which he uses to "handle the situation." The policy of some police departments dictates that drunks and others be arrested. But in most such cases the foot patrolman has a great deal of discretion. This discretion, however, applies only in the area to which the cop is assigned to work and therefore is usually exercised on society's "lowest" mem-

---

* The history of the distinction between the "order maintenance" and "law enforcement" functions of police is briefly outlined in James Q. Wilson, *Varieties of Police Behavior: The Management of Law and Order in Eight Communities* (New York: Atheneum Publishers, 1970), p. 16.

bers—on people who the patrolman himself may feel need varieties of help that simply are not available. In dealing with the same alcoholics week after week (in New Haven, one alcoholic alone was the subject of 140 separate arrests) and with juveniles whom he painfully watches turning into criminals, he is often struck by the futility of the approaches he must take to these problems.

The cop soon learns that on the whole the public is not to be trusted. He finds that many people who call police want to manipulate them for their own purposes. This recognition closes him more completely into the brotherhood of his fellow police officers.

The cop learns that many people who have grudges against others want to use the police to take care of them. And after he has been asked to write a number of theft reports, he realizes that many reports that he writes in good faith are phony ones and that people are using him to defraud insurance companies.

The cop eventually reaches a point where he trusts no one. At this point the notorious secretiveness of the police profession becomes a part of his way of life.

When the rookie cop first comes onto the police force, he typically wants many things. When he first puts on his uniform, he is proud of it. He thinks it is the mark of a group that provides essential services to society which only special kinds of people can perform.

But he finds out that he is not allowed to perform these services. He finds that the policeman's uniform is a mark of low social status to some and the uniform of a hostile army to others, the vast majority of whom are not the criminals who legitimately should fear him.

So his ambitions change. His honest desire to catch criminals is replaced by a practical desire to leave the boredom of the walking beat and get into a squad car. His desire to wear a uniform is replaced by a desire to shed his uniform as soon as possible and get into plainclothes.

The first advancement a cop usually makes is from the walking beat to the squad car. He does not get this advancement by being a good foot patrolman. He does not get it by refusing free meals and cigarettes, nor by staying out of holes while his fellows are sleeping. Ringing fire alarms in the middle of the night and carrying boxes of doughnuts up and down streets do not hurt him. No one does any of the things that he joined the police force to do anyhow. The way the cop gets from the walking beat to the squad car is by going to see his political "hook." If his political connections are still sound, if he has waited long enough, and if he has not arrested the wrong bookies or failed to provide courteous service to the right store owners, he will make it.

Once he is assigned to a squad car, the cop is prepared to go into action. He knows that if he gets tired he has a rolling bedroom and that he doesn't have to look around for holes any more. He also knows that if things get dull, his options for entertainment are unlimited. One of the favorite occupations of New Haven cops was to take extra boxes of shells out to the garbage dump and shoot rats.

But what the policeman still wants is to be a policeman, and when he is first assigned to a squad car he eagerly awaits the radio calls that tell the story of crime throughout the city. Through the dispatcher, he can now arrive in seconds or, at most, in minutes wherever help is needed in his district. When he hears the click of the dispatcher's mike opening, he knows that some incident requires a police response. He hopes once more that he will be the kind of person he thinks a cop should be—one who brings legitimate order to chaotic situations, handles crises decisively, earns the respect of his fellow citizens for his efficiency and flexibility, and ultimately keeps society free from crime.

But as the calls come in, the cop finds himself in the same situations he handled less frequently as a foot patrolman. He sees the same drunks, the same addicts, the same traffic violators, the same car accidents. The tempo of his activity is stepped up, especially in the evening during high crime hours. Occasionally exciting signals will come, telling of fugitives or robberies in progress. When they do, the drama and excitement they provide make him remember

17

his reasons for becoming a cop. But the excitement of these occasions must last a long time to justify the interminable daily rounds of domestic quarrels, barroom fights, traffic violations, report writing and plain waiting that rule the cop's life.

Of the assignments given to the cop in the squad car, one of the most common and typical is the call to intervene in a domestic dispute. To many police officers, these are the most unpleasant and the least satisfying of jobs. A cop cannot win in a family fight. As he walks up the steps of what is often a ghetto apartment building, the cop has no idea what awaits him.

A disproportionate percentage of police injuries come in handling domestic disputes. A husband often feels that he is being challenged in his own house. He may well have been drinking, and he resents the intrusion of a policeman into his personal affairs—even though he may have threatened, beaten, or even knifed his wife. If there are children around, they add to the noise and confusion, and at times they themselves may turn on the policeman. In this kind of situation anything in the house becomes a weapon—a kitchen knife, a hammer, a chair, a vase. Good cops never consider using their guns, but rely on experience, wit, perseverance, and if necessary their night sticks, to control such situations. In fact, some policemen, while they feel that the gun is a necessary protection as a last resort, know how completely its use is blocked from their minds and at times fail to use it when they are in mortal danger. This was the case with one Yale graduate who was a patrolman in New Haven. After he and his partner had been seriously stabbed, he found himself fumbling for a can of MACE while the assaults continued. Finally, however, he resorted to his gun and shot and wounded the assailant.

If one of the disputants—usually the wife—has made the call to police, the spouse will be hostile. Emotions have been aroused, there may already have been physical violence, and the policeman is walking into a potentially dangerous situation.

The instinct of most policemen intervening in domestic disputes is to avoid arrest. Arrest only alienates the husband (who almost always is the one arrested) and aggravates the marital problem that led to it. It causes the officer time and trouble, and the wife, who soon realizes that having her husband in jail is not to her benefit, is seldom satisfied with it. In addition, the policeman who makes an arrest on a wife's complaint often finds that she has changed her mind by morning and that he is left with a prisoner but no complainant.

If a neighbor has called the police, the disputants are even more likely to resent the cop's intrusion. In fact, the policeman may be walking into an ambush as he climbs the stairs. It is a cliché of police work that nothing unites warring parties, temporarily at least, more effectively than a common enemy, and the policeman is nearly always seen as that enemy.

Quite often, if the wife has called the police, she demands that the officer remove her husband from the house. But the policeman cannot legally do this without making an arrest. Consequently, he usually tries to pacify both parties. Sometimes he fails and must drag the resisting husband down several flights of stairs in the presence of his friends and neighbors, who may then become a threat. If the cop has to resort to his night stick, the wife may transfer her anger to him and attack him from behind. Even if he succeeds in calming the parties and avoiding arrest, there is nothing he can do to make this fragile calm more permanent. While more affluent couples call lawyers or go to psychiatrists to resolve their problems, the people who must call police cannot afford such luxuries, and usually the cop knows when he leaves that he or a fellow officer is likely to be climbing the same steps again in another night or two.

But the domestic dispute is only one in an almost limitless number of situations the policeman must face every day. He must break down the doors of apartments whose residents have not been seen for weeks. When he does, he may well find a "sudden death," which usually means a decomposing body. He must guard the scene and wait for a medical examiner to arrive.

The policeman gets to the scenes of serious crimes—robberies, rapes, and homicides—after the perpetrators have fled. In most cases, his task is to guard the crime scene so that all evidence will still be there when detectives arrive to investigate.

Very rarely, if at all, will the patrolman himself follow up on the investigation of such cases. When the detectives arrive, he fills them in on what he knows of the situation, perhaps writes a report, and then is sent back out on the street again.

The patrolman comes to see the Detective Division as a ceiling to his work. Detectives are people who take him away from the "real police work" and throw him back out on the street to deal with drunks and derelicts. It often galls him that although he is the first to arrive on the scene of the vast majority of crimes, he rarely gets credit for the role he plays. If he sees a newspaper story about one of his cases, he will almost always read the names of detectives and high-ranking officers in the department rather than his own.

The patrolman's function in the vast majority of situations is to write a report. He becomes a clerk in a squad car. Since he responds to calls about something that has already happened—a purse has been snatched, an apartment has been burglarized—there is little for him to do but listen to and record the victim's story. He knows that most cases of theft, robbery, and burglary will never be solved, and this is frustrating to him. He may feel that if he did not have to spend 90 percent of his time waiting, cruising, writing reports, and appearing in court in connection with relatively petty cases, he might be able to solve some of the more important ones. Instead he turns them into paperwork that will be filed and forgotten.

The patrolman soon finds that pettiness and insensitivity pervade most agencies that are supposed to serve the public. He lives with it, but occasionally even the most hard-bitten cop gets involved in a situation that arouses his emotions. Once as a young patrolman I was riding in a squad car with a cop who had a reputation for toughness that at times turned to brutality. We were sent to an apartment house where a baby was reportedly very sick. When we arrived, the baby was choking and gagging, unable to breathe. Without immediate attention it would die. My partner took charge; he scooped up the baby and we took off with red light and siren on the most frightening ride of my life. When we arrived at the hospital, the baby was still breathing but was close to death. With the child in his arms the cop rushed up to a doctor and begged him to save it. But the doctor refused to look at it and ordered him to sit in a waiting room. Desperate, the cop cornered a nurse and screamed at her that the baby was dying. She told him to lay it on a table, and then she left.

The cop tried everything he knew, including mouth-to-mouth respiration. Now, in the halls of the hospital, the baby died in his arms. Enraged and heartbroken, on the verge of tears, he screamed at the doctors and nurses until I thought he would attack them. Fighting my own emotions, I found myself restraining him.

Occurrences like this are not the rule. But the policeman who sees various degrees of neglect all around him can hardly help becoming callous and bitter, and eventually he feels his own sensitivity being destroyed.

The frustrations of the cop in the squad car are multiplied by his dealings with the courts. Here, the effects of neglect destroy whatever pride he may have in his job. For if he has managed to retain his honesty, he often finds that the courts have not managed to retain theirs. It is quite common for a policeman arresting a bookmaker or a narcotics pusher to be told by the suspect that there is no point to the arrest because the case will only be "bagged" in court. When he finds that cases for which he has built what he considers (often correctly) solid evidence are repeatedly thrown out by prosecutors or dismissed by judges, he begins to wonder why he makes arrests at all. At best, he will keep making the arrests, feeling that he has done his job and that prosecutors and judges have nothing to do with him. Too often, however, he simply gives up on arresting people he knows to have court connections.

But because of the pressures on him, it is difficult for him to retain his own honesty. He finds that a town's "regular criminals" are among the few people in society who are willing to show even superficial respect for the police. After he has been on the force for a number of years, he knows that he cannot go into the restaurants and bars that policemen are expected to frequent, because of their low social status, without meeting his town's regular criminals. He does not have to seek them out. He has only to sit on a bar stool and order a drink, and he can expect a hand to reach over his shoulder and pay for it. It's a bookie. Before he can order another drink, he will find it sitting in front of him—another bookie, or perhaps someone who plays the horses regularly. There will be friendly words, smiles, and slaps on the back. There will be offers of favors. Since few other people treat him this well, and since the policeman knows that where he receives small favors the town's more powerful politicians and some of its more "respected" citizens receive larger ones, there is no reason for him to rebuff these people or to reject their friendship. This is especially true if the policeman comes from their social stratum and if, as is likely, he sees nothing wrong with gambling in the first place.

The cop may even know that the gambling operations or the narcotics rings these people run are syndicated and that in becoming involved with these people he becomes peripherally involved with organized crime. He may be well aware that as public pressure for increased law enforcement grows, he will go elsewhere to make his arrests; that he will drive out the syndicate's competition, help to ensure its monopoly, and to perpetuate its political strength. But there is little he can do about it, even if he wants to, and if he is getting tired of the meaningless, endless rounds of duty in the squad car, he may look upon such friendship and support with relief.

The policeman often finds the courts unwilling or unable to support him on a case he feels is a good one. If it is not a good one, he may find them equally unwilling to point out to him where he has failed in gathering evidence. Yet those same courts seem all too vulnerable to political influences and therefore too willing to condemn him after the fact for his conduct in ambiguous or delicate situations. Together with a politically sensitive police chief, who has at his disposal a limitless set of departmental regulations to use as he sees fit, the courts can effectively trap the cop even if he does want to enforce the law fairly. Consequently, as the years go on, the cop, no matter how good he is, must reach some kind of compromise with these forces.

As he reaches these compromises, the dangers of his work begin to wear on him. Although there are a few occupations—among them those of firemen, mine workers, and agricultural workers—that are statistically more dangerous than police work, the cop is constantly in potentially dangerous situations, and this fact weighs heavily on him. He is aware that he is most likely to be injured when he least expects it. Added to this emotional strain is the strain of knowing that if he is injured or killed it will probably not be by accident but by intent. In view of these facts, the statistical danger has little to do with the emotional toll that the cop's job exacts on him.

As he ages under these constant threats, the cop becomes more inclined toward violence himself. He may not have been particularly violence-prone when he entered the force, but the highly physical nature of his job tends to brutalize him. He finds that the rhythm of his occupation, dominated by long sedentary periods occasionally broken by short bursts of frenetic activity, is not conducive to staying in good physical condition. He begins to rely more heavily on his night stick. Some older cops have told him that the way to handle trouble is to "get in a good shot with the stick" first and "take the starch out of" potential resisters who may be tempted to try his strength. Unfortunately, he is likely to find the philosophy of the "stick man" vindicated often enough. The policeman deals with the same people week in and week out. They know who he is and how he operates. The cop who cracks a few heads the minute he arrives on the scene is eventually "respected," and after a time he seldom meets resistance. Policemen who seek to avoid brutality, on the other hand, consistently find themselves in full-blown brawls with "cop fighters"—people who have heard of their "weakness" and

23

who want to make their reputations by beating up cops. The courts are far away, and justice is farther. As long as he confines his technique to lower-class areas, the stick man has little reason to fear that his conduct, although patently illegal, will ever be censured. At least on these matters the courts are likely to be sympathetic. It is only when public opinion against police brutality is aroused that the courts do an about-face and condemn the cops for tactics that they have protected or condoned all along.

Because the cop deals every day with the same people—either because he can go nowhere else to enforce the law and obtain convictions in court, or because the ghettos and poverty areas are most in need of order maintenance—all of his latent prejudices are confirmed. The abstractions of economics and sociology are likely to mean little to him if they conflict directly with his day-to-day experience. He knows that the rate of observable and violent crime is higher in these areas than anywhere else. Still, in the face of all these factors, although the stick man may be respected by many cops, most cops are not stick men themselves, and in general those who are truly brutal are ostracized by their peers—if for no other reason than that they are likely to touch off riots or violent reactions that will endanger other cops.

But the cop who is brutal—or even the cop who is blatantly corrupt—is never exposed by his fellows. He is protected, although perhaps uneasily, by the group. The sanctity of the group becomes more important to the cop than the often hypocritical views of outsiders. Even if a policeman wanted to expose a brutal or corrupt fellow officer, he would seldom know which of his superiors was "on the take," or the full extent of the brutal or corrupt cop's political connections.

It would seem that a cop interested in exposing the defects of his police department could turn to the public through the press. But newspapers themselves may be indifferent to police problems, and in the long run a cop who has thrown away his job and violated the trust of his own social group can benefit little from a flurry of publicity that soon dies away.

As his years in the squad car wear on, the endless cycle of shifts takes its toll, and the cop's frustration increases as he sees that he is running hard but getting nowhere. He arrests drunks and sees them thrown into jail, where the causes of their alcoholism are compounded. He knows he will arrest them again. He refers juveniles to juvenile courts and sees them on the streets again with the same lack of support and direction that led to their delinquency. He knows he will arrest them again too, when they have grown, through neglect, into full-fledged criminals. He sees everyone on the take and no one giving. He tires of being trapped between his superiors and the courts, between prosecutors and the public. He tires of making instantaneous judgments on the street that are meticulously analyzed *ex post facto* by people who have no idea what the street as he sees it is like. He becomes exhausted with climbing endless flights of stairs and knocking on the same doors, with finding himself in the middle of fights and brawls, with treating endless problems for which there is—for him—no solution.

Many times he thinks of getting out of police work. But one look at his situation convinces him that there is no place to go. He is likely to have overextended himself financially. He probably has a wife and children and a large mortgage on a home which is his first step toward membership in the middle class. Many times he tries so hard to be middle class that he loses sight of what that class typically thinks of him. At any rate, he needs his steady job, he needs the off-duty work which comes to him through the police department (even though that work is always more police work, and he is seldom thought fit to do more than guard private parties or dances or direct traffic around hazards)—and perhaps most important of all, he is unwilling to give up the promise of his pension. He has already made substantial payments toward it which he will lose if he leaves the police department. Even if, after realizing all this, he still wants to leave police work, he finds that he is prepared to do nothing else. He has no marketable skills. And in addition, he is looked upon with suspicion by prospective employers, who assume that if he wants to leave police work he probably was not a good cop. All these things combine with social and peer-group pressures to keep him where he is.

A cop trapped in police work, however, finds that advancement is excruciatingly slow. The New Haven Police Department is not atypical, and after joining it I waited ten years as a patrolman before the opportunity arose to take a sergeant's examination.

Whether or not he advances in rank, the patrolman's ambitions after a few years in a squad car are likely to be even narrower than they were when he first got behind the wheel. If he is still interested in what he considers police work, he wants at least to get out of the hated blue uniform and into plainclothes. He wants to be where the real crimes are solved. He wants to have a prestige job in which he can use his head instead of his muscle and in which he will be free to act on his own initiative. In most departments, this means the Detective Division.

A policeman is transferred into the Detective Division for the same reason he is transferred or promoted anywhere. If his hook feels that he will function well there, and if enough other important people agree, he has a chance. If he does get into plainclothes, he finds that his job is even narrower than before. In one sense this is a relief, as he is less open to arbitrary condemnation. It probably does not surprise him that he is no more effective than he was before. He finds that, even more than the patrolman, he spends his time writing reports—this time follow-up reports—and filing them where they will be buried forever. He finds that the big law-enforcement problems are too big for him to handle. Organized crime is too subtle and too complex for him to attack even if he wants to. And its power is so often entrenched in City Hall that he finds that wanting to can hurt his career.

The detective also finds, if he does not already know, that the

26

scientific methods of crime detection that he and everyone else has seen on television are a fraud. Fingerprints are the prime example. The detective may go to the scene of a robbery and he may return with a perfect set of fingerprints which he is certain are those of the suspect. But when he sends them to the F.B.I. laboratory, he must send with them a list of the names of ten suspects against which the Bureau can check them. If he has guessed wrong, he may be able to send in ten more names. It is a public myth of some currency that the Bureau checks sets of prints sent to it against all the prints in its files. This is completely false. In fact, unless the detective has an excellent idea of who committed a crime, the Bureau's fingerprint files are useless to him.

The detective finds that his resources have not been augmented in decades. Although he may call in victims and ask them to search through endless sets of mug shots, this is almost always a futile exercise. So he resorts to the most common method of solving crimes—the use of informants.

In order to be successful, the detective must have connections with the underworld. He finds that the best informants are prostitutes, small-time gamblers, and other hangers-on. He is forced to allow certain kinds of crime to continue in order to detect others. It is not uncommon for detectives to work at cross-purposes, with some protecting narcotics violators in order to catch burglars and others protecting burglars in order to catch narcotics violators. When detectives begin arresting each other's informants, the situation can become chaotic.

It is in the plainclothes division, and especially in the gambling and narcotics squads, that corruption is the biggest temptation and the strongest possibility. Here, and in the higher policy-making positions in the department, links to the city's "regular" crime machine may involve substantial sums of money. In these positions, cops can make decisions to ignore one gang and wipe out another. Consequently, appointments to these positions are most likely to be influenced by crooked politicians and underworld figures.

POLICE IN TROUBLE

There are some cops who resist these pressures. But, ironically, they do it not by becoming open, by breaking out of the closed fraternity and widening their perspectives; they do it by closing themselves off within it and by concentrating on cases that come their way. These are the people who love the crime-fighting aspects of police work. They never stop investigating. They work while they are off duty, running from one end of the city to the other to question witnesses again, to follow up leads, to listen to rumors, to piece evidence together. They work on cases which others have ignored. They develop theories or hunches and pursue them tenaciously. They cannot sit at home while there are nagging questions to be answered or criminals running loose on the streets. They see a game, a puzzle, and they are challenged. They maximize the excitement and the drama of their work. If they are touched or bothered by particularly serious or disturbing crimes, they cannot rest until they are solved.

Other policemen may see these men as overly ambitious. But on the whole they are accepted and even admired—as long as they go after the right people and do not rock the boat. These people are happy in police work because they have succeeded in squeezing satisfaction from it. They are oblivious to its handicaps, or they stubbornly fight to overcome them. They present cases so well documented that prosecutors cannot ignore them, and judges cannot throw them out of court. They make sure that witnesses appear on time, time after time, and that their own testimonies are coherent and convincing. When they fail or are thwarted, they try again.

Other cops may be moved to action by other kinds of problems or crises. The cop who is not willing to work overtime on a criminal case may go several nights without sleep in search of a lost child. For many, police work is a series of small satisfactions. But they are seldom enough to lead to satisfying lives.

If the cop in the squad car does not want to become a detective, he is likely to be left with one ambition: to get a steady day job indoors. He does not care where it is. It may be in the Training

The Closed Fraternity

Division, or it may be in some supervisory or clerical job that places him at a desk. At this point he wants little more than to survive. If he can move up in the ranks as he grows older, he will be more than satisfied. Wherever he ends up, his primary function will be to do favors for people. As he does, he finds himself building political walls that cement him into his own position. He gets paid a little more, he works a lot less, and he is as happy shuffling paper as he can be within the structure of the police department. If he is lucky, and if he does not make too many enemies, he may become a chief inspector, an assistant chief, or even chief of police. If he does, he will have received little or no more training or education than the cop on the walking beat, and he will have gained no wider perspective on the police department and its role than a decade of street experience and another decade of "indoor" work have given him. Although there are some notable exceptions, especially in larger cities, most chiefs of police are no more than fifty-year-old patrolmen.

Whether he is a fifty-year-old chief or a fifty-year-old patrolman, the cop who has been on the force for twenty-five or thirty years has long since ceased to question or doubt the ways of the closed fraternity. He has been taken care of or absorbed by the hierarchy. He is no longer climbing three flights of ghetto steps wondering whether someone is waiting behind the door to smash his skull in. Although he sympathizes heartily with the men who still do climb the stairs, his primary attitude is usually hate for those who may be standing behind the doors. He is unwilling and unable to speak out for meaningful police reform that will alleviate the conditions under which he worked when he first joined the force and under which the majority of his fellows still work. He cannot comprehend a larger social perspective which, were he able to adapt and articulate it, might in the end give him some of the support he so desperately needs.

So the policeman continues to hold a position in society analogous to that of a janitor in an office building. He sweeps the same drunks and junkies and deranged people off the streets time after time. He gives out parking and traffic tickets *ad infinitum*. His job is to make sure that society's ground floors are clean enough so that others can walk on them without tripping. Although he may have an idea of what goes on in the offices above him, his life has been defined by those below him. He may indirectly be getting a cut of the profits that issue from the vast factory of white-collar and organized crime that he indirectly helps to protect, but it is a small cut and not even in monetary terms worth the price he has paid for it.

For some, the cop's job has put a severe strain on his marriage over the years. He may have a drinking problem. And he finds that it is difficult to communicate with his children. His "profession" has closed him tightly into a defensive circle from which it is all but impossible to escape. If the cop who sits in front of his suburban house on a summer evening watering the lawn does not believe all the clichés about "niggers" being on welfare, if he is not certain that Communists are responsible for the nation's problems, if he does not have a strong distaste for "hippies," and if at times he does not lash out at every force that threatens what little idealism he has struggled to retain, he has resisted incredible pressures toward evil with virtually no encouragement or support from society.

2

May Day:
Crisis in Focus

MOMENTS OF MASS confrontation reproduce, on a grand and sometimes tragic scale, the thousands of petty frictions and confrontations that police deal with daily. Such moments bring to the surface every force that is capable of influencing police, but too often we cannot see these forces. Too often they remain invisible. We seldom trace their causes: The methods seem too tangled, the process too long and difficult.

We watch mass confrontations like spectators at games. The moment when rocks and bottles fly across no man's land and fall into police lines, we film, we write in notebooks, and we remember. The moment when police charge and shoot tear gas or fire their guns we also keep. The moment when they do nothing—when they stand gauging the dangers and weighing all the complex factors of their responsibility—is not capturable. The moment when they act well is lost.

Perhaps it should be. Perhaps acting well is to be expected. But

31

more often, acting badly is to be expected. And again, it is enough to say, "They acted badly," to see the end of the game, and to leave.

Chicago, Orangeburg, Kent State, Jackson State, Attica. These are frightening new names for police failure as it goes on every day in all American cities. There is a pattern behind these names for failure. It defies the pure simplicity of blame and dissolves for a moment the rigid patterns of resentment and hate. A crisis, a confrontation bring this pattern close to the surface. For a moment, all the sins of the past are crowded together with all the vague hopes for the future. All the pressures are there. From Presidents and Attorneys General to Governors, National Guard generals, and commissioners of state police forces, to Mayors and local politicians, the country's officials and administrators exert their influence. Behind the façades of rhetoric, delicate balances and calculations are going on, power struggles are being waged, and decisions are being made. They are the everyday processes of government, intensified and dramatized. New public figures grow up. Communities take sides. Hidden feelings and long-buried antagonisms are revealed. Strange alliances are made. Congressmen and businessmen and university presidents, laborers and students, all push in their own directions— some motivated by greed, others by ambition, others by idealism. People with their selfishness and their heroism, society with its broad sweep of influences are mixed together. All hang in a tense and uneasy balance, waiting to be resolved.

Sometimes it is an accident that resolves them. Sometimes, despite excruciating planning and meticulous care, things go badly. Sometimes, despite callousness and carelessness, things turn out well.

May 20, 1969, brought an uneasy evening. The New Haven Police Department had received information that members of the New Haven Black Panther party had kidnapped a New York Panther and were holding him in the Orchard Street apartment of Warren Kimbro that was functioning as party headquarters. We did not have enough information to make arrests, but we had the apartment under surveillance. As I grabbed a bite to eat at Leon's Restaurant, my portable police radio told the story.

The phone rang. Something was happening at Panther headquarters; there was a great deal of activity. But we decided there was still not probable cause for arrests. We agreed, however, that more unmarked cars should be brought into position. The call went out, and they were on the way.

But before they could arrive, the gathering at Panther headquarters suddenly broke. Knowing that they were being watched, the Panthers split up into four cars and left in different directions. The radio was crowded with noise as our men sorted the cars out. Three were followed. In the confusion, the fourth slipped away.

That car had to be stopped. We put out an all-points bulletin on it for suspicion of kidnapping. Somehow it wound its way twenty miles up Interstate 91 to Middlefield and back, escaping the notice of state and local police. The next morning a motorcyclist who had stopped to walk by the banks of the Coginchaug River found the body of Alex Rackley lying in the muck, bullets in the head and chest.

The account of our subsequent arrests of eight Panthers (the total eventually reached thirteen) hit the newspapers the next day. It was a big story. Rackley's body showed signs of having been tortured. Along with the murder weapon seized in a raid on the Orchard Street apartment, detectives found a tape recording of an interrogation designed to prove to the Panthers' national leadership that Rackley had been a police agent.

Ten months later, in March 1970, as the pretrial hearings in the Rackley case dragged on, the New Haven Panther trial had become a national political issue. Lieutenant John Maher, the head of the Intelligence Division, brought a report that a massive demonstration was planned for May Day in support of the Panther defendants. Soon afterward police departments from major eastern cities, including Washington, Boston, and Philadelphia, called with information that radicals in their cities were distributing leaflets advertising the demonstration and that many were planning to attend.

The Panthers may be dormant and perhaps dead as a movement now in the wake of the bitter feuds that have torn their national leadership. But at that time their rhetoric, emphasizing their right and need to defend themselves with guns, had sent shock waves across white America. Arnold Markle, state's attorney for New Haven County, had astonished me in the Rackley murder case by asking for an indictment of Black Panther party chairman Bobby Seale.

Although the New Haven Police Department had evidence that Seale had visited the Orchard Street apartment while Rackley was there, we had no solid evidence to link him to Rackley's death or torture. Despite my personal feelings about the case, it was a fact that there was not sufficient hard evidence against Seale, and the New Haven Police Department never requested an indictment against him, nor did we expect that Markle would ask for one. When he did, however, and Seale's name was added to the list of defendants, the trial was provided with all the notoriety that had accompanied the Chicago conspiracy trials.

Since the trial of the New Haven Panthers had become a national issue, it seemed likely that the New Haven Police Department would need help in handling the coming pro-Panther demonstrations, especially if extremist rhetoric and threats of violence continued to be heard from both the radical left and the radical right. I requested a meeting with state police and National Guard representatives.

Connecticut, like most states, has for years operated under a rigid escalation of force policy that governs the handling of emergency situations. Under it, a local police chief in need of assistance is required to turn first to the commissioner of the state police. Only if state and local police cannot control a crisis will the state police commissioner request that the Governor mobilize the National Guard. So it was to State Police Commissioner Leo J. Mulcahy, a solid, scrupulously honest, hard-nosed cop of the old Irish school, with whom I had previously clashed over various issues at the state level, that I had to turn first for help.

The first meeting between myself, Mulcahy, and E. Donald Walsh, Adjutant General of the Connecticut National Guard, produced an instant disagreement between Mulcahy and myself over tactics and responsibilities. In the past, the state police had never been called to intervene in local situations unless they had already become violent. In line with the previous demonstration experience of the New Haven Police Department, and with tactics that we had developed through observing other departments' methods of handling demonstrations, we wanted the state police to act in a preventive, peace-keeping role, to help us in covering the routes of dispersal after the demonstration had finished. And we felt that there was a pressing need for central coordination of all the forces involved.

But Mulcahy's experience and his general attitude toward what he considered to be a racial problem led him to think differently. Because of the dramatic press coverage the Panther trial had received, and because of a general atmosphere of violence that the issue had generated, he believed that confrontation was a foregone conclusion. His attitude was that "this is war." And his position was "we'll come in and help you. But don't tell us how to do it." He suggested that he bring in 300 of his 900-man state police force to occupy half of the New Haven Green, where the rally was to be held, that local police occupy the other half, and that each force be independently commanded. The meeting ended with a commitment of 300 state troopers, but with no agreement on the far more substantive issues involved.

Meanwhile, however, the New Haven Police Department had to begin its own planning. With the demonstrations three weeks away, there seemed to be time. But a great many things had to be decided in an atmosphere of rapidly increasing hostility and hate. The leadership of the police department assumed that the police role would be one thing, but large segments of the New Haven community and many of the policemen themselves believed it would be another.

35

POLICE IN TROUBLE

The department's position was that if people were coming to burn and loot (and we had some intelligence to that effect), we would have to stop them, whether individual policemen were sympathetic to Panthers or hated and feared them. If people were coming to demonstrate, we would have to protect them, whether individual policemen supported right-wing vigilante groups that were forming, or thought such groups a greater danger than the out-of-town radicals themselves. Above all, if people were coming with nothing concrete in mind, with the potential to be either peaceful or violent, we would have to tread a delicate tightrope. While avoiding capricious shows of strength that might incite the crowd to riot, we would have to be prepared to react with force and flexibility if the crowd threatened to get out of hand.

Getting the rank and file of the police force to accept this position was difficult amid the powerful emotional crosscurrents generated by a political issue of national scope. Whatever resentments individual policemen had developed by growing up in the city and serving on the police force were aggravated. Racial hostility, hostility toward Yale students, and hostility toward liberal and radical political figures threatened in some to explode. And this threat was increased by the very nature of the demonstration. The fact that it was sponsored by the Panther Defense Committee meant that Black Panther theories about police would be part of it, and policemen understandably react strongly to being called pigs, or to being characterized as members of an occupation army subjugating the black ghetto by force.

Against these and other powerful negative forces that were operating both in New Haven and across the country, we developed a set of strategies and plans for the May Day demonstration that we felt would diminish their effect and bring the individual policemen to see themselves as more or less neutral monitors of the rallies. I think it is worthwhile to trace the development of these plans and strategies in some detail. Because we did have time to work them

36

out, we were able to prepare for this particular demonstration in a way that I believe has few if any parallels on the national scene.

The earliest concrete decision was an organizational one. For although we were determined to instill a sense of professionalism and an attitude of personal responsibility in the men during the weeks before May Day, it was the control of behavior and not of attitude that was paramount in the short run. Above all, we needed a tight chain of command that would keep the department's ranking officers—and ultimately the chief—in direct control of all operations, and especially in direct control of the use of force.

To accomplish this, we adopted a squad system, dividing approximately 250 men into eight-man groups, commanded by a sergeant who was assisted by a squad leader. The sergeant, or in his absence the squad leader, was directly responsible for the conduct of each of his men at all times, and the squad was to act without exception as a unit. If police were to face strong provocations, from insults to flying rocks and bottles to possible sniper fire, we felt that the squad system as we used it would keep a lid on individual emotions, allow the men both to support and restrain one another, and assure strict accountability up through the ranks of the department. This was to be our most powerful tool in preventing the kind of behavior that has marked police performance in so many crowd and riot-control situations—most notably that of the Chicago police at the 1968 Democratic National Convention—in which individual policemen, either panicking or allowing their emotions to overflow, act on their own without protection or the direction that they need. In Chicago, the chain of command and therefore the formal coercion for responsible behavior broke down, and a department whose outward improvement had gained it a steadily rising reputation ran wild. We were determined not to allow the slightest chance of a "police riot" in New Haven.

The squads were chosen and balanced with excruciating care. We put men whose tempers might flare up into squads dominated by the department's coolest, most competent, most reliable patrolmen. Those men who were older or more inflexible were assigned to duty in the forty-eight squad cars that would keep police service at full strength in the outlying sections of the city throughout the whole weekend. Men we considered hot-headed were put on guard duty at fixed positions away from the center of town.

The attitude of the police-department leadership was that the vast majority of the demonstrators should be considered peaceful protestors whose right to dissent had to be protected. Therefore, our major efforts to prevent serious violence were focused on the possibility of isolated sniping or bombing attacks by either side, which would not only injure or kill people but which might touch off a major riot.

In order to be prepared for this threat, we designated a small number of carefully selected special-weapons squads. These were made up of men who had become weapons experts and whom we felt would be able to isolate snipers and eliminate them with the control and discipline that would ensure the safety of innocent bystanders. These squads were armed, equipped, and dressed like the others, and it was decided that they would be used just as the others were. Only if ordered would they retreat to armory vans and receive appropriate weapons, from tear gas to shotguns. They were the only officers who were to handle such weapons in any circumstances.

After we had decided on the squad system, we began to consider concrete tactics. Here our own experience proved to be valuable. In the spring of 1968, while Washington, D.C., was burning in the wake of the assassination of Martin Luther King, Jr., a large demonstration had been held in New Haven. The mood had been tense and the speakers inflammatory. The night before I had rushed policemen to the predominantly black Hill section of the city and they had made sixty arrests in three minutes to squelch a building disturbance. The town, which had experienced major riots the previous summer, seemed on the brink of another explosion.

The King demonstration had been held on the Green, a large grassy area of four square blocks in the center of town. We had decided that while the demonstrators were there, little or no visible police presence was needed. We had felt that the most dangerous period would be after the demonstration was over, while the crowd was dispersing. We had wanted to communicate a sense of trust to the leaders of the rally and to avoid inflaming the group or threatening them with a concentration of police power. Consequently, we had kept police off the Green during the speeches but had lined the dispersal routes with them. The tactic had worked.

The importance of attention to dispersal routes was illustrated even more dramatically a few months before the May Day demonstration when a gathering of 75,000 rallied on the Boston Common. Boston provided 500 policemen for the rally, all of whom were concentrated downtown. When the speeches were over and the crowd dispersed, some 5,000 protestors marched back to Cambridge. By the time police could be moved there in significant numbers, a riot was under way that the Cambridge department could not possibly control. It resulted in an estimated $400,000 worth of damage to stores and offices and took several hours to contain.

In the light of this experience, we felt that the May Day rallies would require not a massive show of police power that would threaten the demonstrators and lend credibility to their "police state" rhetoric but a police presence removed from the demonstrations and virtually invisible while they were in progress.

Since our most urgent tactical requirement was for mobility, deliberations on how the squads should be deployed were begun early. As we looked for ways to deliver instantaneously large numbers of men to trouble spots, a pattern began to emerge which made "low visibility" even easier to carry out.

Policemen usually work alone or in pairs, spread out over their cities in individual squad cars. We needed to bring them together and yet keep the mobility of the squad car, or increase it. Putting policemen in vans rather than individual cars seemed to accomplish this. Individual cars would arrive at confrontation scenes at various times and might therefore increase the vulnerability of policemen. They would have to be parked; they would multiply communication problems and cut down on the cohesion of the squads. The most minute details of our deployment pattern were worked over again and again, until we were convinced that we could match trouble spots with measured and yet adequate police power wherever they occurred. The emerging pattern placed police vans strategically around the Green, either parked on side streets with the men concealed inside them (and most of the vans were unmarked, rented ones) or in garages with the men nearby.

This plan assumed that there would be no need for uniformed men on the Green. Aside from trees and grass, there was little to damage there—except for the churches, and those had been opened up as shelters for the demonstrators themselves. Uniformed men in the crowd would be vulnerable and provocative. The possibility of entering the crowd to make arrests for possession of marijuana, indecent exposure, and other such offenses in instances where we had no complaints was never considered. The plan did call for eight or ten uniformed officers around the edges of the Green to give directions or summon ambulances in case of emergencies. But aside from these men, there were to be no police visible to the demonstrators from the Green.

The other side of the "low visibility" theory was containment. One of our most vital concerns was that if trouble started, we avoid dispersing the demonstrators in a way that would scatter them throughout the city. As long as we could neutralize the crowd and minimize violence, as long as we could assure that they would not be provoked, and as long as we could keep them from isolated acts of arson and vandalism in the city proper, we felt there was a good chance of things turning out well. Fortunately the demonstrators themselves chose the immense area of the Green for their rally. The Green adjoins the Yale campus, to which they could be directed if trouble broke out. On the Green, hot tear-gas canisters could not start fires, we would not have to fear that gas would affect innocent people who might be trapped in their homes or cars, and there was always a viable escape route for those who sought no confrontation.

In order for containment to be successful, there must be a minimum of physical contact between police and demonstrators, there must be areas which can act as buffer zones between police lines and the lines of demonstrators, and there must be some area into which demonstrators can retreat which offers them relative security. The New Haven situation provided us with many of the necessary ingredients for this formula, and we attempted to supply the rest.

Shortly before May Day, policemen and civilians from the New Haven department traveled to Washington, D.C., to observe recent innovations in their crowd and riot-control training programs. Washington, a city that has to contend with dozens of demonstrations every year, had previously exhibited a philosophy similar to ours. But as we watched their trainees dodging rubber bricks and learning the use of new equipment, we found that we disagreed strongly with policies they had recently developed. They held that police handling disturbances should make as many legal arrests as possible once a crowd became unruly. In rejecting this policy for our May Day demonstrations, we disagreed as well with a portion of the mob-control textbook, which advocates the arrest of an unruly crowd's leaders. This tactic may prove appropriate in dealing with small groups in which guilty parties can be identified positively. But in dealing with large masses of people, many of whom are potential leaders, we felt this policy would be unwise. Arresting a few demonstrators on minor charges like abusing a police officer or disorderly conduct would make martyrs and would give agitators in the crowd an opportunity to focus anger on police. It hardly seemed worthwhile.

The "politics of confrontation" dictate that, in a game that can turn deadly in seconds, restraint and balanced judgment are the keys to neutralizing violence. In this case, we were willing to ignore police baiting in the interest of keeping the crowd confined to areas where we could handle them. Especially in cases where identification was

41

difficult and pursuit dangerous, we felt that we should refrain from making arrests of people who shouted insults or threw debris.

These tactics required extremely mature behavior on the part of the policemen. Most experienced officers know that arrest is not the best solution to the majority of the ambiguous human situations they face every day. They know that they usually do not make arrests when people scream insults or throw things—even when, in the heat of an emotional situation, these activities may be directed toward them. This is a simple function of the necessity of making delicate judgments as to what is and what is not a crime and of the impossibility of enforcing all laws at all times. But when police feel they themselves have become the enemy, this insight, and the calm ordering of priorities that should go with it, is likely to be lost. Especially when policemen do not agree politically with the people they are policing, they are likely to justify making all the arrests they possibly can on the abstract ground that ideally all laws should be enforced at all times. And when they see offenses taking place in front of their eyes, especially if those offenses are directly challenging their authority, they are likely to react in a manner not in keeping with their everyday behavior. So, in a situation like May Day, few policemen realize that their primary function is not to make arrests but to preserve life and property and to avoid escalating the level of violence, which inevitably radicalizes a crowd and makes them a greater danger than before.

For police to succeed in the "politics of confrontation," they must keep physical contact with hostile groups at a minimum. Refraining from making unnecessary arrests is part of the minimum physical-contact policy, since an arrest always requires some contact. Keeping together in squadlike groups so that demonstrators cannot attack them singly is another important factor. But there are times when police must advance to clear strategic areas. When these advances are accompanied by the use of tear gas—as they often should be, in order to create a buffer zone between police and demonstrators and, once more, keep physical contact at a minimum—crowds will become dangerous unless they have someplace to which to retreat. A mob on which gas has been used must not be trapped, choking and bleary-eyed, cut off from shelter, and forced to break through police lines to escape. Violence is the inevitable result of such entrapment. In New Haven, we were fortunate in having the Yale campus available on the west side of the Green, as a place to which the crowds could be driven when they became too hostile. This meant that the campus became a *de facto* sanctuary.

The concept of sanctuary became a volatile issue with the New Haven policemen, who justly felt that no one who has committed a serious crime should be permitted to escape. While departmental orders made it clear that no sanctuary would exist for people who committed serious offenses, police were to cease pursuit when such suspects entered Yale grounds, to regroup their squads and await instructions. This seemingly contradictory order meant simply that barging into the relatively closed compound of the Yale campus with squads of uniformed officers was not the way to make necessary arrests. The risk of such pursuit was greater than the need for immediate apprehension, and if an arrest proved necessary on review, it could be arranged by plainclothes officers or campus police.

The importance of the *de facto* sanctuary lay in the fact that the demonstrators, feeling at home in their centrally located shelter, and able to get first aid for burning eyes if they needed it, were not forced out into the city proper. Minimum physical contact, buffer zones, and *de facto* sanctuaries in effect became vital techniques for crime prevention over May Day.

Although adherence to these policies had to be ensured by a chain of command that would not break down under pressure, it would have been absurd to attempt an authoritarian imposition of them without trying to gain acceptance for them. By establishing the squad system and by building strong systems of accountability, we had done all we could to control behavior. We also did all we could to instill an attitude of professionalism and detachment in the men. The police department's training program in general had been directed toward making the policeman a more effective peacekeeper as he attempted to ease the frictions of city life. Now our job was to apply these ideas about handling individuals to a theory about handling hostile groups.

This responsibility fell to the New Haven Police Department's trainer, John Heaphy, and the vehicle for it was our in-service training program. I sat in on the sessions, one afternoon each week for four hours. They were open and freewheeling.

In the beginning, the talk in these sessions centered around better equipment: more guns and bigger sticks. In fact we had purchased some equipment—radios and pepper foggers, portable dispensers that could send out steady streams of tear gas, and the men had been trained in their use. But it was more important in the in-service training sessions to make the men reflect on their attitudes and on their role in situations of dissent. Some of them realized that the demonstrators who were converging on New Haven had a constitutional right to dissent and that to attack that right would be to attack their own rights—rights which they would find highly important when it came to organizing police unions, picketing and protesting for redress of their own grievances. But others simply could not understand such a philosophy. They saw the coming demonstrators through the eyes of many townspeople and envisioned them through the eyes of newspaper reporters who almost without exception were predicting the outbreak of guerrilla war. To them the dissenters were an invading army, and they were New Haven's militia. Their attitude was epitomized by the remark of a young patrolman who said at one of the sessions that the answer to the May Day challenge was to "get tough."

I entered the discussion to ask him exactly what he meant. Since it seemed that there was no way to get him to agree to the philosophy behind our plans, I appealed to more pragmatic considerations. It turned out that he could not articulate what "getting tough" meant. He was unwilling to admit—at least to me—that such a phrase might mean making illegal arrests or beating people. And as far as

44

arresting everyone who committed a minor offense was concerned, he could not answer where all the policemen could be found to carry out such a policy, or what it would mean for an individual cop to enter a hostile crowd in pursuit of someone who had called him a name, or how New Haven was to be protected if half of the police force was busy loading people into vans and booking them for petty violations.

During these in-service training discussions, we asked more of the members of the New Haven Police Department than is usually asked or expected of police officers. They were to be deaf to name calling and profanity. They were to duck rocks and bottles. They were to maintain their assigned squad positions unless ordered to do otherwise, and they were not to obtain or fire tear gas except on the direct order of a ranking officer.

In return for what we asked, we tried to assure the men that they would never be trapped without support or left out on a limb. We gave them specific assignments and clear, unambiguous orders. They had access to a long and thorough document detailing all of the department's basic plans and policies, and they knew that they would see the department's ranking officers, including the chief and assistant chiefs, at any potentially dangerous disturbance. This meant that the pressure of making many delicate and crucial decisions would be absorbed through the regular apparatus of the department's command structure. They would not have to make *ad hoc* decisions on the basis of partial views of the situation. By the same token, if they did take it upon themselves to make such decisions, their actions would not escape notice. They knew that the May Day challenge would be difficult, but at least they knew what was expected of them.

The result of all this was a somewhat different conception of what a policeman is in a mob or riot situation. This conception grew out of the work which we had tried to do in the department over many preceding months. Many of the men of the New Haven Police Department came to feel that they were referees and not—as many had previously felt—protagonists in an essentially political situation. Their job was to keep order, to keep demonstrators from hurting New Haven and New Haven from hurting the demonstrators, without involving themselves, and without becoming political tools of either side. This conception of the "referee role," which was the fruition of our concrete plans, came sharply into focus over May Day, and its success, dramatic in its juxtaposition with most policemen's conception of their role in society, made a deep impression on many of the men. It went a long way, coming as it did at a period of intense crisis, to further define what we meant by a highly controversial ideal that we had been struggling to realize and define—police professionalism.

But while the New Haven Police Department was going through these intricate internal processes of preparation, the problem of external support was becoming more acute. Mulcahy, Walsh, and I met again, but this second meeting, far from clearing up minor difficulties, brought major ones more dramatically into the open. Mulcahy renewed his offer to divide the Green in half, and I renewed my objections to a visible police presence on the Green and to a divided command structure that would obscure lines of responsibility and accountability.

Mulcahy then offered to police a section of the city rather than half of the Green. I asked him what section he would take, and he replied that he would deploy his men on the Hill.

The Hill, a fairly small section of New Haven, housed Panther headquarters at the time. Mulcahy's choice of it indicated more clearly than ever that he saw the coming demonstrations as a racial issue. I felt that race had little to do with it and knew that the black community was making its own plans to cool tensions. The New Haven department plan called for no more than a dozen cars to patrol the Hill over the weekend, and the idea of saturating it with hundreds of state troopers who were not familiar with the area and could not be sensitive to its problems seemed highly dangerous.

May Day: Crisis in Focus

Mulcahy and I had reached a stalemate. But it soon became plain that General Walsh of the National Guard, who had listened carefully to my description of the New Haven department's plans, approved of them. Walsh, a short, stocky man of approximately Mulcahy's age, with a professional military manner, could have been expected to have an outlook similar to Mulcahy's. He proved, however, to be flexible, enlightened, and willing to experiment. He saw the need for dividing what would essentially be a police force into individual, highly mobile units, and he recognized the need for clear lines of authority and a centralized command. He suggested that he bring in the Guard and said he would be willing to deploy them for the preventive function that our plan required.

But the Connecticut escalation of force policy specifically blocked the use of the Guard except at the request of the commissioner of the state police, and Mulcahy, infuriated at what he saw as an attempt to circumvent his authority, refused to go along with Walsh's suggestion. Confident that Governor Dempsey would follow his advice, Mulcahy challenged us to appeal to him.

While these crucial negotiations dragged on behind the scenes, New Haven and the nation were becoming increasingly anxious over the prospect of May Day. It seemed that the Black Panther trial would succeed in bringing the most militant and desperate offshoots of the civil-rights movement together with the most radical and violence-prone segments of the antiwar movement over a highly explosive national issue. Images of shoot-outs between Panthers and police merged with images of Weathermen bombings to produce a hysteria almost impossible to re-create. It seemed that the protections of civilization were being stripped away, and in such an atmosphere the most deeply hidden fears showed themselves. The ancient white fear of blacks invading the suburbs combined with the newer one of white crazies killing and maiming in the lurid rites of drug-sex cults to dredge up nightmares of violence. Guns and explosives were stolen. The Minutemen were reported ready to strike. Merchants feared for their property, and citizens envisioned the police

47

being swept away and overpowered at the first rush of the protestors, leaving the town to the mercies of rabid revolutionaries. From the streets of New Haven to the highest levels of the national government, the coming demonstrations were acknowledged to be a crisis, and pretensions were dropped as people's most basic instincts were revealed.

Amid the confusion bred by such an atmosphere, the problem of outside help for the New Haven Police Department was not resolved until two days before May Day. New Haven's Mayor Barthlomew Guida is an old-line ward leader who during his twenty-two years as an alderman had won prominence for his opposition to redistricting schools to achieve racial balance. New Haven Democratic boss Arthur T. Barbieri chose him as a successor to Mayor Richard Lee, whose independence and honesty had proved an embarrassment to the machine for nearly two decades. Barbieri had placed Guida in what was now an extremely delicate and critical position. Guida had been slow to make decisions for May Day on such critical items as extra police radios, tear gas, police overtime, rental vans for the squads, and even food. His attitude toward protestors was summed up in his statement "It's too bad we can't just get the bastards." Now, although the New Haven department had already decided to take the necessary steps to prepare for May Day and risk the consequences, there were other things to discuss—among them, the issue of outside assistance.

As I waited to see the Mayor, Guida received a call from Governor Dempsey. Moments later a call came through for me from the same source. Dempsey was summoning us to an important meeting in Hartford to formulate plans for New Haven's protection.

The meeting was held at state police headquarters. Governor Dempsey, Commissioner Mulcahy, and General Walsh were there with their aides. Guida and I were introduced to a Presidential strike force consisting of Clarence Koster, associate director of the federal Law Enforcement Assistance Administration (L.E.A.A.), William Ruckelshaus, who was then Assistant Attorney General of the

48

United States, and several others. The strike-force concept came into being after the Detroit riots of 1967, during which there was an enormous gap between the time when Mayor Jerome Cavanaugh requested federal troops and the time when President Johnson sent them. Strike forces are supposed to keep the President informed on situations that may require federal assistance, to assess critical situations and recommend concrete courses of action.

Ruckelshaus brought with him a confidential report that had, he said, been compiled by the F.B.I. and various other law-enforcement agencies. The report, according to Ruckelshaus, indicated that New Haven was "in for a very bad time." The meeting was already quite emotional, and the impact of his statement was considerable. He then announced that the President had made available over 3,500 infantry and paratroopers, many of whom had been flown into Connecticut, Quonset Point, Rhode Island, and Chicopee Falls, Massachusetts, from faraway bases.

On the basis of the intelligence that the New Haven Police Department had gathered, this seemed to be a gross overreaction, and in view of the fact that New Haven had not been consulted or informed beforehand, the news came as a shock. Evidence that the Nixon Administration anticipated enough violence to justify such moves could only aggravate public hysteria. And the troop movements could certainly be interpreted as a threat and a provocation by those demonstrators who were coming to demonstrate peacefully and within the bounds of the law. I wondered what was in the F.B.I. report, and I asked to see it.

Although New Haven's security was principally the responsibility of the New Haven Police Department, the strike-force members at first refused to let me see the report. It was only by pointing out that ignorance of its contents could seriously hamper the operations of the department and by holding out the possibility that I might have information to add to it that I was surreptitiously able to obtain a copy.

What I read when I finally did get the report was alarming, but

49

not in the way I had expected. It raised serious doubts about the quality of information that results in crucial government decisions. The report was almost completely composed of unsorted and un-evaluated stories, threats, and rumors that had crossed my desk in New Haven. Many of these had long before been discounted by our Intelligence Division. But they had made their way from New Haven to Washington, had gained completely unwarranted credibility, and had been submitted by the Director of the F.B.I. to the President of the United States. They seemed to present a convincing picture of an impending holocaust.

During the crush of May Day preparations there was a constant flow of "information" into our Intelligence Division. Sources ranged from reliable informants to phone calls from the public to generally circulating rumors.

People who offer information in the context of politically con-nected activity do so for diverse and varying motives, with varying degrees of frequency and reliability. Some are contacted by police and may offer information on only one occasion. Many of them offer information when they fear a situation is likely to lead to vio-lence or other criminal activity. They usually want a situation dif-fused. Many of them also offer information for sale out of simple mercenary greed. And there are some who participate in political activity simply because of such motivations, who may operate with-out police encouragement.

Although gaining information through informants may seem a questionable tactic, and although it is obviously subject to abuses, in many situations police must have information on organizations that may be a threat to life or to the law. This way of gaining in-formation proves more palatable than mandatory interrogation, un-limited searches, and other less acceptable alternatives. However, unless police are as assiduous in sorting out intelligence, in corrobo-rating it, and in using it for legitimate purposes as they are in gaining it, it can be dangerous. The New Haven Intelligence Division at-tempted to lessen this danger by sorting raw May Day intelligence according to specificity and verifying it through independent channels. If it could not, the information was discarded.

Meanwhile, however, we forwarded "raw intelligence" to other law-enforcement agencies such as the F.B.I. which might have other sources for checking it, and the F.B.I. provided us with some "raw intelligence" in turn. Somehow, with May Day information, F.B.I. field offices, undoubtedly under pressure from Washington for information, sent the national office unsorted and unverified material. And F.B.I. officials in Washington, who should have known the difference between rumor and intelligence, endowed it with a stamp of authenticity by submitting it formally to the President.

Let me cite a few examples from the strike-force report, whose heading read:

> To: The President.
> To: The Vice President, attention Mr. Kent B. Crane.
> To: Director, Central Intelligence Agency.
> To: Director, Defense Intelligence Agency.
> To: Department of the Army.
> To: Headquarters, U.S. Secret Service, attention, PID.
> To: Attorney General (by messenger).
>
> From: Director, FBI

On page 3 of this document there appears the following paragraph:

> THREATENED ACTION BY RADICAL GROUP. A SOURCE ADVISED THAT HE HAD HEARD THAT SOME MEMBERS OF THE WEATHERMAN FACTION OF THE ANARCHISTIC STUDENTS FOR A DEMOCRATIC SOCIETY (SDS), NEW YORK CITY, WHO WERE INVOLVED IN THE NEW YORK BOMBINGS, WERE DEFINITELY GOING TO NEW HAVEN FOR MAY ONE, NINETEEN SEVENTY, RALLY TO TAKE ACTION AGAINST "BANK AND COMMERCIAL BUILDINGS ONLY."

We had received this report in the New Haven Police Department. It came to us from the New York Police Department, which furnished us with excellent information on potentially violent individuals during the weeks before May Day. The New York department sent it, and we received it, with the implicit understanding that it was not yet "intelligence"—that it was merely a lead to follow up, a possibility to be aware of. There is no assessment in the F.B.I. version of the reliability of the source. The individuals in question are unspecified. The presence of the word "definitely," which seems to make the report authoritative, is meaningless, as are the references to specific targets which seem to lend the story plausibility. As it stands, this report could have been genuine. But it could also have been the result of a casual conversation in which one person said he was definitely going to New Haven, and another discussed bombings in general, and a third said that such actions should be taken against banks and commercial buildings only. Without further verification, a report like this should be discarded. In fact, we asked the New York department to check further on this story for us, and in the end their assessment was that the people coming to the May Day rally from their city were unlikely to instigate trouble, although they might well be involved in trouble if it did start. There was, in the end, no evidence whatsoever to link them with the New York bombings.

Directly below this report on page 3 of the strike-force document appears the following paragraph:

> A SOURCE ADVISED THAT THE YALE FACTION OF THE SDS WAS THINKING OF TAKING OVER A BUILDING ON THE YALE CAMPUS TO-NIGHT. SDS MEMBERS MENTIONED THAT THEY WOULD HAVE A "THRASHING" [SIC] AT A NEARBY SHOPPING CENTER WHICH WAS "RITZY" AND CONTAINED TWO BANKS. THEY STATED THEY WOULD DO NOTHING TO DAMAGE THE PANTHERS AND WOULD "SAVE THE ROCKS FOR THE COPS."

We also received this report in the New Haven department. We checked on it through sources at Yale, which revealed that although building takeovers and trashing had been brought up at a relatively open SDS meeting, the tactics had been sources of heated controversy, and no plans had been made. In fact, the advocates of these

tactics seemed to be on the run. I had been wary from the beginning
of the possibility of groups fanning out to nearby communities like
Wallingford, Branford, and West Haven, and we had communicated
with them about it as well as warning our own men to be vigilant.
But once more, suggestions that fly about in meetings and are set
aside or rejected out of hand hardly deserve to be couched in terms
like "source advised," supplied once more with details that make
them seem authoritative, and included in official reports that suggest that concrete plans for such activities exist.

A third example comes from page 5 of the report. It is even less
comprehensible:

> SOURCE REPORTS PLOT TO ATTEMPT BLACKOUT OF NEW HAVEN
> AT TIME OF PANTHER TRIAL. YESTERDAY INFORMATION WAS RE-
> CEIVED FROM A SOURCE THAT THERE IS A PLOT AFOOT TO ATTEMPT
> THE BLACKOUT OF NEW HAVEN BUT HE WAS UNABLE TO ELABO-
> RATE ON THE INFORMATION.

There have been few major demonstrations in this country in the
last five years that have not been accompanied by this particular
rumor. It is a favorite. It did not have to be picked up "yesterday."
It could have been picked up anywhere, on any day, from any one
of a thousand "sources," all of whom would have been "unable to
elaborate" on it. Its credence was probably heightened in the case
of May Day by the Panthers' repeated threat that if Bobby Seale and
his codefendants were not freed, they would "put out the lights"
in New Haven. No one knew, even as inflated rhetoric, whether this
was meant literally or figuratively. In the literal sense, this contingency had been allowed for. There were extra guards on power
stations and other strategic utilities, and in a concerted effort by
New Haven's utility companies, every manhole in the city had been
welded down.

In the F.B.I. report, the wording of this rumor is repeated, which
adds to its impact but hardly to its content. This rumor is like those
that surrounded the demonstrations at the 1968 Chicago conven-

tion that the water supply was going to be poisoned, or that LSD was going to be thrown in the reservoirs, which were largely the result of Yippie jokes. It is too vague to be checked, it is impossible to guard against, and it is hardly intelligence, despite the phrase "he was unable to elaborate," which seems to imply that details of the plan existed but simply were not available. If police and governments are not to be made fools of by the wild imaginings of a very imaginative group of people, the most that should be done with stories like this is to forward them—as rumors—to other agencies and to hope that if one in a hundred such rumors is actually grounded in fact, a combined effort will result in hard data as to which one.

The last example I will cite is perhaps the most blatant instance of a story that could have been checked rather easily but was not:

> HARLEM, NEW YORK, BPP LEADERS INFORMED THE COMMITTEE [the Black Liberation Committee of the American Communist party] THEY HAD RESERVED FORTY-FIVE BUSES WHICH ARE LEAVING THE HARLEM AREA FOR NEW HAVEN ON MAY ONE TWO THREE, NINETEEN SEVENTY.

In conjunction with the other "information" in this report, stories of whole ghettos being moved from one location to another cannot help but evoke pictures of all-out race war. When the New Haven Police Department received this report, we called bus companies in New York and found, as we had suspected from our knowledge of Panther organizational strength in the East and especially in New York, that it was false. This, however, like so many other bits of myth and fable in the report, also ended up on the President's desk.

The content of the strike-force report made it clear that, consciously or unconsciously, the publicly announced decision to move elite combat troops to within striking distance of the May Day demonstration had been based in part on a combination of deception and willingness to believe the worst that is a danger to all intelligence operations.

In fact, I would speculate that the deception in this case began as self-deception. The F.B.I., undoubtedly faced with demands by the White House and other branches of government for information about the New Haven situation, must have leaned hard on their field offices to produce intelligence overnight. This pressure led agents to put everything they received (and, contrary to popular opinion, the F.B.I. receives most of its information from local police forces) on the wire to Washington. Since the director of the F.B.I. had honored the Panthers shortly before by calling them the greatest internal threat to the security of the country, the usual tendency of law-enforcement agencies to overestimate the potential for violence in a given situation was heightened. There appears to have been a premium on showing that the situation was critical. Somewhere in the pipeline between the hectic New Haven rumor mill and the President's desk in Washington, the pressures for hard, unqualified information must have become intense. At that point, the subtle semantic changes took place that turned a group of disjointed and largely unverifiable accounts into a coherent and convincing picture of an emerging guerrilla war. The danger of the situation was magnified rather than analyzed, precipitating a federal overreaction.

But even on the basis of the exaggerated picture presented in the F.B.I. report, it seemed to me that the response had been excessive. This was especially true in view of the fact that there had been no effort to determine from local and state agencies how elaborate their own plans were to be. This action may be attributable to a desire on the part of the Nixon Administration to make political capital out of the event by "getting tough" with protestors. It seemed ironic that while we were having acute difficulty getting 300 state policemen to use in preventing violence, the federal government was willing to bring in over 3,500 troops for use once violence had erupted. It was also ironic that Mayor Guida, whose office overlooked the battlefield and who was on top of the situation, was unable to take action but that President Nixon, from his office in Washington, felt compelled to take extreme action.

POLICE IN TROUBLE

The large commitment of federal troops can perhaps be explained by the fact that President Nixon, juggling a volatile combination of international politics and domestic crises, knew he would be announcing the invasion of Cambodia at the very time that thousands of radicals were converging on New Haven. The invasion could not help but be a challenge to the powerful antiwar movement at a delicate moment. It seems possible, on the basis of his information, that he or his advisers fully expected this combination of events to explode into "war" in New Haven. And his reaction was to be ready with overwhelming mobility, manpower, and fire power.

While it was the feeling of the New Haven Police Department that the vast majority of people in any given demonstration should be regarded as neutral or nonviolent and only a few as desiring violence, the Administration obviously regarded almost all of the projected 35,000 demonstrators as enemies. Actually that figure turned out to be a gross overestimation, as many potential demonstrators left New Haven or decided not to come because of the threats of violence. In the face of the massive commitment of heavily armed combat troops, this attitude threatened to become a self-fulfilling prophecy.

The faulty-intelligence syndrome was not unique to New Haven. In fact, according to the Walker Report, faulty intelligence contributed to the trouble at the 1968 Democratic National Convention. As rumors filtered unchecked through the Chicago Police Department, they made individual officers see themselves as combatants in a war.

At any rate, the federal troops had been committed and a public announcement made. There was nothing to be done about it. The Hartford meeting continued. Mayor Guida asked the strike force exactly what it was going to do for New Haven. When he was told that federal troops were to be used only as a back-up for state and local forces, he began to expound on the subject of the cost of May Day to New Haven and asked that the Marines and paratroopers be moved into New Haven prior to the demonstration. He seemed unaware of the dangers of such an action. Governor Dempsey, somewhat surprised at this request, patted the Mayor on the shoulder and eventually managed to calm him down.

After the strike force had left the meeting, the Governor, Mulcahy, Walsh, and I met to discuss arrangements for state assistance to New Haven. It seemed that Dempsey had originally told Mulcahy and Walsh to come to New Haven and cooperate with whatever plans our department had made. Now he was surprised to find that there were, to say the least, uncertainties.

I requested that the National Guard come to New Haven prior to the demonstration to act in a preventive role as an extension of the New Haven Police Department. Delegating such wide authority to a local chief of police was a political risk for Dempsey. If there was widespread violence in New Haven, he would be in an embarrassing situation. But I outlined our strategy, and he approved of it. He asked Walsh's opinion. Walsh said he felt it was logical and that it was sound from a military point of view.

The meeting ended with Governor Dempsey ordering Mulcahy to conform to our plans. Dempsey, following his instincts in a critical situation, had overturned the formal escalation-of-force policy for the state of Connecticut, an action that saved our entire May Day strategy and philosophy from foundering. In this decision, Walsh had played a critical role, for he had made it clear that there should be one person in command of the operation and that in this case it should be the local chief of police. Together, Dempsey and Walsh had made it possible to proceed—now at a breakneck pace, as May Day was less than thirty-six hours away—with the whole complex set of plans we had worked out. I placed a call to New Haven to get the process started.

While the New Haven Police Department entered into an intensive period of preparation, the city of New Haven was preparing also. In the midst of the paranoia, there were many who were responsible and cool. New Haven's black community pulled together a complex set of preparations. Many whites, including one store owner who cornered me in a barbershop the night before the rally and wanted to know what I was doing to protect his particular business from the blacks, assumed that the Panthers would draw in legions of gun-toting ghetto radicals. But no one who knows the extraordinary mobility of white youth and the corresponding difficulty with which ghetto people go anywhere doubted that the crowd would be white students. The black community knew this and made it clear that it would not pay the price for the hit-and-run attacks of white radicals. Rumor-control centers were set up, community patrols were organized, and weekend-long activities were arranged to keep children from becoming involved in, or swallowed up by, any trouble that might break out.

The Yale University administration, faced with the threat of a potentially hostile invasion, had made the courageous decision to open its doors to the demonstrators, to host them rather than repel them in a fashion that might cause the walls of Yale—or the walls of the city—to come tumbling down. Now students went about setting up logistical systems, coordinating teams of medical and legal advisers, and sending out a stream of information that, in line with the Panther party's own releases, called for a nonviolent weekend.

But some of New Haven's citizens did not act quite so rationally. Many store owners went to extreme lengths to protect their property. Trying to head off a massive shutdown of New Haven, I went before the Chamber of Commerce to urge them to keep stores open over the weekend. I felt it was important to preserve an air of normality. But by Thursday, the day before May Day, virtually every downtown store had boarded up, and by evening New Haven looked like a ghost town, a shanty village of plywood. It looked as though the inevitable riot had already happened.

At 6:00 P.M. on the evening of Thursday, April 30, I walked out the door of my office. The final staff meeting was over. The preparations for May Day were complete. The long weeks of intricate planning and training were over. The agonizing task of imagining and allowing for every conceivable contingency was done. The last small detail had been a change in assignments. General Walsh of the National Guard had come up with a few more men than we had counted on, and they had been detailed to guard gas and electric facilities, freeing a few more regular New Haven policemen for downtown duty.

Now there was a lull. In the emergency communications center in the basement of the Hall of Records, I watched state police and National Guard radio networks being patched into ours. Then, carrying the portable radio that kept me in constant command of the 430-man New Haven police force, as well as of the 4,000 National Guardsmen who were moving into the city and turning the Goffe Street Armory into a military bivouac, I headed home.

For the first time in weeks there seemed to be nothing to do, and I tried to eat supper and relax. As I walked from room to room of my house alone, the phone rang incessantly, and I realized sleep would be impossible. I gave up and drove downtown, this time to the police department's weekend headquarters at the Park Plaza Hotel, a seventeen-story steel and glass structure that overlooks the New Haven Green. I joined my closest advisers in a suite on the top floor. In the Park Plaza too, emergency telephone lines were being installed in record time. I stared out the window at the empty Green. Ordinarily I would have seen three colonial churches, a wide expanse of grass, ancient elm trees, a flagpole reaching up into the gathering dusk. But now I saw dispersal patterns, buffer zones, milling crowds, traffic flows, undercover agents—and every contingency that we had dreamed of over the previous weeks.

In a matter of hours, New Haven would be a pressure cooker. Police and demonstrators would begin facing each other in a confrontation very much like those experienced by police departments all over the country during the sixties and now into the seventies. There was no guarantee that any of the systems that we had set up would function. There were too many variables on both sides to be certain. If radicals, either right-wing or left-wing, set off a bomb in a public building close to the center of town, it might well do the two things we feared most: arouse the crowd to action and trigger reactions by town vigilantes.

We did not expect this to happen. But several days before, detectives had raided a bomb factory on Elm Street and confiscated some explosives. I was thankful that, over May Day, trained Army bomb squads attached to the National Guard would be available to deal with such problems.

But still, we had to worry about dangerous individuals. One suspect from the Elm Street raid was still at large. We had eight detectives trying to locate him. A last-minute inquiry on the case revealed that there had been no progress.

We had been more fortunate with regard to other potentially violent individuals. A black extremist suspect in the bombing of the Berkeley Police Department was under arrest in California. He had been in New Haven a few weeks before, reportedly to share his skills as an explosive expert with local radicals, and had been apprehended on his way to an airport for a return flight to New Haven. He was being held with two companions for possession of marijuana. He had been a concern of our Intelligence Division for several weeks, and his arrest would allow them to direct their energies elsewhere. From now on, we would almost be able to time the arrival of potentially dangerous contingents on whom we had information. I hoped that luck and hard work would allow us to keep track of them.

Thursday night, firemen drove a ladder truck onto the Green. As arranged, they tied the halyards on the flagpole twenty feet in the air and applied a thick coat of grease to the metal below. Among our many pre-May Day imaginings had been that a riot would be touched off by demonstrators hauling down the flag before the eyes of infuriated townspeople.

By eight o'clock in the morning, the crowd was already building on the Green. Watching the influx of people from the far side of Chapel Street, I walked down toward police headquarters. On the

60

way, I saw a police lieutenant walking to his assignment. Although most of the men had at least tentatively absorbed the spirit of our strategy, he had not. Instead of his regular police uniform he was wearing blue combat fatigues. He looked as though the war had begun. We had forbidden the use of sirens—police, fire, or ambulance—in the city over May Day to avoid triggering crowd reactions. I was not about to let unprofessional conduct by my men produce such a result. I ordered the officer to change back into his proper uniform and made the unauthorized alteration in dress the subject of an official reprimand.

But an hour or so later, it was obvious that he had been an exception. The New Haven police were in position and out of sight. A few blocks away, observers from the National Guard were checking their deployment locations along the dispersal routes. Now things were under way, and we would see how the department would react under pressure.

The first near miss of the weekend was precipitated by the state police. We had decided to hold some of the available state troopers in a few downtown staging areas as reserve forces. My agreement with Mulcahy was that they were to enter the buildings—the Superior Court Building, site of the Panther trial, at Church and Elm, and City Hall, on Church Street, also facing the Green—from the rear doors. They were to arrive early, before the crowds had gathered, and they were to be as unobtrusive as possible.

At ten o'clock, after many thousands of demonstrators had gathered on the Green, a state police bus pulled up at the front entrance to City Hall. The troopers filed out and marched into formation, opening and closing the breeches of their shotguns and slamming metal around. A stream of militaristic orders echoed across the wide expanse of grass. Mulcahy had always believed in shows of force, and whether planned or inadvertent, this was a show of force *par excellence*. It looked like a deliberate challenge, and it brought the demonstrators surging to the fence of the Green, yelling and spilling into the street.

POLICE IN TROUBLE

Tense moments ticked by. Were there guns in the crowd? A single shot from the crowded Green could bring a deadly response from the troopers. I had no idea what instructions Mulcahy had given his men, but I knew that they were armed with lethal 00 buckshot, and I knew the effects that a volley of it would have on the wavering lines of protestors. Or perhaps a few insults, a rock or a bottle, would send the troopers across the street and into the crowd.

But there were no shots, and there were no provocations. The state troopers filed into City Hall and disappeared. From then on, the Friday demonstration went smoothly. Student marshals and Panthers themselves acted as buffers between police and demonstrators, and we listened to the speeches with equanimity.

During the afternoon rally, the one visible threat of trouble came from small groups of motorcycle-gang members who roared down Church Street alongside the Green, stirring strong reactions in the crowd. In Connecticut, motorcycle gangs are generally right-wing, and some of them are often eager to start trouble. Later in the day we received word that gangs from all over the state were on "runs," headed for New Haven. We dispatched cars to the New Haven exits of the Merritt Parkway. The officers stopped the cyclists on the exit ramps. They made careful inspections of the motorcycles and found motor vehicle law violations in almost every case. They informed the bikers that they would be subject to arrest if they did not turn back.

But if the motorcycle gangs were the only outward threats to the security of the rally, there were internal dangers that were not quite so evident. Over May Day a great many undercover agents from other cities, most of them from the Alcohol, Tobacco, and Firearms Division of the U.S. Treasury Department, traveled to New Haven to offer their services. John Wadduck, head of A.T.F. in Connecticut, worked closely with local law-enforcement officials, realizing the critical role of federal gun law enforcement and the necessity to share information gathered by his agency with all other agencies involved. His agents, complete with long hair, beards, and intimate knowledge of the internal workings of radical politics, circulated in the crowds and furnished us with excellent information to supplement what we received through our regular channels.

It soon turned out that some of the Black Panthers, despite the party's public nonviolent position, were trying to stir up trouble. We knew this not only from our informers and agents but also directly from the Panthers themselves. The Black Panther party had purchased two-way radios with which to direct their May Day operations. As we watched the crowds from a command post on top of the Union Trust building, on the northeast corner of the Green, we monitored their frequencies. Ironically, our frequencies were also being monitored at the time—not by the Panthers but by federal agencies who had contracted with Motorola for equipment so that they could listen to New Haven police bands in Washington and keep the White House informed.

While we watched the Panthers and listened to their radios, we heard them sending orders over the air: "Go over [to X] and see if you can get something started." A Panther would detach himself from his group and make his way to a designated location. By the time he had begun his speech, an undercover agent would be there. If the rhetoric seemed to be stirring the crowd toward violence, the agent would attempt to diffuse the situation by yelling "I thought you guys didn't want any trouble!" and "What do you want to do, get us all killed?" Whether the attempts of these agents were successful, or whether the demonstrators themselves were ready to listen but not to act, we never knew. And although several highly placed Panthers were among those giving the orders for agitation, the New Haven Police Department never challenged the Panthers' reputedly nonviolent role over the weekend. It was to everyone's advantage to have them maintain a credibly nonviolent image before the crowd. Their position, no matter how insincerely held by some of them, was absorbed by the demonstrators because it made sense. The party held publicly that although nonviolence was an absurd tactic in the face of an overwhelmingly violent government, revolutionaries would have to pick the time and place of their actions to be successful. But privately, their "politics of confrontation" seems to have taken into account that many of the demonstrators over May Day were not as radical as they would have liked and that a violent confrontation with police would do more to radicalize them than any number of inflammatory speeches. Part of the reason that the Panthers were not successful was undoubtedly because of a persistent rumor among radicals that the government had hatched a grand plot to trap every extreme leftist in the country on the New Haven Green and, as the saying went, "mow them down."

By Friday evening we were well into the weekend. The New Haven police had responded well. They had been vigilant, patient, and calm, and the pervasive fear that had taken over New Haven in the preceding weeks was beginning slowly to ebb. Those of the department's ranking officers not on duty returned to the Park Plaza, and we ordered dinner.

As it arrived, darkness was starting to fall. On the Yale campus, bonfires turned Gothic courtyards into primitive villages shining with dark faces, long hair, and bare torsos. Representatives of the Chicago Eight, and others, were speaking, chanting, and performing. In one Yale dormitory complex, the indefatigable Jerry Rubin was holding forth with his standard "We've got to burn white suburbia down" speech.

Suddenly someone, jumping to the stage and grabbing the microphone from him, shouted that Panthers had been arrested in downtown New Haven. Whatever the source of this completely false story, and whatever the intention of the *provocateur* who spread it, a crowd was on the streets in minutes. It was all harried marshals could do to turn it several times at strategic corners before it swelled to unmanageable proportions and headed inexorably toward the Green and, behind it, City Hall.

May Day: Crisis in Focus

We had just begun dinner when I glanced out the window. The sight was a shock. Hordes of angry protestors were streaming down Chapel Street.

As usual, there were no police visible around the Green. But fortunately, the squads had been held in their positions on its outskirts. We barreled into the elevators and moments later spilled into the street.

The call for men had already gone out. Instantly the squads responded. Pouring in and forming up in disciplined ranks, they turned the demonstrators slowly onto the Green, setting up lines along Chapel Street.

Minutes later, the rocks and bottles started coming. Student marshals were no longer able to function. Thousands of people who had been attending a dance at Yale's Ingalls ice-skating rink poured downtown, drawn by reports of action. The barrage of debris grew, and the mood of the crowd became intense.

Tear gas was brought up. The first volleys forced the crowd back toward the waiting and open gates of Yale. From then on it was cat and mouse. One store window and one bus window had been broken, but there were no injuries and there was no serious property damage.

As it turned out, it was fortunate that all but a few dozen of the people in Ingalls rink had come downtown. Shortly before midnight a bomb exploded in a basement locker room in the rink, tearing up chunks of concrete in an entryway that a short time before had been full of people. The blast warped metal and threw showers of broken glass sixty or seventy feet into hedges across the street.

We did not know then, and we do not know now, whether a member of the radical right bombed the rink trying to kill demonstrators and retaliating against Yale for harboring them, or whether a radical leftist did it in an attempt to destroy Yale property and stir the demonstrators to counteraction. It is an indication of the nature of extremist politics that although the situation would point to the radical right as the most likely suspects, this terroristic tactic could have been used by either side. Although we could prove nothing, our most likely suspect was a member of the radical left.

Friday night faded into Saturday morning. As the time stretched out slowly, our hopes for a successful weekend began to grow.

By Saturday at one o'clock in the afternoon, the Green was strewn with bodies lounging in the sun. People played games, smoked marijuana, and waited for things to begin. After the confrontation of the night before, they perhaps felt that they had in some small way encountered "the enemy." Now they relaxed and enjoyed their comfortable position in the center of occupied New Haven. Here and there they built human pyramids or gave guerrilla-theater performances. By this time it was obvious that the demonstration as such was a played-out form, a form without a concrete function. The gathering itself had emerged as its own *raison d'être,* and individuals had emerged more important than any of the speakers or "leaders." Isolated groups of blacks moved through the crowd cautiously, holding themselves aloof.

A game of "buck-buck" began at a tree just inside the Green, across the street from City Hall. An anchor man, long-haired and naked to the waist, bent over and wrapped his arms around the trunk of a tree. His teammates did likewise behind him, until they formed a human caterpillar ten bodies long. Another team lined up twenty yards away, and, running one by one, leaped onto the caterpillar's back—the object, if there was any, being to crawl to its head and break it down.

Cheering grew, and bodies smacked together. Fingernails left scratches that colored the heaving pile of bodies, and onlookers pressed in. More sweating bodies could be seen nearby, joined in a circle. Others tried to break out by hurling themselves against the ring. Was this practice for breaking through police lines?

Suddenly there was a roar of voices. The Yippie yell rose above it, and the crowd convulsed like a giant nerve net, surging over the fence past two soft-hatted cops and pouring out into the road toward City Hall, shaking their fists and screaming, several thousand strong. Stragglers came running from blocks away.

In a flash the mood of the afternoon had changed from peaceful to tense, baiting, ugly. A few shirtless bodies reached nearly to the lines of police that filed out of City Hall and formed up on the side-walk, helmets on and visors down.

This was it. There were squads of policemen stacked up inside the building and around the corner. Guardsmen filled the court-yard in the rear of the building. Squads of cops and units of the Guard were waiting around the Green, capable of sealing off three sides of it in an instant.

An orange soared out of the crowd, and then a tin can. There was a tear-gas unit hidden in the doorway of City Hall. It stayed where it was while we waited for the student marshals to react. They had been scattered around the Green and caught off guard by the sudden surge. Now they streamed to the front of the mob, placing themselves between protestors and police, their yellow headbands forming a thin line against the background of seething bodies. Black faces appeared among them, shouting, "The Black Panther party doesn't want this! Now is not the time! You'll only get your-selves gassed and shot! Now is not the time for a confrontation!"

I couldn't have agreed more.

Minutes went by, with cops standing quietly in formation. We let the traffic increase slowly, making it harder for the demon-strators to cross the street now that debris was no longer being thrown. Chants grew up: "Free the Panther Twenty-one; free the Panther Nine," referring to the New York as well as the remaining New Haven defendants. It soon became clear that if there were weapons in the crowd, they would not be used. And for once, the supply of rocks and bottles seemed to have run out. Confronted by the marshals, forced to see human beings instead of blue-uniformed "pigs," they shouted at them and cursed them; but their violence remained verbal. I wondered whether the police department's performance over the weekend would go some of the way toward making them see policemen as human beings too.

The buck-buck game had nearly turned into a spontaneous riot. Tired of playing, the group had decided to fake a rush at City Hall. Their movement had intentionally or unintentionally set off the rest of the crowd. For a long time the tenseness hung in the air.

But by two o'clock the crisis was over. A Black Panther party sound truck, a Volkswagen bus with a speaker projecting through the roof, drove up to the edge of the crowd. "All power to the people!" yelled the voice at the mike. "When the Black Panther party says 'off the pig' we mean 'off the pig.' We mean to leave him dead in the street. But we never said to do it like this!" He reiterated the Panther position that anyone who tried to stir up trouble was a *provocateur,* and a *de facto* pig. I had to admire the way in which —if it was planning and not simply internal inconsistency—the Panthers played their dual role over the weekend. "We don't want a situation," he said, "where there's a massacre." And he went on, "A riot is not what's happening. The only thing that's happening is an organized group with guns shooting these fools!"

Whatever their motives, the Panthers somewhat belatedly helped cool things off. The afternoon went by, and the speakers spoke— but I couldn't help dwelling on the reaction of my men under pressure. I remembered with pleasure one sergeant in particular, whom I'd disciplined just a week earlier, standing calmly and professionally in front of his men. Even he seemed to have absorbed the mood. By Saturday the men were starting to be proud of themselves, and there was a pervasive feeling of confidence and competence. One newsman who had observed the carefully controlled movements of squads in and out of City Hall in response to the threat, sometimes in helmets, sometimes in soft hats, but always matched to the mood of the crowd at the particular moment, had rather amusingly captured the excruciating care which went into every small decision. "My God," he had said, "they're orchestrated!"

May Day: Crisis in Focus

The demonstration broke without incident, and the city remained peaceful until early evening. Around 8 P.M., however, a storefront called New Politics Corner was gutted by fire. The New Politics Corner, a reform liberal office on one corner of the New Haven Green, had served as McCarthy headquarters for the 1968 Presidential primary and later as headquarters for black mayoral candidate Hank Parker. The fire brought crowds of spectators down from Yale. They streamed down Elm Street, spread out along Church, threatening damage to stores and offices, and occupied the steps of the courthouse. The situation was critical.

I spied a young marshal and called him over. He was slim and baby-faced—an extremely unlikely-looking candidate for mob control. I asked him to try to clear the courthouse steps. Incredibly, he managed to gather a few other marshals and, with them, to cajole and coax the hostile crowd back onto the Green. His efforts had brought things under control again.

Once the mob had been confined to the Green, they stayed there, throwing things and yipping and cursing. We waited a long while, dodging rocks and bottles, hoping the demonstrators would tire or run out of ammunition. Finally it became obvious that they were doing neither, and the barrages of debris flew at us more heavily. I was on the verge of calling for tear gas when a huge bottle—it turned out to be a champagne magnum—struck me in the chest. The officers near me saw me stagger back and catch my breath, and they surged forward angrily. I put off calling for the gas for a moment, because I wanted to avoid giving the men the impression that I had reacted out of personal anger.

The evening wore on, and the crisis spots shifted. But by now the policemen were feeling that they knew how to handle things. And the demonstrators almost seemed to look on their rushes and sallies as games. The Green was clouded with gas that drifted in the treetops, and the streets reeked with it as the wind blew it up. But no one was dead, and no one was injured, and no property damage had been done by the crowds. The time got late, and the

69

crowd thinned, and then the sky lightened, and New Haven was quiet. It was Sunday morning, and May Day was over.

There were over 600 newsmen in New Haven over May Day. So many came to report on the beginning of the revolution, on the decimation of an American city, on police brutality, on Black Panther insanity, on guns and bombs and fires, that sorting them out and accrediting them all—from representatives of the "underground press" to national magazines, radio and TV reporters, and even foreign television—had been a major task for Tom Brunner, one of the department's civilian planners. When the weekend was over, there was nothing for them to report but why those things they had come to observe had not happened. One reporter got a partial answer when Brunner's wife drove him to the train station in a battered car covered with flower decals. Others analyzed the reasons in other ways.

The police department got a great deal of credit for preventing violence. I told the press quite truthfully that the performance of the men of the New Haven department over May Day had given me my proudest moment as chief.

I was well aware that other factors—the enlightened policy of the Yale administration, the cool, dedicated, and sometimes heroic efforts of the marshals, the strongly nonviolent stand on the part of the demonstration's organizers, and the actions of the Panthers themselves—had been as decisive as we had in preventing violence. I knew that sheer luck had played a huge part. Although I had no sympathy with the stated object of the May Day demonstrators— to free the defendants in the Rackley murder case without trial— I wondered how much longer the nation's leaders, by refusing to respond to widespread dissent on the issues of war and race, and on the broad range of underlying social problems that aggravated them, would continue to depend on police to keep apart segments of society that never really needed to be set against one another.

But for the time, it was enough for the New Haven Police Department to look back over the weekend and take pride in the fact that it had done its job well in the face of tremendous challenges. There had been more pressures on them—as there are on any police—to act badly than there had been to act well. The President, who termed student protestors "bums," and the local politicians, who were always ready to bring out the worst in people for their own ends, had sent strongly negative signals that had pervaded the atmosphere. Community pressures and peer-group pressures had added to these.

The national recognition that the department received for its May Day performance reinforced the good instincts that had begun to develop. In training programs after May Day, we were to hear little of the "bigger sticks and more guns" rhetoric that is so common to police. When that rhetoric did come up, it was countered by suggestions that there were other ways to do things. Many cops began to believe that nonviolence could, in some senses, be the policeman's first line of defense and perhaps his second as well. People began to believe that intelligence and sensitivity really could work more effectively than night sticks and guns. A great many things seemed suddenly to have become possible.

But all this was tempered by the knowledge that none of the fundamental realities of police work had changed. Sensitivity, although it can break through in the course of a profound experience —and I do not think it is too much to say that for most police forces a challenge as intense as that offered on May Day would be a profound experience—must be nurtured, encouraged, and rewarded if it is not to be lost. In most police departments, this simply is not possible. There are too many people, and too many forces, working against police for sensitivity and professionalism to have a chance. Many of those people and forces surfaced over May Day. But then they disappeared—and their exposure was lost.

The recognition that the police department received for its May Day performance had made it a greater threat than ever to the New Haven political machine, reinforcing a set of antagonisms that although by no means unique to New Haven, have been operating there for years. It was, in a way, ironic that a police department had been so lavishly praised for giving the kind of service that, after all, should have been expected of it all along. The simple fact, however, was that cities and towns get the kind of police service they demand and pay for and that the New Haven department had been the exception rather than the rule.

Days after the May Day demonstrators had left New Haven, the violence that had been avoided there erupted at Kent State and Jackson State to sear the national conscience and divide the country more deeply than it had been divided in a century. In a sense, the exception was obscured, and the rule reasserted itself. Although major demonstrations and confrontations lay bare for an instant all the forces that influence police, and although they force police departments to reveal their true characters, they do not show what gives the "rule" its force; they do not show police departments from the inside. To recognize what a police department is, what its problems are, and what attempts to improve it are up against, we must look at the department through the eyes of the man who runs it: the chief of police.

3
Chief of Police

IT WAS BUILT IN 1874. Walking through the dilapidated doors past Victorian formations of reddish stone, you had a feeling that its architect had grandiose notions. When you learned that he had been an alderman and this had been his first creation, the structure began to make some sense. The stairwell, arching up past peeling paint, filled with dirty illumination that spilled from oversized windows onto dirtier steps, seemed to gut the building of useful space. A knowledgeable stranger, asked what city agency would be likely to have its offices here, would almost certainly have answered, "The police department."

Police in America are appropriately thought of as society's servants. As such, however, they have usually inherited the servants' quarters. Shoving them into the grimy back rooms of municipal architecture too often shoves them into the grimy back rooms of politics and corruption as well. Perhaps the best functioning part of the building that housed the New Haven Police Department

POLICE IN TROUBLE

prior to 1968 was the second-story back door to the Mayor's office. Directing traffic through that door was sometimes more complicated than directing rush-hour traffic in downtown New Haven.

I was sworn in as chief of the New Haven Police Department on March 12, 1968. Serving an East Coast city with a major university, a trade and manufacturing history reaching back to Colonial days, and a complex tangle of racial and ethnic groups, the department had been around for over a hundred years.

A new police chief is faced with an overwhelming crime problem in his city. He knows that citizens are not safe on the streets; that there is widespread fear everywhere; that robberies, muggings, and burglaries are occurring at every moment; that narcotics use is threatening the lives of addicts and that their crimes alone threaten the security and property of vast numbers of his city's people; and that organized crime or criminal organizations are widespread in their activities and many times unchallengeable in their power.

A conscientious, ambitious, honest, and intelligent police chief wants to fight back at crime. He wants to combat street crime, strike hard at organized crime, rid his city of narcotics, and attack white-collar crime on a broad basis. On his first day at the job, however, he is likely to find that he can't get a letter typed, an order given, or a request made. His office is staffed with inefficient clerical help and often furnished with castoff chairs, desks, and cabinets from the Board of Education. The shabbiness extends from the office of the chief to the streets, where policemen drive dented cars with hundreds of thousands of miles on them and use battered, defective equipment. Even in cities like Kansas City, Missouri, and Los Angeles, where money is available, police facilities are new, and equipment is the finest money can buy, material things are often but a gloss over dehumanized structures that remain after years of neglect. Negative attitudes, obsolete procedures, and rigid policies are hidden behind the modern buildings whose existence betrays attention to the symptoms, but not the causes, of the low position of police in society.

74

Chief of Police

The material things by which policemen are surrounded have a great deal to say about that position. Almost without exception, a new chief of police is a product of the department he will head, and his twenty years or so in it are likely to have made him cynical. His attitude is likely to be tacit acceptance of his position.

Many of the problems which hamper police in their day-to-day activities and which often make them unable to begin meaningful attacks on crime are a function of police-department budgets. Nearly every police department in the country has to go begging at budget time. When they do, the volatile issues of crime are likely to be manipulated rather than solved, as police chiefs must exaggerate and dramatize, often by inflating crime statistics that may be deflated again in election years, to pay for the smallest improvements. Consequently, a new chief usually spends his tenure trying to rectify the problems he sees when he first walks in the door.

When I took office in New Haven, the departmental budget was coming up for approval before the Board of Finance in four days. I called the clerk of the department, an elderly man who had long been breathing the stale air of police headquarters, and asked to see it.

Like any other bureaucracy, police bureaucracies, left to themselves for years, divide into small, jealously guarded fiefdoms. Protecting his, the clerk informed me that the budget had already been "made up."

When I got a copy of the "made-up" budget that was supposed to rule the operations of the New Haven department for the fiscal year 1968-69, I was faced with a combination of waste and inadequacy that was, and is, typical of police-department financing.

The building that held our offices was scheduled for demolition, but the budget contained $30,000 for an intercom system for it. As it had for years, the budget also contained money for a departmental tailor, who although he drew the salary of a ranking officer in the department, had largely ceased to function. And then there were little things like six power lawnmowers. Our downtown station was entirely surrounded by concrete. The lawn of Station 2, several miles away, the location of training operations, was the responsibility of the parks department. I eliminated the intercom, the tailor, the lawnmowers, and many items like them. When I finished, I had red-penciled $100,000. Although this was not a large percentage of the total budget of approximately $3.5 million, it *was* a large percentage of the money that had not already been committed for salaries, which represented the great bulk of the total. I hoped that the Board of Finance would be impressed with the cuts, because I planned to ask them for the $100,000 back, plus an additional $400,000. Some of that money would go toward alleviating the most obvious material deficiencies of the department, but the great bulk of it would be used for personnel—to create new staff and support positions.

As in Kansas City, Missouri, a few departments do not have to beg quite so hard at budget time. The police department of Kansas City operates on a budget that is allocated by a Board of Police Commissioners appointed by the Governor. It is, by law, a fixed percentage of the city budget. If the city spends more money, the police department gets more money.

But police departments that do enjoy such financial support have been unable to alter the quality of their personnel or to make changes that would alter the way their men interact with the public, so that they become more human. In investing most of their discretionary money in computers and other hardware without primary attention to the police who must use them, they have been unable to attack the basic problems of police work.

Even a police department like Baltimore's, which has been one of the nation's most innovative in its use of personnel, falls into the "material trap" occasionally, as a statement by one Baltimore planner indicates. While making out an application for funds for a helicopter, he was asked what the department would do with it. "Hell if I know," he replied. "We'll worry about that when we get it." This attitude is typical. Police chiefs know that those who appropriate their money are more likely to do so for hardware and gadgetry than for more intangible benefits like the improvement of personnel.

With these dangers in mind, I made out a new budget and submitted it to the Board of Finance. I had the full support of Mayor Richard Lee. New Haven under Lee was a dynamic city. He had superimposed a powerful redevelopment agency, and the nation's first antipoverty agency, Community Progress, Inc. (CPI), upon the old structures of city government, and these allowed him to move forward independently of the city's political machine.

Lee was one of the few mayors in the United States with a clear vision of what a city ought to be, and following the riots of 1967 he turned his attentions to the state of the police department. Lee commissioned a study of the department which showed it to be nonfunctional in many respects. He knew how badly the money in the proposed new budget was needed. So, along with a few sympathetic Board of Finance members, he succeeded in winning approval for it. After less than a week on the job, I was already in a better position than most chiefs of police.

The study Lee had commissioned had been done in 1967 by Dr. John Herder, a telephone-company executive on loan to the police department. As a lieutenant, I had been assigned to work with Herder and therefore was intimately aware of the problems cited in his report. They are typical of the problems of most police departments.

Since about 90 percent of a police department's budget is normally spent meeting payrolls, the effective use of personnel is the most pressing need in police work. But prior to 1968 the New Haven Police Department, with approximately 430 men and an annual budget of over $3 million, could keep only twelve to nineteen cars on patrol at a given time. Of course, there were detectives and traffic-enforcement personnel, but the patrol division, the heart of the police department, had largely ceased to function.

Much of this inefficiency was the result of inadequate leadership and management within the department. As the Herder report said, "The main problem appears to be a state of immobility. The men who run the department appear to be dazed and demoralized. The department seems to have lost its capacity to initiate and sustain administrative action." It went on to say that "The men of the department are stunned by the increasing magnitude of the task facing them. They are sobered by the limited resources available to them. Clearly, there is little the department can do about these circumstances."

Officers who have worked their way up through police-department ranks to become assistant chiefs, chief inspectors, and captains find themselves in middle-management positions in multimillion-dollar enterprises without the training, and often without the inclination, to handle management and planning problems. In most police departments ranking officers have become clerks or petty bureaucrats by default. Often the administrative structure is cluttered with leftover paper figures from previous political situations. The result is that the bureaucracy runs itself, but little else.

This difficulty often extends to the chief of police himself. As the Herder report pointed out, "An important cause, however, is the management climate of the department. The Chief of Police apparently does not see himself as an administrator. Rather, he appears to see himself as the 'head cop.' He is far more sensitive to interpersonal aspects of his role than he is to the executive aspects." The report went on to say, "The basic executive functions of planning, organizing, directing and controlling are not being carried out adequately in the department at the present time."

Most police chiefs find themselves in this situation initially or eventually fall into it. Even with armies of paper-pushers below them (who have few functions other than to receive reports from subordinates and forward them to superiors), chiefs often end up performing their functions. For instance, the New Haven Police Department had become the victim of an *ad hoc* system of responsibility whereby the dog warden, the armorer, the departmental tailor, and the maintenance superintendent reported directly to the chief. These inefficiencies illustrate the administrative confusion and waste of personnel that pervaded the department at all levels. The chief did what the ranking officers were supposed to do, who in turn did what secretaries and clerks were supposed to do, and the men in the street ended up without leadership, without support, without supervision, and without discipline. If they ever knew what was expected of them, they certainly were under no compulsion to do it.

The Herder report had found that "police supervision is one of the weakest features of the present department." It was clear that the department's officers were needed not in the station house but on the street. Toward this end, the new department budget contained allocations for clerical and paraprofessional personnel that allowed sixty sworn officers—12 percent of the force—to return to patrol work in a period of three months. It was obviously far more efficient to hire paraprofessionals at $6,000 a year, in order to get sworn officers into the streets, than it was to hire more policemen at $10,000 a year and continue to allow the clerical functions to be performed badly.

With more officers on the streets and with the clerical help in the station house to back them up, we began to get supervision and leadership in the department. Unfortunately, however, there were even more acute problems with using personnel efficiently that could not be cleared up by a slightly higher budget. Like most police departments, New Haven's operated on rigidly fixed shifts, with one-third of the department working the midnight shift, another third coming on at eight in the morning, and a third taking over at four in the afternoon. Since criminals do not work such regular hours, having the same number of people working at five o'clock in the morning, when there are virtually no crimes committed, as are working at nine at night, when the switchboards are flooded with all kinds of calls, is an immense waste of money as well as a handicap to crime fighting.

POLICE IN TROUBLE

In some cities this arrangement is stipulated by law. In others, as it was in New Haven, it is a matter of union agreement. It was not until the police union contract came up for renewal that we were able to have this pattern altered—and only then by focusing on incoming recruits who had no representation in the union as yet. It was agreed that for their first two years, new patrolmen could be used on any shift. Since the New Haven Police Department had begun to demand far more of police officers than had previously been asked, there was a large turnover in the department at that time, and we were taking in as many as ninety recruits a year. These were used to augment patrol during the high-crime periods, and we were able to deploy as many as fifty cars during those periods. These men worked the day shift at times but were rarely used on the midnight shift. Since we felt these were better working conditions than those produced by the old, rigid pattern, we hoped that before the turnover rate lowered and the system became unworkable, the rank-and-file patrolmen would perceive their own self-interest and agree to greater flexibility.

This rigid shift pattern of inefficient distribution is not the most basic police manpower problem. Americans have less police protection in terms of man hours per capita than they had in 1940. At that time policemen in virtually all cities were working under atrocious conditions. New Haven's schedule of six-day weeks and ten-hour days was typical. When policemen began to react against these unbearable conditions and make contract demands on cities, the city's reaction was inevitably to avoid giving away money. So instead they gave away police service. Department budgets stayed the same, but work hours went down, and with them police protection. In 1940, New Haven was squeezing approximately 3,000 man hours of work a year from its beleaguered policemen. In 1970, the figure was just over 2,000.

In the wake of the riots that struck many cities in the 1960's, police salaries began to rise. New Haven experienced riots in 1967, and from a base salary level of around $6,000, police pay rose to

Chief of Police

$9,606 a year for a starting patrolman in 1970. Faced with such increases, cities could not—or would not—increase over-all department size, and increased efficiency, which in many cases could obviate the need for such increase, likewise proved impossible. Even given some overtime, greater mobility, and better communications, it should not be surprising that shrinking police departments are unable to keep up with rising crime.

In addition to these institutional handicaps, the police chief is almost always hampered in his effort to use his few men in treating problems of serious crime. One of the most widespread of these hindrances takes the form of public demands for unnecessary service. Policemen are expected to stand guard, for instance, at funerals and ceremonial occasions. The excuse for the presence of a policeman at a funeral is usually that he must direct traffic. But the real reason is invariably that the family of the deceased is politically important to the party in power. They may be influential voters, party workers, or generous contributors. In any case, the policeman is a symbol of official sympathy and concern and not a necessary functionary.

Another typical request that debilitates police departments is the request for a foot patrolman in a given neighborhood. The foot patrolman is valuable in extremely high density areas, but for the most part he is an anachronism and a romantic myth. Almost without exception, he is little more than a watchman.

At times citizens who demand unnecessary police service are strikingly inconsistent in their attitudes toward police operations. While many people like to have relationships with police departments that allow them to ignore traffic tickets and commit other petty infractions with impunity, these same people sometimes present police chiefs with demands for harassment of people who have violated no laws. In one case a New Haven lawyer who had gained a liberal reputation for his civil-rights activities came to me and asked me to clear the "hippies" out of a section of the downtown business district. He intimated that I should stretch loitering and breach of the peace statutes because store owners felt that their businesses were being hurt by the presence of young people who frequented the area. These people are inclined to wink and pat you on the back, as if a tacit understanding existed about this kind of police behavior. Making them see that police departments cannot serve as their own private armies is often impossible. Such demands, in addition to being degrading to the policeman, greatly hamper efforts to prevent and detect serious crime.

As the New Haven Police Department administration began to resist public requests for unnecessary or illegitimate police service, and as the department's supervisory personnel returned to the streets in order to give support and leadership to men who had in many cases been relieved of mechanical and clerical duties, the effective size of the patrol and detective forces rose sharply. Over a period of two years, the number of cars on patrol during peak crime periods rose to quadruple that of the 1967 figure. But increasing the effective size of the department's manpower was only half of what we needed. The other half was the management and planning that in fact had never been done. The department's ranking officers —lieutenants, captains, inspectors, and assistant chiefs—were the only people who had been in the position to do it, and they had never been educated or trained in management techniques. In New Haven all positions up to the rank of captain are Civil Service appointments. This means that in effect the chief of police, as in most cities, has no staff within the formal organization of the department. The new budget contained money for a civilian planning division that would provide the staff and the management expertise that the department so desperately needed. To head up this new operation I brought in Jay Talbot, the head of planning for New Haven's pioneering antipoverty agency.

Bringing civilians in at a high level of the department was, understandably, threatening to many of its ranking officers. It took some time for them to realize that the new division's purpose was not to shove them aside but to relieve them of responsibilities they had not been equipped to handle and to create a dynamic tension within the ingrown structure of the department.

I had contended to the Board of Finance that this division would more than pay for itself in streamlining the department, in researching new developments in police work, and in applying for grants from outside sources to implement them. Once the department's ranking officers saw that in fact this was what the division was doing, acceptance and eventually enthusiasm for it followed. The overwhelming majority of police departments have not been willing to experiment with the use of civilians, and because their own ranking officers have received virtually no management training, they are inefficiently run and planning is nonexistent.

The lack of such planning manifests itself directly in such areas as patrol methods and deployment. In most cities beat plans—the plans by which walking patrolmen or squad cars are distributed—are framed not around data on the intensity or frequency of crime but on the basis of vague geographical notions which divide cities up like pies. Busy street corners and congested arteries where crime seldom occurs are often patrolled heavily with no perceptible benefits. Although occasionally an alert supervisor may change the pattern, there is no systematic way for him to tell whether his changes are warranted by the actual crime pattern.

The lack of planning is reflected in detective procedures as well. The Herder report said of the New Haven department in 1967 that "even if some physical evidence is left at the scene of the crime, the Detective Division has neither the manpower nor the skills and equipment to analyze it thoroughly. Only one or two men handle scientific crime work for the entire division."

With regard to other methods of investigation, the Herder report went on to say: "For most common crimes—burglary and larceny —investigation is perfunctory. Burglary investigation amounts to little more than cataloging the losses, noting the point and method of entry of the burglar, assuring the homeowner that the department is working on the case. For the detective, this procedure is routine.

83

POLICE IN TROUBLE

It is conducted with little attention to detail, on the assumption that nothing much will come of it. Many times the investigation duplicates the work of the patrol officer. A few interviews constitute the total procedure for larceny investigations. At the end of the shift the investigating detective returns to the division room, writes a report, and files it along with hundreds of others which probably will never be looked at again." With practices like these ruling the operations of most of the nation's police departments, it is not difficult to see why police are unable to cope with crime.

One of the glaring deficiencies which the New Haven Police Department had in common with virtually all others was its antiquated system of record keeping. The analysis of records is vital to a police department if it is to process the large quantities of data it gathers and keep up with changing patterns of crime, if it is to solve specific cases, and if it is to be able to identify suspects or arrestees. Yet in virtually all departments, evaluation of records is impossible, and the records system itself is a shambles.

In addition to these planning and management problems, there are a variety of police functions whose quantitative evaluation is crucial. For example, when a person needs a policeman, he usually needs him in a hurry. "Response time"—the time between the reception of a complaint at police headquarters and the arrival of a squad car on the scene—is one measure of police adequacy that can be made objectively. It is possible to have bad police service with good response time, but it is impossible to have truly good police service with bad response time.

Before the spring of 1968, when the New Haven Police Department received a call, it was routed to one of two precinct desks, where the information was scribbled on a piece of scrap paper by the desk sergeant, who performed numerous other duties as well. When he was free—and when he was so inclined—he would telephone the message to a dispatcher, who in turn wrote it on his own scrap paper. When the dispatcher got around to it, he assigned a car to the call. If the men didn't like the sound of a particular complaint—a barking dog, for instance—the scrap usually ended up on the floor. At the end of the night all the scraps ended up there anyhow and were thrown away. There was no way to check response time. In fact, there was no way to tell whether a call had gone out unless the policeman receiving it had remembered to enter it in his log. This arrangement operates in many cities, especially smaller ones. In cities of all sizes it may be policy to "stack" calls—that is, to wait to give out assignments until patrol cars are free. When this happens routinely during high crime hours, response time is atrocious and the chance of apprehending criminal suspects virtually nil.

The New Haven department instituted a system whereby phone operators receiving complaints recorded them on standard forms, stamped them with the time, and dropped them onto a rapid conveyor to the dispatcher a few feet away. The dispatcher in turn stamped the form with the time he assigned a car to the call, the time the car radioed that he had arrived, and the time the car returned to patrol. No calls were stacked. If patrol cars were busy, supervisory or detective cars responded to complaints—including those involving barking dogs. The response time on such relatively insignificant calls was naturally longer, because priority was given to serious cases, but in the end the average response time for all calls—checked by computer—was under three minutes.

While improving response time and measuring it objectively added to the quality of police service, there were still other problems and possibilities that had to be dealt with. For example, to increase police visibility and therefore heighten the effect of our limited man hours, we installed bright green lights on the roofs of police cars. These could be seen for many blocks, and therefore greatly increased the deterrent effects of patrol. In addition, since they were so wired that they could not be turned off except by turning off everything else in the car—including the radio—they made it more difficult for men to sleep on the job.

But a police chief's problems transcend these technical areas, and better management and more effective use of the people he has will not in themselves make his department either more humane or more effective in fighting crime. The ultimate limitation on the police department is the recruitment base with which it operates. A chief is likely himself to be an example of his own problem. Because the policeman's job is not prestigious, because until very recently it was abysmally paid, because working conditions are usually atrocious and advancement is prohibitively slow, few people with more than a high-school education are attracted to police work. Because only a very specific kind of person is recruited for and welcomed by police departments, they are on the whole ingrown and defensive, and therefore both educated people and minority-group members are hesitant to join them. Police recruiting is usually non-existent. Departments wait for prospects to come to them, or to be brought by politicians. This policy—and these low standards—apply to recruitment for every position on the department, police departments being virtually the only organization of their size to take every level of their management and administration from the same recruitment base. This is why leadership is almost always non-existent. The situation is analogous to IBM being run by management teams selected from among the janitors, or the chairman of the Joint Chiefs of Staff being selected from a group of draftees with only high-school education and basic training.

Even those recruits who want to be good policemen are seldom given the training which would prepare them to do their jobs well. A new police chief will find that training is an area in which he has relatively wide discretion and in which he can make rapid innovations at a relatively low cost. Unfortunately, almost nowhere is the attitude of the public or of state or city administrators conducive to making police training more meaningful. In Connecticut, this attitude is reflected in the state law, which, although it requires 1,200 hours of training for a licensed beautician, requires only 200 for a policeman. It is difficult to believe that lawmakers feel that it is more important for beauticians to know how to curl hair than for policemen to know when to use their guns, how to make legal arrests, and how to mediate in domestic quarrels.

This sorry situation is reflected in the scandalous state of police training throughout the country. In most police departments, the Director of Training is an officer who has been transferred into the job from another position and forced to become an overnight expert in an unfamiliar field. The exceptions are equally inefficient: retired military officers or F.B.I. agents who, in addition to lacking general knowledge about training procedures and educational theory, know little or nothing about the problems a patrolman faces from day to day. Very few training directors have a perspective on the police role other than the one that is gained from long years within the system itself. Consequently, training in most American police departments —whether it is limited to a week of following an experienced officer around, as in many small departments, or whether it is supposedly sophisticated and takes as long as six months—is worse than worthless. Using the old-fashioned lecture technique almost exclusively, it teaches the mechanical use of weapons without teaching when to use them, and policemen come to see themselves as little more than extensions of their guns and night sticks. It teaches—or tries to teach—what laws are, without allowing for sensitivity or a sense of priorities in enforcing them, and policemen come to see themselves as bloodless extensions of the legal code, remaining unaware of the dangers of unconscious—or conscious—"selective enforcement."

Before 1968, training for the New Haven Police Department was ten weeks long. It included a week on the firing range, a week of first-aid training, and a week of lectures on the law. The head of the Traffic Division taught traffic control, and foot doctors were brought in to lecture on the care of the feet. In such a program there was no attempt to make recruits aware of the complexities of the social situations they would be entering, no effort to unearth their underlying prejudices and capabilities, and no provision for teaching them nonviolent ways of handling potentially violent situations. Neither was there any frankness about the dangers of corruption, nor any mention of the absurdities and frustrations the cops have to put up with. There was no sense that any policy or order could ever be changed or even questioned, no reflective discussion among the recruits about what it meant to be a cop, and no speculation about what they would do in certain hypothetical situations. Old cops simply taught young cops what they had learned, and that ultimately boiled down to how to cover themselves, how to stay safe, how to do the minimum of everything and get away with it. The training was geared to the lowest possible mentality. What idealism managed to creep in was laughably simplistic. Everyone made it through. No one was washed out. Two weeks after graduation, any recruit who had taken the training seriously could see that his ten-week experience related neither to the realities of the street nor to the realities of the department.

Among my most urgent requests was for the authority to hire a professional Director of Training. The new director was a civilian with a Master's degree in educational psychology who had been the director of the Neighborhood Youth Corps in New Haven. Besides his skills in psychology, he brought with him experience in curriculum development and teaching, which allowed him to experiment with a number of techniques ranging from psychodrama, role playing, and audiovisual aids to discussion groups and other techniques. In addition the training program was expanded to twenty weeks.

Because police departments operate from top to bottom with a narrow variety of underqualified, undereducated, undertrained, insufficiently motivated people, supervision and discipline in police departments are almost always inadequate, and accountability is virtually nil. One concrete manifestation of this situation is a police department's written policy. Of the forty thousand police departments in the United States, twenty-five at most have clearly defined written policies on crucial issues that can mean life and death, or success and failure, in the day-to-day running of the department. The policies of other departments are agglomerations of petty rules that are impossible for any human being to obey. Consequently their function is highly negative. Because very few rewards are available in police work, punishment is the only form of control available. Departmental rules virtually assure that if a supervisor does not like someone beneath him, he can "legitimately" discipline him for some infraction of a petty regulation, such as one forbidding smoking on the job, or one pertaining to minute details of the officer's uniform. From the slim but devastating volume of departmental regulations that rookie policemen received in New Haven before 1968, to the seven-inch-thick manual of the Oakland Police Department containing two full pages on how the braid is to be arranged on the uniforms of the chief and the assistant chiefs, police-department policies are virtually all oriented, effectively if not consciously, toward this technique of negative control.

New Haven had no written policy on the use of guns, nor on when policemen were to engage in hot pursuit (which is one of the most frequent causes of serious injuries to policemen), nor, in fact, on anything of importance regarding the conduct of a police officer. Decisions on these matters rested, as they do virtually everywhere, on the individual cop's instincts, limited—where enforceable—by state law. In Connecticut as in most states, for example, it is legal for a policeman to use deadly force to halt a suspect when he has reason to believe a felony has been committed. Since the law requires clear probable cause, not mere suspicion, for an arrest, a Connecticut policeman could conceivably shoot someone whom he could not arrest. The New Haven Police Department modified and tightened this policy several times, at first prohibiting the use of guns in cases in which the felon was suspected to be a juvenile and later confining the use of guns for the most part to situations in which it was absolutely necessary to save life.

Other determinations were more difficult. For example, shortly after I took office a policeman was pursuing a stolen car when it stopped in a neighborhood of low-income high-rise buildings and the suspect fled on foot. The officer fired a warning shot into the ground. The bullet ricocheted up, hitting the suspect and injuring him. He was a thirteen-year-old boy.

I considered forbidding warning shots. But before issuing such an order, I called the Dixwell Legal Rights Association, a group that offers legal aid to people unable to afford lawyers, and asked the advice of its director. He convinced me that a suspect was entitled to a warning shot if the officer felt he would have to use deadly force in the situation, and he offered the obvious suggestion that warning shots be fired only into the air.

In formalizing policies like these, the objective was to give policemen guidelines that would help them rather than burden them with endless petty regulations that were basically nonfunctional. Police badly need such general statements that will define the areas of their responsibility and clarify priorities. If they do not have them, they are largely directionless and are subject to all kinds of diversions and manipulations. The policeman on the street has enough instantaneous decisions to make and enough opportunities to be second-guessed. He needs written assurance that if he acts in accordance with certain guidelines, the hierarchy of his department will back him to the limit. At the same time, these policies can act as important deterrents to peer-group or public pressures to be "tough" or political pressures to be heroes in the defense of a particular set of interests or way of life. In addition, written policies made available for public inspection and influence are an indirect way in which citizens can review police behavior.

4
Politics and Police

THE CONDITION OF THE New Haven Police Department in March 1968 was almost identical to that facing most police departments today. Its problems were staggering, and its limited resources had never been utilized effectively. A police department in a situation like this is vulnerable. Its weakness dictates that it cannot deal effectively with crime, and it is left open to the influences of more powerful individuals who would use it for their own purposes. The problems that I have talked about so far are difficult enough for a police chief to handle. As difficult as they are, however, they are not the most important explanation for the abysmal state of police service in the United States today.

There is, essentially, one issue on which every police chief stands or falls as a professional, one issue which decides whether his department is going to enforce the law fairly, effectively, and honestly. But it is a virtually unknown issue.

In his book *Keeping the Peace*, Herbert Jenkins, chief of the At-

POLICE IN TROUBLE

lanta Police Department for the past twenty-five years and one of the nation's more successful and dedicated chiefs, makes the following statement:

> Respect for the law is the policeman's Hippocratic oath. It is his guiding star of survival in a democratic society. The newest police recruit can never hope to move forward as a career policeman without this fundamental principle. Respect for the law.*

This is the kind of statement that police chiefs, no matter how principled and dedicated, are constantly making. Police chiefs, like all policemen, are defensive within their own circles and mistrusting of the public. Some make statements like this for the reason that Jenkins undoubtedly did—in the hope that a new type of policeman will come to believe it and that it will become a self-fulfilling prophecy. But as a generalization about the state of law enforcement in America today, it is simply not the case. In almost no department in the country does advancement depend on respect for the law. Leaving respect aside, it does not even depend on enforcing the law. In fact, it often depends on particular varieties of the opposite. This fact is virtually never treated by students of police problems. The fourteen-volume study of the President's Commission on the Administration of Justice, undoubtedly the most comprehensive survey of the law-enforcement process ever done in America, completely ignores the greatest threat and detriment to fair and effective law enforcement. This threat is illegitimate political interference, often intimately connected with corrupt and criminal interference.

Some months before May Day, 1970, when mounting pressures for political interference in the administration of the New Haven Police Department were already beginning to make the situation untenable, I had been contacted by the office of Cleveland Mayor Carl Stokes. Cleveland was without a police chief, and the Mayor wanted to interview me for the job.

Several days later I was met at the Cleveland airport by a Stokes

---

* Herbert Jenkins, *Keeping the Peace* (New York: Harper & Row, 1970), p. xi.

aide. In our preliminary talks about Cleveland, he admitted that the city's problems were phenomenal. He outlined a picture of political manipulation and corruption similar in many ways, and identical in many others, to that of New Haven before 1968.

A visit to Cleveland's Public Safety Director confirmed the aide's estimation of the city's problems. He painted a picture of a department riddled with corruption and torn by open racial hostility.

After these discussions, I was dropped off at a large Cleveland hotel where I had been registered under a fictitious name. The choice of a police chief would be a delicate and possibly dangerous one for Mayor Stokes, and rumors were already filling the police department.

In my hotel suite, I had not finished hanging up my coat when the phone rang. "You'll make a good chief, but you're not black," said an anonymous sarcastic voice.

Later, I went downstairs to one of the hotel's bars. Someone was waiting for me. I had never seen him before, but he was not a total stranger. Cops, no matter how far apart, usually manage to recognize each other. I had no sooner sat down when he began—without identifying himself—to outline the situation in the Cleveland department in his own way. He was there to let me know that I might talk to the Mayor, but I would have to deal with the cops, and they were ahead of me.

He began by asking questions that showed that he knew a great deal about my background. He knew that I had been in a Catholic seminary for a time. He asked me whether I knew a certain priest. He asked me other questions having to do with the Church. Then, sounding a familiar note, he said, "They'll like you here." The talk was evasive and vaguely threatening—but the point was clear: I would have to reckon with them if I became chief of police of Cleveland, and they were very certain of their strength.

The next morning, I met with Mayor Stokes. He went into greater detail than the others had on the problems of the department and proved completely aware of the complex tangle of problems that face police chiefs. He said that the department was in very bad shape, and that he was determined to do something about it. The police crisis in Cleveland had reached such proportions that he was considering extreme action, even to the point of calling out the National Guard to take over the department's functions. He reported that without being diligent in the pursuit of it, many officers in supervisory positions found graft amounting to three times their pay in their desk drawers each week. Policemen habitually went to drive-ins and watched movies through their tours of duty. In one instance, cops had beaten up a supervisor who ventured into a drive-in to get his men out. White cops refused to patrol the ghetto. They routinely parked one two-man patrol car and rode four in another. Discipline was nonexistent, public accountability was nil, and the department had, in fact, become a danger to, rather than a guardian of, public safety.

Many of Stokes's conflicts with the department stemmed from his handling of a Cleveland riot during which black community leaders had urged him to pull white policemen out of the ghetto. They had promised to restore order themselves, with the aid of black cops. Taking an immense political risk, Stokes had heeded their suggestion, and the tactic had worked. But the department's latently racist attitudes had been exacerbated, and since that time white cops had all but refused to police the city's ghettos.

I told Stokes that were I to be offered the job, I would need many new civilian positions created within the police department. Cleveland shares many of New Haven's problems—problems that are common to the vast majority of police departments. The chief there is completely alone, surrounded by Civil Service employees and others who owe their allegiance not to him, not to law enforcement as a profession or to departmental policy, and not necessarily to the Mayor, but to politicians who work behind the scenes and to the crooks paying them off. Stokes agreed that the positions would be needed but observed that they would have to be approved by the City Council.

In addition to the staff issue, there was another disturbing aspect to the Cleveland situation that had not been a problem in New Haven. The police chief there serves at the discretion of the Mayor. He is the only person in the police department not protected either by Civil Service or by the security of an appointment for a fixed term. This means that, as sincere and competent as the Mayor may be, if he is faced with severe public pressure with regard to the police department, there is only one person he can remove in order to pacify opinion: the chief. In Cleveland and in most cities, the police chief must fight the influence of politicians with underworld connections who control the lower levels of party politics no matter who controls the upper levels. He has the aid only of the Mayor, who is in a similar position. In such situations new chiefs can do little more than announce programs and policies that they suspect can never be carried out and hope that they are offered positions in bigger and better departments or somewhere outside the field of local police work before it becomes obvious that their departments are going nowhere, or before major scandals or incidents of brutality blow up in their faces.

I maintained contact with Stokes over a period of weeks. He was having trouble getting the City Council to agree to create the civilian positions I had mentioned. As much as the prospect of the job itself and the prospect of working for Stokes appealed to me I had to keep reminding myself that to go into the Cleveland situation all alone would be suicidal—and since without support and resources I could not hope to improve the department, I gave up consideration of the job.

In the end, Stokes hired a new chief from the Detroit Police Department. The new chief had been in office just three days when he was charged in the Detroit *Free Press* with taking bribes from an alleged abortion clinic. After his departure Stokes hired someone from within the Cleveland department. Not long afterward, he lost his Public Safety Director, Benjamin Davis, who quit to become head of the federal sky marshals.

The problems of the Cleveland Police Department are the problems of the New Haven Police Department, and they are the problems of most police departments. The structure of the department and the politics of its city ensure that a police chief will be unable to make fundamental institutional changes leading to lasting reform and professionalism. Police chiefs are politically vulnerable, and especially so if they serve at the discretion of their mayors. Since they do not have control over promotions in their departments, and since they are isolated from the command structure below them, they can offer no rewards to good cops. Any experimental steps they wish to make place their careers in jeopardy. Unlike people in other professions, unemployed police chiefs have few places to go. This leads to personal insecurity, which makes chiefs even less willing to take risks.

Most police chiefs, however, having come up through the ranks of their own departments, alleviate their insecurity—as much as possible—years before they become chiefs. They protect their own, they play politics, and they survive. If they serve in cities where crime machines hold the real power and lubricate police departments with illicit funds, the chiefs function in ways that perpetuate machine power and cut off police from broad democratic controls. It is only when they are threatened by ghetto riots or student unrest, or when gambling and narcotics activities become so widespread as to incite a public reaction, that they stand a chance of being exposed; and even when they are exposed, the staying power of the crime machine is usually far greater than the power of those political leaders who are borne upward by brief surges of public indignation. Consequently, the years come, and the years go, and nothing changes.

There is nothing more degrading or demoralizing to a police department than the knowledge that every favor or promotion within it is controlled by hack politicians and outright criminals. And there is nothing more nearly universal. Five years ago, anyone with the most superficial knowledge of the workings of the New Haven Police Department could point to the political power behind every captain on the force. Every cop who wanted to get ahead had his "hook"—or, as they say in New York, his "rabbi." Everyone owed his success to a politician—from the Town Chairman on down—or to an influential underworld figure. Needless to say, in a situation like this there was no chance whatever of the department functioning in the public interest.

A day after I had taken office, I closed the second-story back door to the Mayor's office and issued a renewal of a long-standing and long-ignored departmental order prohibiting any police officer from seeing the Mayor without the authorization of the chief.

Given the incredible tangle of grimy politics that still existed in the lower levels of government and in the structures of the city's political parties, this action was largely symbolic. But as a gesture it was necessary. It would be immediately evident to everyone in the police department that if I would not permit the Mayor who had appointed me to influence departmental promotions or assignments, I certainly would allow no other politicians to influence them.

Mayor Lee was aware of the connections between politics and police. As Allan R. Talbot points out in his book *The Mayor's Game*,* Lee himself was capable of intervening in the affairs of the police department to advance cops whom he considered honest and effective who otherwise would have been buried. Riding home with the Mayor in a car one day, I showed him a draft of my order. He frowned slightly, nodded, and then approved.

But this order was only the opening shot in the war to end political interference in the police department. The far more substantive challenge was to make clear in every way possible, to every man in the department, that political influence of any kind was out. There was only one way to handle the problem, and it was somewhat heavy-handed. The men were made responsible for stopping interference themselves. They were warned that if politicians or underworld figures approached me with requests for promotions, transfers,

* Allan R. Talbot, *The Mayor's Game: Richard C. Lee and the Politics of Change* (New York: Harper & Row, 1967).

97

or easy assignments for cops, the officers in question would be barred permanently from those positions.

The immediate reaction among the cops was total incredulity. Political maneuvering had been the basis for advancement in the department for so long that it was doubtful whether they believed there was another way to be promoted. I would not be surprised if they thought that promotions in the department would freeze until I resigned or retired. But they did believe me. And they did convey the message to their hooks. For the time being, political interference in the department all but stopped.

At the same time that I issued the order forbidding policemen to see the Mayor without my authorization, I issued another forbidding policemen to sell any kind of tickets or to have testimonial dinners held for them. It is common practice in many police departments for organizations such as the Police Athletic League to hold testimonials for others who are being promoted. As innocent as these affairs may seem—and as innocent as some of them may be—they are often occasions for practicing petty corruption. In the first place, whenever a town's "regular criminals" have a chance, they give cops money. Policemen will go into bars selling testimonial tickets and meet local bookies there. The bookies will purchase and pay for fifty tickets. They will then return forty to the policeman, who will sell them elsewhere and pocket the extra money. The bookies breathe easier.

But the real difficulty with testimonials is that the dinners themselves may be regularly attended by underworld figures or by people who require police favors. Typically, tickets for testimonials will sell for $7.50 or $10. The meals may cost $3 each, or less if the testimonial is given in a restaurant where the owner occasionally requires police favors. The difference between the ticket price and the cost of the meal goes into a purse for the officer who is being honored. It can sometimes come to a great deal. The present chief of police in one Connecticut city received eight thousand dollars upon being promoted to his position.

Politics and Police

This was another order that puzzled old-time policemen in the New Haven department. It was not merely that they had become accustomed to collecting purses swelled by the presence of crooks and gangsters at testimonials. They could not see why they were being singled out for deprivation, since the testimonial is a widespread phenomenon throughout local government and since prosecutors, judges, and many political figures continued to benefit from them after they had been forbidden to policemen. The danger of policemen selling tickets and promoting other enterprises is that such activities may become tantamount to shakedowns. Citizens may feel they have to contribute, and policemen may feel the same way.

There is great temptation for police to profit from their positions. The testimonial example illustrates the ease with which police can come to associate with underworld figures on acceptable social levels. But these examples only begin to explain the complicated interconnections between petty criminals, big-time criminals, and police. When connections like these exist—as they do in many more cities than we would like to imagine—police departments are worse than ineffectual; they are dangerous weapons.

These connections are invariably realized through subtle chains of control and reward that include not only the police but also politicians and the courts. Although some cities suffer only purely political interference, criminal elements often operate through the political structures themselves. Sometimes, for all practical purposes, they bypass them and virtually make appointments and promotions in police departments themselves. New Haven, where three different organized-crime syndicates have, for many years, operated a broad spectrum of criminal activity which characterizes organized crime, is by no means an extreme example of these forms of control. In New Haven, as elsewhere, organized-crime money is traditionally moved covertly into the coffers of both political parties —especially the party in office. This means that organized crime and politics are intertwined in an inextricable—and usually impenetrable—fashion.

Cities that have recently suffered scandals uncovering the influence of organized crime in politics are not exceptional for experiencing this kind of interference. Newark, Jersey City, and Seattle are exceptional only in that the interrelationships have recently been uncovered. The New Jersey scandals were exposed only because intensive federal investigations run by honest prosecutors intervened at times when corruption had become so widespread as to be impossible to conceal completely. In Seattle, a web of corruption was uncovered that eventually brought indictments of nineteen city officials.

Perhaps the best way to begin an exposition of the way in which police departments are controlled is with the figure around whom the various systems of control revolve: the political boss. Although political bossism was supposed to have gone out of style years ago in the wake of reform efforts that have swept nearly every city at one time or another, most cities are in fact ruled by men or groups of men who function covertly as bosses in much the same way as did the infamous figures of the past.

The primary strength of the boss lies in his political machine. Whether or not he has ever been elected or appointed to public office, the boss is the lynch pin of the machine, the focal point of all its various interconnections.

The machine consists of people who can get votes. It consists of strategically placed people in various communities who can remind voters of their obligations to the machine, who can publicize candidates, who can produce campaign contributions and make sure that people do not forget to go to the polls on election day. It functions as the basic source for candidates for patronage jobs in governmental agencies and can ensure that large groups of people in close-knit communities can be obligated to the machine—whole families through a single job, whole blocks by special favors such as extra police protection or street cleaning, whole neighborhoods by new public-works projects.

Patronage jobs must be approved, however, by the machine's officeholders. If the boss himself holds office, he decides, and he controls the grass-roots organization. They need his political image to survive, because they need a candidate who can win. If the boss does not hold office, he controls those who do to one degree or another, and he functions as "director of patronage." If the boss does not hold office, by definition the candidate who does is so weak that he needs the machine more than it needs him—at least at the outset—and so must give away power to be placed on the party's ticket.

If the political boss has control of the appointments to a city government, he has control over those who hold such appointments. He can replace them or have them replaced, he can embarrass them in various ways, or he can render them powerless by giving real control over their functions to someone else.

This means that political bosses control chiefs of police, who usually serve at the discretion of the mayors under whom they work and who therefore are highly vulnerable. Since bosses also control the boards that administer Civil Service examinations and determine advancement under that system, they are able to subvert Civil Service. Through the chief they can control who is assigned to such vital areas as vice, gambling, and narcotics investigation, and whether the department's Detective Division attempts to combat organized crime. Since they control promotions, the chief owes his to them more often than not, and any deviation from their policies or desires is sure to handicap the career of any officer in the department.

This arrangement assures that the political boss can do numerous favors for politically important people. He can have parking and traffic tickets fixed, he can assure that minor violations of numerous laws—from obstruction of public streets to liquor-law violations—are ignored, and he can deliver extra police protection for favored neighborhoods. He can do a great deal more as well.

101

POLICE IN TROUBLE

Political bosses control courts and prosecutors—or at least some of them—just as they control other segments of city governments. Whether elected or appointed, judges come by their positions politically. If they are appointed, the connection is direct. If they are elected, someone must agree to put them on the party ticket, and that person is the boss.

Judges are typically faithful party members who have run for other offices and failed, or who have been willing to serve the machine's interests in private law practices or in business capacities. This means that, below the federal level, they are seldom first-rate legal talents; they have had to make their way by means of influence rather than by legal brilliance or even legal competence, and they are compromised before they begin. The judge has considerable power to do favors for people which in turn lubricate the boss's machine.

Prosecutors are in much the same position as judges. However they come by their positions, they are seldom first-rate talents, and often their activities will be more or less controlled by the bosses who put them into their positions. They have virtually unlimited discretion as to which cases to prosecute and which to drop. Prosecutors often have political ambitions on which bosses can play and tend to use their public positions as steppingstones to higher office.

Often prosecutors are part-time officials and have their own private practices. Public business takes second place to private business, and when the two come into conflict, as they may, justice may not be served.

With the courts and prosecutors controlled by these webs of political influence, even when they are honest they seldom dispense justice. This is evidenced by the policeman's day-to-day interaction with prosecutors, which is frustrating at best. Policemen who know that they have built solid and well-documented cases against dangerous criminals are forever astonished at the process of plea-bargaining, by which prosecutors change serious charges to relatively minor ones to which defendants will plead guilty. From the prosecutor's point of view, it saves him the time and trouble of trying the case in court, it keeps cases off the crowded court dockets, and it does not hurt his conviction record.

In fact, given the incredible case loads with which prosecutors are burdened and the inadequate staffs they are given, plea-bargaining is often the only way to move cases forward. In some sense, therefore, the "revolving door justice" dispensed by our courts is comprehensible in terms of a lack of support for the criminal justice system, and with regard to some prosecutors it would seem that they have little choice but to employ it. To that extent, it may seem excusable.

What is not excusable, however, is the discriminatory way in which plea-bargaining operates. Because of public pressures for "law and order," prosecutors must gain maximum penalties for some serious offenders. These maximum sentences are virtually always given to the poor and to those without influence who cannot afford good lawyers. The reason is simple. The prosecutor, like any other political figure, gets along—and gets ahead—by doing favors for people. The people for whom he does favors are invariably people who will some day be able to do favors for him. Among this group are lawyers. They are not, however, legal-aid lawyers or others who deal habitually with the powerless. They are lawyers who have ties with the political machine and who can wield political influence.

A "good" lawyer in our criminal justice system is seldom one who is intelligent, hard-working, and dedicated. He is almost always one who knows the prosecutor and whose personal relationship with him ensures that his clients' cases are not among those very few that ever come to trial.

When politics systematically exert such illegitimate influences on a city's (or a state's) criminal justice system, the stage is set for politicians to paralyze police if they are good and control them if they are not. It is usually set for them to control those that they have paralyzed.

The party boss who controls politicians, patronage jobs in public services, and governmental agencies like police departments, along with the courts, is at the hub of a vast wheel of power that he can turn at will. But as yet we have not discussed perhaps the most important factor in the turning of that wheel in the processes of government: money.

The boss himself, at the wheel's hub, typically sees vast sums of money revolving around him, and he controls their direction. Because a boss or a group of bosses is primarily interested in power and not in money, the boss himself may not become extravagantly rich—and if he does, he may not show it. If he is a lawyer, it is true, his private practice will flourish. If he is an insurance agent or real-estate agent, he will do well. People find that doing business through politically powerful people makes things easier. Lawsuits are more likely to be won, zoning variances are more likely to be granted, government contracts are more likely to be awarded. As a recent account of the financing of New York's political boss, Carmine De Sapio, points out, "the political elite, in order to make anything from a comfortable living to a sizable fortune, go in for businesses which by their nature offer a front for the selling or lending of political influence. For a long time the most popular fronts were law firms and insurance companies. They have been joined in recent years by architecture and public-relations firms. All have in common the fact that their services cannot be arranged for by competitive public bidding, their fees cannot be based on what the traffic will bear, and there can be no probative evidence why one firm was selected in preference to another." *

But on the whole, the boss is concerned with maintaining his political machine, and consequently this is where the greatest flow of money comes. People in patronage jobs are expected to kick back part of their salaries to the machine in the form of campaign contributions. They may even be assigned a given percentage of their income to give. Businesses that receive favors from the machine also contribute, and money regularly flows from the public treasury

* Warren Moscow, "How Carmine De Sapio Made Ends Meet," *New York* magazine, October 11, 1971.

into the treasury of the party in power. This in itself is enough to pervert a city's resources and make good government impossible. It is enough to make a police department so much a part of the machine that it cannot possibly enforce the law fairly, efficiently, or honestly. But it is not enough to account for the state of police service in those places where it is at its worst.

A glance down the contribution lists of political parties in most cities will reveal the names of many convicted criminals. Gamblers will be especially prominent. The amounts that these people admit giving in public are, as a rule, only a fraction of what they give under the table. And there are usually underworld figures contributing to political parties who are so infamous that their names could not appear on the contribution lists at all. A look at such a contribution list begins to show the pattern of criminal involvement with boss-run politics that in its most advanced stages takes over police departments and the rest of the criminal justice system.

Gamblers are the most frequent contributors to political parties for two reasons. First, gambling is more widespread and enjoys greater public acceptance than most other crimes, and second, gamblers can profit more greatly from police connections than can other criminals because their businesses are relatively public.

The political boss who is in control of the police department, who determines who is placed in what divisions and who is promoted, is in an excellent position to help gamblers. Not only will police refrain from arresting gamblers who work for the political machine and who contribute to it; they will go elsewhere to keep up their arrest quota and drive out the competition. When this is possible—when gambling grows up and continues under police protection—other crimes begin to come into the open as well; prostitution becomes more widespread, and the drug traffic increases.

Under these conditions, organized crime moves in. It syndicates police-protected operations—or syndicates independent operations and then buys them protection—and often deals directly with the political boss in assuring that there will be no interference.

Gambling has long been the basis for organized crime's operations, because it provides a predictable volume of income whose source is so widely based that it cannot dry up. Gambling money is used to finance organized crime's entire complicated set of operations. This financing is big business. In the New Haven area alone, the yearly profit from gambling operations has been conservatively estimated at $3 million. Since the majority of Americans probably do not consider placing a bet to be a crime at all, and since those who do gamble resent being forced into illegal behavior by the law itself, people seldom consider themselves conscience-bound to take into account where their gambling losses go. But since they know they are breaking the law as it is written, they will be unlikely to turn against their bookies or numbers runners and expose them. Often, in fact, a neighborhood bookie is thought of as someone who is providing a service to the community at a risk to himself, and occasionally he is looked on as someone a little more clever than his fellows. If this is the case, bookies themselves may become minor political leaders, and the criminal hold on the government is strengthened.

With this well-protected access to the pocketbooks of the American lower and middle classes, organized crime is assured of a reliable financing for such operations as shylocking. Shylocking, or lending money at exorbitant and illegal interest rates, realizes a high percentage of profit. It can also drive fundamentally honest people into criminal activities in efforts to pay back loans, and many times it can set the stage for organized crime to take over legitimate businesses.

The typical shylock loan may be made at 20 percent per week, and it is made on Monday morning and must be paid back by Friday at noon, with interest. If the borrower cannot meet his obligation, he may find himself in physical danger. Or, if he has something that the mob wants, the loan may be "refinanced," allowing him to put up his possessions, or perhaps his business, as security.

If a legitimate businessman happens to run an enterprise—the restaurant trade is the best example—that banks and finance companies do not consider a good risk, he is often forced to go to underworld sources for loans in times of hardship, or to take credit from mob-owned restaurant-supply businesses. If he does, he often has put himself into a situation from which he cannot possibly escape. When he defaults on his payments, his restaurant falls into the hands of organized crime. It is not uncommon for businessmen to hasten this process by building up gambling debts to the underworld, then paying them back with shylock loans using their businesses as security, and end up losing them to the mob.

Once organized crime has taken over legitimate businesses, it turns them into fronts for other criminal activities as well as money-making enterprises in their own right. They provide receptacles for money from illegitimate sources. They are ideal media through which to filter gambling, narcotics, and other profits, as their books can be manipulated easily. And they allow mobsters to surface as seemingly respectable members of communities.

Money from gambling ends up financing the narcotics traffic as well as shylocking. Although it is rare for mobsters to deal in narcotics at the street level, they effectively control the wholesale heroin and cocaine markets and have made inroads into others. On the wholesale level, immense profits can be made from the narcotics traffic with relative safety by well-connected criminals with the cash necessary to finance narcotics import operations. Police are free to arrest addicts and small-time addicts-turned-dealers, but they are barred by a lack of resources and by various types of interference from striking at those who deal in narcotics on a larger scale.

Organized crime is not confined to running such wholly illegal activities. Mobsters will move into any area, from jukeboxes, vending machines, garbage collection, and pornography, to labor unions, wholesale produce, and entertainment, where they think they can make money. As they do, their respectability grows—and so do their contributions to the political machine in power. They may

107

branch out into such areas of white-collar crime as embezzlement and fraud, or they may operate rings that perpetrate more traditional crimes like auto theft or hijacking on a massive scale.

When organized crime and political bosses work closely together, or when bosses tolerate organized-crime activities and tacitly approve of them by making police, prosecutors, and courts ineffective in combating them, the machine has reached the proportions of a crime machine—and it has become capable of running itself for years or decades. In order to keep arrest rates up, police literally arrange large-scale raids on small-time bookie joints and other locations with the big-time criminals who control them. The police are safe because they are protected from all sides, and they may be making money as well. The small-time operators who are arrested do not care; they are well treated in court, and the mob pays them a bonus for submitting to arrest. The public is convinced that the police are trying to eliminate crime, and the statistics back them up.

The effects of such a syndrome can be devastating. Immense amounts of money flow from governments to organized crime through various enterprises and into the coffers of the party in power, and the city's progress is paralyzed. Its citizens are made the victims of unfair gambling odds, enormous rates of interest on shylock loans, and fixed prices on many mob-controlled commodities. In the end, there is only one way for the mob to enforce external cooperation and internal discipline, and that is through violence or the threat of violence. In this kind of situation, police are powerless to fight the crime machine and more often than not become a part of it. They are pinned down, manipulated, and coerced from all sides. Although the entanglement of the police department in political struggles and criminal operations in New Haven had certainly not reached the proportions described above, the essential elements were present: political figures willing to intervene in the internal affairs of the department, and sophisticated gambling operations whose leaders had the desire and the resources to influence departmental promotions and assignments.

Politics and Police

New Haven has a political boss, Arthur T. Barbieri, who was perennially involved in Democratic party politics and eventually became Democratic Town Chairman. By 1959 he had been appointed Public Works Commissioner, a job that carried with it the power to make many patronage appointments. In that year, as Allan R. Talbot relates in his book on Mayor Lee, the Board of Assessors in New Haven had been involved in a scandal. "The Republicans had charged, and their charge was valid, that the board had illegally reduced assessments on some 125 residential properties, several of which were owned by friends or relatives of Barbieri's." In connection with this scandal, says Talbot, "[Lee] took another bold step. He dumped Barbieri from his Public Works job. During the 1960 campaign, Barbieri had been charged with running the department like a private club. These charges, plus the disclosure that Barbieri's relatives had received 'illegal' assessment reductions, made him a liability in Lee's judgment, so he privately asked Barbieri to resign. Barbieri did not like giving up his job (he still harbors a grudge over it), but he knew the rules of the game." *

Barbieri may have been out of his job, but he was far from out of party politics, and in fact his strength as New Haven's boss continued to grow. Among his powers was to create a judge of probate, Charles Henchel, who was elected to office when Barbieri put him on the same ticket with Richard Lee. In Connecticut, although they are given city office space, probate judges pay their own staffs and run their courts like businesses. Rather than earning salaries from the city government, they collect percentages of the money they handle. The amount they can make is virtually unlimited. In addition, as Talbot points out, ". . . the judge of probate is a dispenser of considerable patronage. . . . The appraiser jobs and high fees which go with them are handed out to party faithfuls. Henchel's Republican opponent had campaigned to reform the court, which he claimed was corrupt. He had even charged that

* Talbot, pp. 55–56.

109

Henchel and Barbieri had received appraiser fees from the court in the past." *

In addition to these political figures who would later demonstrate their eagerness to intervene in departmental policy-making, there were also gambling figures who had a greater interest in departmental promotions and assignments. During the early fifties, when a member of a New Haven city commission owned a bar that booked bets, the operation was so secure that the bar opened on Sunday mornings as a service to its betting customers, even though no liquor could be sold until afternoon. Eventually detectives raided the bar. It turned out, however, that the case could not be successfully prosecuted. Shortly thereafter, all supervisory officers in the Detective Division were transferred. It was an object lesson to the department.

A later incident involved a neighborhood bar in New Haven which was a front for a well-known bookie operation. Its owner boasted for years about his influence on the police department, which was considerable. One day a New Haven detective arrested him on a gambling charge. This particular error led to the detective's transfer out of the gambling and narcotics squad. The chief of police at that time, however, managed to resist strong pressures to transfer him out of the Detective Division altogether and into patrol.

The constant attempts of political figures to make department policy and the efforts of prominent gambling figures to influence departmental promotions and assignments convinced me that an effort had to be made to shield the department from outside influences. The frustration of these efforts made it increasingly difficult to perform the duties of chief with integrity and eventually led directly to my departure from the department.

The first clash arose over a seemingly minor issue: my effort to

* *Ibid.*, p. 231.

place a restaurant off-limits to police officers. The establishment involved had been identified by federal, state, and local authorities as a gathering place of major organized-crime figures and the location where many violent crimes had been planned. Although the restriction was not publicly announced and had a negligible impact on the tavern's business, the owners retained Judge of Probate Charles Henchel, intimate associate of New Haven Democratic boss Barbieri, to challenge my action. On the Board of Police Commissioners the two members with the closest ties to the Barbieri machine, one of them his brother-in-law, supported the challenge. Although a majority of the board ultimately upheld my action in this particular case, the symbolic significance of the episode was graphically clear. It was evident that the Barbieri machine, now that it controlled city hall, intended to make basic decisions affecting the integrity of the department and that it was insensitive to the power organized crime could gain over the police through this process. The second round of the emerging struggle for control of the department began shortly thereafter. It concerned Civil Service.

Down through American history there have been major systematic efforts to insulate political structures from illegitimate interference. With regard to police departments, the most comprehensive effort in this direction was the institution of Civil Service. Civil Service is common to most large city departments and is expanding to smaller cities. Its purpose—to give government employees job security (which is one way of fighting interference) and to make advancement dependent on merit rather than on political or criminal connections—is unassailable. But its lack of success within police departments particularly has been spectacular.

Advancement under Civil Service in the New Haven Police Department depends on performance and written tests, along with "efficiency ratings." Officers with the highest combined totals of written test scores (55 percent of total) and efficiency ratings (45 percent) are promoted first when openings arise within the department. Civil

111

POLICE IN TROUBLE

Service as it now functions in New Haven, as in most cities, is a cynical joke. Policemen do not trust it, and no honest or intelligent politician respects it.

Before 1968, the written Civil Service examinations were made up by a three-man board appointed by the Mayor. The board served without pay and had no expertise whatever in the field of police work. Tests were essay examinations, but officers received grades like 98.765 percent. As if that were not absurd enough, examinations regularly took as long as two years to grade. Sometimes this was simply because of neglect, but more often it was because of behind-the-scenes political maneuvering, which was more effective as the time between the administration of the examinations and the posting of their results increased. It was not at all uncommon for the results of written tests to be withheld for many months pending the outcome of an election.

No policeman could ever see any written examination but his own, and there was no way to determine whether the tests had been objectively graded. The written test scores were open to all kinds of manipulation. At any rate, they were completely unsuited to the jobs they tested for. The captain's examination—which should have tested for management skills—typically asked questions about the motor-vehicle laws.

But the truly corruptible element in the Civil Service system was the efficiency rating. Whether a policeman received a high or a low rating was without exception determined by the power of his political connections. Before the departmental order forbidding policemen to see the Mayor without my authorization, it was common for policemen to go to City Hall at the time of Civil Service examinations and request good efficiency ratings. In addition, they would go to their "hooks" and ask them to use their influence in obtaining good efficiencies. In fact, the power of a strong "hook" invariably increased under this system, as policemen who had missed promotions would try to determine which political figures had been behind those policemen with the highest efficiency ratings and would make it a point to approach them at the time of the next examination. With this kind of institutionalized begging going on, the Civil Service system acted as a cover for the very manipulations it was supposed to eliminate. It functioned perfectly to make the public *think* that the system was objective and shielded behind-the-scenes machinations of politicians and crooks.

Shortly after my appointment as chief, after we had made an effort to ensure that efficiency ratings would be determined from within the department, I indicated to Mayor Lee that I did not trust the written Civil Service examinations. With his approval, the city hired a national testing firm that had developed batteries of examinations for police departments around the country. The tests were not ideal, but they were far better than anything that had preceded them and helped to eliminate some of the cynicism that had previously surrounded the written examinations.

As a second stage in reforming promotional practices, the department developed a new system for determining efficiency ratings which placed principal reliance on the supervisory structure. Under this proposal an officer would be evaluated by several of his immediate supervisors who were directly familiar with his work, and that evaluation would be reviewed by higher commanders. Officers would be furnished with written evaluation reports to assist them in improving their work performance. In addition, formal reports and elaborate appeal procedures were intended to preclude unfairness or arbitrariness.

Precisely the same configuration of political figures, including the two commissioners involved in the off-limits episode, moved to block this proposal, which, when combined with honest written exams, would have effectively removed patronage from police promotions. Over the course of many months I was unable to get action on this proposal from the Board of Police Commissioners. Indeed, one commissioner had stated to the department's legal adviser that he expected the efficiency ratings of each man to be determined by the commissioners themselves, who had no personal knowledge of the men but who, in several cases, were tied directly to Barbieri's machine. It was obvious the politicians were moving to assert control of the department. A chief of police cannot long resist such a concerted onslaught in an institutional and political setting like New Haven.

A police department that is backed by strong public support and by honest and dedicated politicians can do many things to improve its internal efficiency, to make itself effective in fighting crime, and to eliminate political interference within its ranks. But cities that do this are usually only islands in seas of corruption and massive criminal activity, and at best all they can do is to build walls around themselves which make them temporarily effective. Some crime problems are by definition problems which cannot be handled by local departments. They are regional or national in scope, and although they may be treated partially on a local level for a period of time, their underlying structures and their pervasive influence can seldom be eliminated.

Thus far state and federal agencies have been completely ineffective in rooting out widespread and subtle networks of crime and corruption and thus have been ineffective in supporting local police departments.

In most cases state agencies—that is to say, state police departments—are unable even to approach such problems. They are primarily traffic agencies. The Connecticut state police force, for instance, is just under twice the size of the New Haven Police Department. Even if state police forces were expanded and assigned to such statewide problems as organized crime and narcotics, however, there is a far more important block to their effective cooperation with local departments that would have to be removed: simple interagency jealousy. This is a problem that *has* been recognized by law-enforcement studies in the past, particularly by the previously cited report of the President's Commission on Criminal Justice. Interagency power struggles and jealousies are quite often politically motivated. They are therefore always concealed from the public. This makes them and their effects extremely difficult for the public to understand. Sometimes such rivalries develop over the allocation of federal funds. At other times they develop over other issues. But whatever their origin, they paralyze state and local police alike and ensure that even the limited resources of law-enforcement agencies are used to inappropriate ends.

The very nature of the day-to-day responsibilities of state police, and, in fact, their jurisdictional limitations, make it unlikely that they would be able to deal effectively with problems like municipal corruption, organized crime, or narcotics, which are invariably interstate problems.

This means that these problems should be attacked by federal agencies. The principal federal organizations able, at present, to deal with interstate crime problems are the F.B.I., the Bureau of Narcotics and Dangerous Drugs, and the independent strike forces set up by former Attorney General Ramsey Clark.

The F.B.I. is limited in these areas by its dependence on local police forces for much of its information. To the consternation of local police departments, the exchange of information with the F.B.I. is strictly a one-way street. Although F.B.I. agents are constantly asking local police forces for information, they virtually never give out information themselves. Consequently, there is no organized national effort on the problem of organized crime. Given the corrupt nature of so many local police departments, this reluctance on the part of the F.B.I. is understandable. In many cases, they could just as well have given their information directly to local criminals.

But local corruption does not account for the F.B.I.'s inability to deal with this serious national problem. While the F.B.I. may have built itself a national reputation for crime fighting, in recent years it has done more to attract publicity to the radical left than to fight the truly dangerous criminals who have pervaded so many

115

areas of the country's public life, and to local police departments it has seldom proved useful. Indeed, the bulk of federal action against organized crime has been taken by Justice Department strike forces in which the F.B.I. does not often participate.

Local police chiefs who are battling to make their departments functional and effective in the most basic areas of law enforcement and order maintenance are, even under the best of conditions, greatly handicapped by their inability to treat these wide crime problems, and they are completely powerless to free themselves and their departments from the negative effects of broad social problems and political deficiencies that perpetuate them.

The structure of the police department and the nature of its relationship to the politics of its city virtually ensure that a new police chief will be unable to make fundamental institutional changes in the department which will lead to lasting reform and professionalism. Most police chiefs are extremely vulnerable politically. Since they do not have true control over promotions in their departments, and since they are isolated from the Civil Service command structure below them, it is exceedingly difficult for them to make reforms and changes. Any experimental steps they wish to make place their careers in jeopardy. And, unlike people in other professions, there is little else that a police chief can do. Given this tremendous insecurity, the most that a chief can do in a bad situation—and most American departments are bad situations—is to come in with a flourish, polish the police cars and purchase new equipment, make a certain number of improvements in efficiency and technique, and hope that these cosmetic improvements will gain him the reputation sufficient to get him out of the department before it collapses like a house of cards around him.

But most police chiefs do not even go this far. Because the crime machine keeps the city sewed up under its own power, these departments usually do not collapse. Inefficiency goes on; brutality goes on; frustration for honest and idealistic cops is the rule. If nations either rise or decline but never stand still, then the United States is declining with regard to criminal and social justice, and the deadly interconnections between crime, politics, and police are helping to pull it down.

5

The Pawns of
National Power

THE POLICEMAN WHO IS ALIENATED from the society he must police is far away from its leaders. To the cop who patrols the streets of our cities, the White House and the power it represents are faraway abstractions. Yet at times, especially in times of crisis, a President can, with a few words, reach down to where a cop walks his lonely beat at midnight, or into the squad car where he listens to the static of his radio.

Why?

Because there is no *profession* of law enforcement.

Above the cop on the beat there is a vacuum of true leadership that exists in few other professions. Into this vacuum the country's most powerful politician can move in times of crisis. The policeman whose ideals are systematically destroyed, who finds that practices that are good one day are bad the next—for reasons having nothing to do with good or bad—searches for the authority behind these shifts of value. When he finds it, he may respect it only as authority.

119

POLICE IN TROUBLE

The policeman who can see no leaders above him comes to understand that there are no true leadership positions in police work. When he realizes this, he realizes that he himself can never become a leader. So he may resign himself to becoming a professional follower. His ambition becomes to escape from pettiness and condemnation, to have security in the face of criticisms that come at him from all sides.

Under these conditions, men whose emotions are strong and whose frustrations are great are capable of being used by politicians —whether it is a President in extraordinary times, or a lesser figure in ordinary times—who see the power of their badges and guns. Because the policeman's weakness can be translated into power, those who deal in power seldom seek to improve the policeman's lot. More often they seek to use his discontent. They say that they are with him, and they are. But they are not with him as he wants to be, as he could be, or as he ought to be. They are with him as he is after he has absorbed the disappointments of his profession. They seek to channel his frustration to their own ends and make political capital out of his defeat. Rather than providing him with the means to overcome his problems and the problems of his profession, they may urge him to lash out—at targets they select. The policeman often loses sight of the fact that when the crisis is over, these same people will feel as they always did, that his low social status and poor image—although there is no reason to change them —make him a person to be shunned.

When the nation is gaping and divided like an open wound, when tensions are so great that something must explode, the policeman, for all his limitations one of the most politically sensitive beings in our society, listens in the vacuum for signals. He knows, better than anyone else, when the political figures in power, of either party, sincerely seek to avoid unfairness and when they will uncompromisingly condemn insensitivity or brutality. While their voices fill the vacuum, he may not be systematically helped, but at least appeals are made to his best instincts.

120

The Pawns of National Power

But if such people are not in power, he receives other signals. He is encouraged to vent his frustrations within the context of his daily work rather than express them in terms that will alter that context. When this happens, the policeman becomes the least that he can be—a hard knot of prejudices, the products of his work, which cannot rationally be untied. If there is anything that he has learned well, it is the game of violence that he is forced to play every day, and so his actions are likely to be violent.

This same dynamic applies to other groups who perform police functions. Although they do not face the institutionalized frustration that characterizes the policeman's occupation, National Guardsmen are likewise sensitive to political signals coming from above. And although the rigidity of the military command structure has allowed them no experience parallel to that of the police patrolman —although they have seldom been called upon to exercise personal discretion in delicate situations—when this leadership fails or is perverted, they are left without the fatalistic patience of the experienced cop. Consequently, their actions may not be covered by the thin veil of subtlety that the policeman's job demands, and the effects on them of national political signals may be more blatant and equally disastrous.

In the spring of 1970, on Monday, May 4, barely a day after the pro-Panther demonstrators had left New Haven, M-1 rifles spoke out in Ohio. A group of bedraggled, ill-trained, poorly led, and hostile people who happened to be wearing National Guard uniforms—an army in a police situation—marched among "the enemy" on the campus of Kent State University, their rifles locked and loaded. Short on sleep and patience, caught in a crowd that they had been assured was antagonistic toward everything they held sacred, a few of them came to see the Kent State campus as a free-fire zone. Assaulted with rocks, insulted and jeered and harried, marched on a fool's errand down a hill and back again, they reached a turning point in American history. They wheeled and knelt in a skirmish line. In their sights appeared figures—people

121

running away, people standing, people lying on the ground. They opened fire.

Tragedy has been the word used by many to describe the killings at Kent State University and later at Jackson State College. Certainly the 1960's, a decade of burning cities, turned to a panorama of divided campuses and spilled over into the 1970's like a tragic play searching for an ending. Abstractly we may wonder whether there are forces moving behind history that make certain events necessary. More concretely we may wonder whether it was inevitable that some time in the spring of 1970, if not in New Haven, then at Kent State, if not there, then at Jackson State, and if not there, then at some other college campus, the surgings of the student protest movement would finally be halted by a hail of bullets.

But for Americans to accept the word "tragedy" as an explanation for the killings at Kent State University and at Jackson State College is to prejudge these questions. It is to imply that those events were written somewhere in the sky and played out by human beings who had no responsibility for them. On the stage, when such events occur, they are rightfully called tragedies. But to talk about historical events in this manner is to talk in a way which, were it taken seriously, would stop society from functioning. When the law is forgotten, and when the sweep of history is made to take the shape of political fiction, the realities of power take over from the ideals of justice, and there ceases to be any possibility of freedom in a free society. To playwrights and some politicians, the events at Kent State and Jackson State might have been tragedies. But if our society has a true commitment to the fair and equal enforcement of the law and to the concept of justice, they have to be called murder.

In the days following the Kent State killings, two questions were raised in the minds of a public that was aroused over this issue to an extent that it had seldom been aroused before. What had really happened? And why had it happened?

The Pawns of National Power

The first question rapidly separated into smaller ones. It was obvious that the National Guard had fired on Kent State students, that they had killed four and wounded nine others. But had the Guard been responding to sniper fire, as first reports indicated? Had they been surrounded by dangerous groups of students, had they run out of tear gas, had their lives been in danger? In the absence of authoritative answers to these questions, the public divided along political lines. People believed what they wanted to believe.

The second question—the question of why the killings had taken place—was a question on many levels. As a police chief, my first reaction was to analyze police and National Guard behavior. It was plain that the National Guard had acted as an independent military force rather than an extension of local or campus police departments and that its liaison with university officials had been insufficient. The Guardsmen had gone onto the campus with loaded rifles. And either their command structure had broken down, or it had been inadequate.

Beyond these observations, unanswered questions lay in two directions. What were the particular facts of the situation? Here the question of why merged into the question of what. And, on a broader level, what were the forces that had caused campus unrest in the first place and necessitated police or National Guard intervention? There was a need for an authoritative, meticulous examination of the circumstances of the Kent State and Jackson State killings and for a broad consideration of the basic questions of campus unrest. It was clearly a problem upon which President Nixon had to act. As it had been so many times in the past, the Presidential reaction was to form a commission.

Probably because of the publicity that the New Haven Police Department had received for its handling of the May Day rally, and perhaps because the Administration felt the commission needed a law-enforcement officer, President Nixon asked me to serve on his Commission on Campus Unrest.

123

POLICE IN TROUBLE

In the preceding five years three separate commissions—the Kerner Commission, the Eisenhower Commission, and the Katzenbach Commission—had been formed in order to look into national problems that, in one way or another, directly involved police. And while one of them had in fact been responsible for much of the legislation in the 1968 Omnibus Crime Bill, I was skeptical of the way in which commissions had been used.

But I did feel that Presidential commissions could perform vital functions, and I especially felt that it was imperative that the overall causes of campus unrest and the specific events at Kent State and Jackson State be investigated. Consequently, I accepted the President's invitation to serve on the commission, although with a certain uneasiness.

I could not help but remember the extent to which our May Day success in New Haven had depended on sheer luck, as well as on the efficiency and good will of such people as the student marshals. I knew that the men at Kent State and Jackson State, and perhaps their officers, had been subject to many of the same pressures and influences that had come to bear on my men in New Haven. And while the hysteria surrounding May Day was far more intense than anything faced in either Ohio or Mississippi, we had had, after all, three weeks in which to prepare.

But when I began my service on the President's commission I knew—and, as the only police officer on the commission, I may have known better than the others—the extent to which individual policemen, or military men acting as policemen, can and must be held responsible for their own behavior.

The chairman of the President's Commission on Campus Unrest, William Scranton, former Governor of Pennsylvania, did a statesmanlike job of pulling the commission together. The commission members were James E. Cheek, president of Howard University; Revius O. Ortique, Jr., a New Orleans attorney; retired Air Force Lieutenant General Benjamin O. Davis; Joseph Rhodes, Jr., a graduate student at Harvard University and Junior Fellow there; Erwin

The Pawns of National Power

D. Canham, editor-in-chief of the *Christian Science Monitor;* Bayless Manning, dean of the School of Law at Stanford University; and Martha Derthick, the commission's only woman and Associate Professor of Government at Boston University.

Our individual prejudices at first nearly led me to despair that the commission would ever reach agreement. When we finally got down to the basic issues involved, however, we found that they were relatively clear and that we could work well together toward a common solution. In the end, we were able to draft and submit to the President a unanimous report. Its general recommendations, and its specific findings with regard to the Kent State and Jackson State killings, are a matter of public record. They need not be repeated. What does need to be considered, however, is the Administration's reception of the report of the commission which it had appointed with such great fanfare and solemnity. That reception has a great deal to say about the workings of national leadership in such situations, both generally and specifically with regard to law enforcement.

The commission was charged with compiling a penetrating and definitive report on a major national problem within a period of three months so that its recommendations could be available before the beginning of another academic year, in time to prevent further disorders. An indication of the difficulty of this assignment is that staff and research people eventually numbering 170 had to be screened, hired, coordinated, and given assignments around the country.

The commission succeeded in delivering its report to the President on September 20. The report was as firm in condemning the tactics of violent students and the deficiencies of university administrations as it was in insisting that the national leadership provide meaningful moral direction and that the police and National Guard be held responsible for any criminal actions they might have taken. But it took the President as long to draft a statement of his reactions to the report as it had taken us to compile it. The only immediate

125

reaction from within the Administration came from Vice President Agnew, who termed the commission's report "pablum for permissivists."

It was widely known that the President found the report politically unacceptable. His feeling was made evident when the Presidential adviser who had been assigned as liaison with the commission came to work one morning to find his office dismantled and his personal effects in the hall.

Not until January—after the Congressional elections of November came and safely went—did President Nixon react personally to the commission's report. And at that time he chose to take issue with the commission's findings that the nation's chief executive had not properly discharged his responsibilities for moral leadership. He implicitly denied that speeches in which he had called college protestors "bums," and in which (after Kent State) he had implied that "when dissent turns to violence" overreactions on the part of policemen and Guardsmen could be expected, might have communicated its own tone of permissiveness to law-enforcement officers. He magnified and publicized only those portions of the report that dealt with the inadequacies of universities and with the intemperate actions of radical students.

To the casual onlooker, it might have been unclear why the President, if he was going to treat the report in this manner, had bothered to impanel the commission at all. While there is no doubt that he was surprised by the commission's findings and recommendations, it now seems that—as many contended when the commission was announced—he had resorted to it only in order to calm public anger over the Kent State and Jackson State issues and to make it seem as though the Administration was taking forthright action. In effect, the commission turned out, as so many commissions have in the past, whether intentionally or not, to be a substitute for substantive legislative action on the one hand or for criminal prosecution of those liable to it on the other. In effect, the Administration had—at least with regard to law enforcement—

clearly opted to maintain the leadership vacuum which would allow it to manipulate the "law and order" issue for its own purposes. Instead of resolving to get to the truth behind campus unrest and to find some way to bring together those whose reactions to Kent State had been "they should have killed more" with those whose reactions had been "the government is made up of fascist murderers," the President ended up effectively maintaining the first position. In doing so, he forced certain commission members to defend their stands concerning moral leadership, police professionalism, and responsibility before the law. This, in turn, had the effect of making the commission itself take sides and of obscuring the original balance of its report. In the heat generated by the subsequent exchanges between Administration and commission members, the commission's long-range recommendations were in danger of being lost and its positive functions of being vitiated.

In June 1971 I was invited to testify before the Senate Judiciary Subcommittee on Administrative Practice and Procedure on the subjects treated in the Scranton Commission report. My thoughts at that time reflected some of the disillusionment that some commission members, and many Americans, had come to feel over the Administration's reception of our report. I told the subcommittee that Presidential commissions could become excuses for neglect and that there was a danger that Presidents faced with national crises —such as civil disorders, political assassinations, or campus unrest —might impanel them not as steps toward substantive remedial action but as substitutes for it. This could be done without attention to the social forces that had caused the crises, which would therefore remain untouched and potentially explosive.

During the period between January 1971, when the President made his first public comments on the Scranton Commission report, and June of that year, it had become increasingly obvious that the Administration was dedicated neither to a broad attack on the social problems that directly affect police work nor to law enforcement with professional leadership free from partisan political interference.

Another season of demonstrations rolled around, and in the face of a new May Day threat—the radical threat to "shut down Washington"—the Justice Department took over the task of defining the tactics and strategies that the Washington, D.C., police would use in handling the demonstrations. These developments—based on the principle of indiscriminate mass arrests—seemed to me to be particularly dangerous. In my testimony before the Senate subcommittee, I observed that the control techniques used at the May Day demonstrations in Washington had caused serious and possibly irreparable harm to the cause of professional law enforcement and that the Justice Department policy of illegal mass arrests was an affront not only to the Constitution but to all able law-enforcement officials who were attempting to provide fair and equitable law enforcement.

The Washington example provided an illustration of the extent to which even relatively powerful law-enforcement officers are vulnerable to political manipulation through the vacuum of leadership in law enforcement. The Washington Police Department, under the direction of Jerry Wilson, had built an excellent and well-deserved reputation for sensitive handlings of demonstrations and disturbances over a period of years. It had handled with success civil-rights and war-moratorium demonstrations consisting of hundreds of thousands of people. Wilson had always insisted upon legal arrests, and he had been among the innovators in techniques of nonviolent crowd control.

But in the face of the May Day challenge, the Justice Department decided that these tactics were too "permissivist." Attorney General John Mitchell and his aides determined that the legality of arrests would no longer be a relevant question. Wilson, caught in the middle, carried out that policy. Then, after his department had swept the streets of thousands of onlookers and passers-by and people who had been breaking no laws, he found himself forced to defend this policy in public.

The Attorney General seemed well satisfied with the mass-arrest technique. After its "success" in the Washington situation, he began widely advocating illegal mass arrests as the best method for controlling demonstrations.

Political slights and partisan maneuvering had to be used to squelch those who, from within the profession of law enforcement, objected to these policies. New York Police Commissioner Patrick Murphy indicated that he would not have used such tactics had he been faced with a similar situation in New York. Shortly afterward, in the face of a public uproar over an alarming rise in fatal attacks on police, President Nixon called a White House meeting with law-enforcement administrators and others to discuss the problem. But Murphy, head of the nation's largest police department and the department that had experienced the largest number of police murders, was excluded from that meeting. The reasons were apparent. It soon became clear that with regard to police murders, the President was ineffective in dealing with this volatile issue and would contribute to the problem rather than solve it.

Although the White House meeting was widely publicized, the only recommendation to come out of it was that the widows of murdered policemen should receive a $50,000 insurance payment. This was certainly not a proposal that promised to save police lives. There was little substantive analysis to come out of the meeting on the question of why people would want to kill police and little attempt to find meaningful measures by which to stop them. In this light it can be contended that in publicly rebuffing a police chief who was and is fighting an almost impossible battle against entrenched corruption in his department, the President had inadvertently done more with his White House meeting to injure the cause of police professionalism than he had done to help it, and in fact had contributed to the very reasons why police are feared, hated, and sometimes killed by segments of American society today.

The Scranton Commission report had made a considerable effort to point to the direct relationship between national political problems and police behavior. While the President may send signals to police causing them to enforce unpopular or immoral policies by illegal methods, law-enforcement administrators are not expected to criticize or judge these policies. *They* are supposed to be apolitical. It is difficult to evaluate the effect of the lack of feedback to the national leadership. Were it not for the leadership vacuum, law-enforcement officers might have been able to communicate to those in high government circles the impossibility of enforcing unpopular political policies through police power. On the other hand, when the flow of power begins to turn so that police or those who look upon police as their primary weapons begin to determine national policy, the road to a police state is short.

The experience of the Scranton Commission brought the connections between large social issues and concrete police issues, and between national political leadership and local law-enforcement leadership, clearly into focus. It attempted to analyze a specific kind of police problem in a broad perspective in commenting on the Vietnam war and civil-rights issues and in developing theories about the relevancy of education which in many cases bear directly on the problems of campus unrest. All societal problems cannot be left to police, and the commission's report, in recommending societal responsiveness to dissent in conjunction with an upgrading and professionalizing of police, recognized this.

The experience of the commission was somewhat frustrating, however, since it had become clear that its report was not to be used to provide new directions in any of these problem areas. Especially vital to the commission itself was its insistence on attention to broad social issues. Yet it was obvious that the Administration was in fact pursuing a conscious policy of "benign neglect." All three of the previously mentioned Presidential commissions had found the provision of social justice essential to the avoidance of continued strife. But none had experienced a more significant response than neglect.

But societal neglect was not the most immediately alarming of the Nixon Administration's web of law-enforcement-related policies. By June of 1971 it was clear that certain of those policies which applied directly to law enforcement were falling into a dangerous pattern, of which the May Day arrest policy in Washington had been only a symptom. Governors and congressmen were coming to believe that their privacy was being violated, that their telephone conversations were being monitored, and that their daily activities were being observed by the Justice Department. Files stolen from the F.B.I. office in Media, Pennsylvania, indicated that it was the Bureau's conscious policy to create this kind of fear among the ranks of the political left. As if the fear itself were not enough, the Attorney General attempted to justify indiscriminate wiretapping to the public on the grounds of Executive prerogative. The suggestion was heard that Americans might have to surrender some of their Constitutional rights in the interests of national security as defined by the Justice Department.

This pattern was most clearly illustrated in an Administration decision that related directly to the Scranton Commission's report: the Justice Department decision not to pursue the prosecution of those who had done the killing at Kent State or at Jackson State.

While the Scranton Commission was performing its investigations, it was enjoined from taking testimony from a number of witnesses and participants involved in hearings before a Portage County, Ohio, grand jury. A similar situation prevailed in Mississippi, although the state grand jury there did deliver their findings before our report was written. Because our activities in investigating Kent State and Jackson State might have prejudiced further prosecution attempts, and because commissions at any rate should not function as grand juries, we made no allegations of personal guilt or innocence, nor did we say directly that a crime as such had been committed. But the commission did find that the deaths at Kent State were "unnecessary, unwarranted, and inexcusable" and that those at Jackson State were the result of "unreasonable, unwarranted

131

overreaction." In addition we made other subsidiary findings, such as that in the case of the Jackson State killings, "racial animosity on the part of white police officers was a substantial contributing factor in the deaths of two black youths and the gunshot injuries of twelve more." And the commission report left little doubt as to our opinion of the "justice" of the findings of the Mississippi grand jury which exonerated state police.

But although the Scranton Commission made no allocations as to guilt, and although it did not say that crimes as such had been committed, there should be little doubt in the public mind that those who fired their guns at Kent State and Jackson State were, and are, liable to criminal prosecution. When people are killed unnecessarily, inexcusably, unreasonably, and unjustifiably, only someone with a deep cynicism concerning our system of justice could assume that they were not killed illegally.

There is a wealth of evidence concerning the Kent State and Jackson State killings that has not been released to the public. The F.B.I. has eight thousand pages on Kent State alone. And a news leak in the Akron *Beacon-Journal* (which won a Pulitzer Prize for its coverage of the Kent State incident) indicated some time ago that—although the F.B.I. emphatically denies ever evaluating evidence—certain members of the Bureau felt confident concerning the possibility of successful prosecution at least in the Kent State case.

The Justice Department, however, chose not to initiate federal action in the Kent State and Jackson State cases. Behavior of this kind on the part of the highest prosecutorial agency in the country threatens to confirm the most radical criticisms of the American system of justice that have been brought against it in recent years. The political motivation in the Justice Department's refusal to prosecute at least the Kent State case seems blatant, crass, and cynical.

In recent years there have been demands to stop criminal trials —the New Haven trial was one—in which some felt that prejudice might rule out fairness. Those pressures were dismissed out of hand as unthinkable in a nation dedicated to live under law, and the outcome at least of the New Haven trial seems to have been fair. It would be frightening if the Attorney General had so little confidence in the American system of justice that he proved willing to submit only his political enemies to it.

But the seemingly unique nature of the Kent State and Jackson State situations must not be allowed to give the impression that political signals from the White House and the Justice Department affect only issues of national prominence. In fact the attitude and policy of the Administration rapidly pervades all levels of the law-enforcement hierarchy. The effects of the Justice Department's strategy for the Washington demonstrations can be seen throughout the country. In a town as small as Waterbury, Connecticut, a town that has recently been wracked by charges of corruption, the signals are heard clearly. Police there broke up a demonstration by Puerto Ricans protesting police brutality. There were charges of illegal arrests. In past years, no police chief in the country would publicly admit to having made illegal arrests, and most attempted to avoid such arrests. But when questioned about the demonstration arrests, the Waterbury chief, who had attempted to improve his department, admitted that some had been illegal and unapologetically allowed that illegal arrests were to be expected in such situations.

Political signals from national figures affect the attitude and morale of a department as well as have visible effects on its policies. In our attempts to build a police department in New Haven that policemen could be proud of, we gave attention to everything connected with such pride—right down to police uniforms. At one point the issue arose as to whether police officers should be allowed to wear American flag pins or patches on their uniforms. This was a delicate point and a highly volatile question on a symbolic level.

The New York Police Department had faced the same problem, and its leadership had contended that the American flag was not part of the police uniform. Officers had been denied permission to

POLICE IN TROUBLE

wear it. The issue seemed settled until a New York policeman wrote to President Nixon complaining of Commissioner Howard Leary's decision. The President predictably wrote back that he felt that policemen should be allowed to wear the flag. Those members of the New York department who wanted to wear it now rallied, and the department leadership, caught between the country's chief executive and many rank-and-file policemen, was forced to give in.

When this development became known in New Haven, we were besieged by requests from policemen to be allowed to wear the flag. We also took the position that it was not part of the uniform. I tried to tell the men that they did not have to turn themselves into walking billboards in order to prove their patriotism. I pointed out that members of the armed forces do not wear flags as parts of their uniforms, that their patriotism certainly is not in doubt, and that the policeman is in a far more delicate situation than the soldier. I asked them whether, if they wanted to wear American flag pins, other patrolmen should be able to wear peace buttons, "Free Bobby Seale" buttons, and other kinds of political paraphernalia. I pointed out that there were many who saw the American flag not as a national symbol but—as it had come to be—a symbol for a specific set of political values. Some of them seemed to realize that to go into a ghetto apartment wearing an American flag was to enter it not as a professional attempting to enforce the law fairly and equally but as a political figure ready to back up his own beliefs with the powers of his office. While this controversy was going on within the police department, a local citizen offered to pay for American flag pins or patches for the entire department. The department declined the offer, and a general order was issued to the effect that flag pins or patches were not part of the policeman's uniform and were not to be worn. Even at that, the flag issue continued to be an emotional one for those who felt that it was a symbol to which all Americans *should* have a basic loyalty and who maintained—somewhat inconsistently, because they had not requested

134

to wear the flag before it had become a symbol for a concrete set of political views—that in that sense it was "neutral."

These issues are significant enough in themselves, because they create emotional turmoil within police departments. But perhaps they are more significant for what they conceal. They allow politicians to make cheap political capital by appealing to emotionalism. They act as lightning rods, attracting public attention away from the need for fundamental structural reforms in police departments which would require profound thought, dedicated effort, and the expediture of money. Thus those who talk most vociferously about "law and order" often prove to be least willing to ask for money to improve police—as in the case with the Nixon Administration, which has initiated no programs and requested no money that had not been approved or authorized under the previous Administration.

Most of the progress that has been made in recent years in law enforcement was initiated by former Attorney General Ramsey Clark. Clark, who was made the scapegoat in the 1968 election for allegedly being "soft on crime," in fact took a number of decisive and meaningful steps toward effective law enforcement. One of these was the initiation of federal strike forces on organized crime, which succeeded in exposing scandals of corruption and involvement with organized crime in Newark and Jersey City.

The Nixon Administration itself has done little but allow the funds of the Law Enforcement Assistance Administration (L.E.A.A.) to be dissipated without federal guidelines or standards in the vast boondoggles of local politics.

The federal strike forces on organized crime are among the few promising agencies that stand a chance of making concrete improvements in police departments on local levels, but their role can hardly be one of leadership. Of the other national or international agencies or associations which have had the opportunity to provide leadership in law enforcement, none has proved capable of doing so for varying reasons.

135

POLICE IN TROUBLE

In other professions, a great deal of leadership comes from professional organizations such as the American Bar Association or the American Medical Association. The only group analogous to this in police work is the International Association of Chiefs of Police (I.A.C.P.). It would seem as though the I.A.C.P. could function as a kind of professional organization. But since it is made up exclusively of police chiefs from among the nation's forty thousand police agencies (each of whom has an equal voice in its affairs), it has in the past done little more than offer technical advice and organizational analysis to individual police departments.

At times, Congress has attempted to provide leadership in law enforcement, but these attempts have been failures. Laws such as the "Rap Brown" act, which makes crossing state lines to incite a riot a federal offense, are often no more than reactions to public demands to "do something" and at times threaten to build ambiguities into the law which are capable of abuse without really solving the problems involved. In past years there has been a marked tendency for Congress to pass laws that are either unneeded or are already on the books in another form in order to create the public impression that a problem is being dealt with. And it should by now be obvious that appropriations in themselves—although they are absolutely vital—do not represent leadership but merely the possibility of leadership.

Some have blamed the Supreme Court for the ineffectiveness of local police departments. Supreme Court decisions upholding the basic civil liberties of the accused are said to hamper law enforcement. These attacks and promises to "take the handcuffs off the police" have encouraged police to believe that they can ignore the Court's decisions with impunity—which is often the case—and have led to sloppy police work. They have further blurred the lines of police responsibility and certainly have added nothing to efforts to reform police departments substantively.

The Justice Department would seem a natural source for police leadership. While effective support for local law-enforcement agencies can come from the Justice Department, in the best of times it is incapable of solving the systematic problems of local police departments, and in the worst of times its political nature can pervert the system of justice drastically. In recent years the Justice Department has become increasingly political. Through many political administrations it was the custom to reward one's closest political adviser with the position of Postmaster General. Now it seems to have become the custom to place these people at the head of the Justice Department. This is a matter of Presidential discretion, but it is difficult to see how an Attorney General who masterminded President Nixon's election to office in 1968, and who will doubtless perform a parallel if not identical function in the next election, can have his sensitivities attuned to the objectives of justice rather than to the realities of political power.

Although the President, who can at times of crisis speak directly and forcefully to the cop on the walking beat or in the squad car, can and must do a great deal to provide moral leadership and to appeal to the policeman's best instincts, systematic changes have to be made before policemen in the United States can function effectively as professional law-enforcement officers whose priorities are identical with the interests of society as a whole. Not long ago President Nixon told a group of graduates of an F.B.I. training academy for local policemen that "the era of permissiveness in law enforcement is over." And he urged them to spread this message to their fellow local law-enforcement officers. Messages like this mean as little—or as much—as phrases like "get tough." If most policemen think to themselves carefully, they will be hard pressed to identify any "era of permissiveness" in law enforcement in this country's history. They will not have to think long, however, to grasp the meaning of the President's words. To policemen they can only signify that politicians are ready to encourage police to act outside the law in enforcing whatever type of behavior is politically expedient. Because to tell policemen that "the era of permissiveness is over" without giving them the systematic means to enforce the law more effectively is to place on their shoulders the burden of stopping "crime." And this they can do only by resorting to intimidation and brutality. Obviously, statements like this made without any real commitment of funds or leadership represent the type of rhetoric that must be eliminated as a minimal first step toward progress in law enforcement.

But a second step must be taken. If we are not to continue to have fiascos such as Operation Intercept, sealing off the Mexican border and harassing tourists in an attempt to cut down the flow of marijuana, while the flow of heroin into New York City continues unabated, independent and dynamic leadership in law enforcement must be developed. This leadership can never be allowed to become independent from democratic controls. But truly democratic controls are possible only when the power and jurisdiction of the people's representatives are as great as the force and scope of the problems they must face. And they are meaningful only when there is an identifiable and responsible leadership that formulates policy and makes it explicit and available to the public for review. If no one can be held responsible for the over-all state of police inadequacy today, it is difficult to see how police service can be improved. But, worse than the impossibility of improvement, without democratically responsible leadership, police leadership falls by default to other powers. The leadership of any function is bound to fall to the most powerful forces interested in that function. If those people are not the representatives of the public, the results can be frightening.

In 1967, while I was a police lieutenant, rioting broke out in New Haven's ghettos. The memory of Watts and Detroit and Newark was still fresh in the public mind. The Newark holocaust—which, in the face of inadequate law-enforcement capability, continued for days—had ground to an end amid a rush of mysterious shootings that claimed dozens of black lives.

The New Haven Police Department was unprepared to handle riot situations effectively and was having a difficult time. While caught off guard, unorganized and underequipped, it did manage to handle five days of rioting without firing a shot, without seriously injuring anyone, and without permanently polarizing the city. At the same time it was able to enforce the law, having made over six hundred arrests.

At one point during the disturbance, however, a New Haven political figure suggested that the police department was not able to control the situation. He intimated that he could bring in some "hit men" who, he said, could take care of rioters "so they wouldn't bother anyone." With that statement he smashed his fist into his hand. When asked why he thought it would work, his answer told much of the story of how police departments fall into—or are forced into—extralegal relationships in the face of the vacuum in law-enforcement leadership. "It worked in Newark," he said. Of course the enlistment of new soldiers was not undertaken, and the city was brought under control.

When organized crime and police departments have interests that overlap to the extent that police end up enforcing the law in ways that help criminal organizations, and criminal strong-arm men can substitute for police with little or no public notice of the difference, it is to be wondered whether the cities involved actually have any police service at all. Newark and New Haven are not alone in experiencing this kind of pressure or performance. There are reports that offers of mob assistance to police departments are often made in riot situations, especially when mobsters have certain enemies within the ghetto that they would like to eliminate under the cover of a civil disturbance. If the police themselves are efficient enough not to need mob help, they may, because of their political orientations, function as mobsters in uniform.

Whether atrocious police behavior in times of crisis is precipitated by inadequate or ill-motivated direction from the White House, or by cynical plotting by local politicians and gangsters, it is an indication of one overriding fact about police: They are extremely vulnerable to political manipulation. This vulnerability, in turn, comes from the lack of meaningful leadership in law enforcement. It is a lack that is felt every day, by every policeman.

Leadership may be the key to the improvement of police service in this country, but leadership will not solve the problem unless leaders have clear ideas of what police can and cannot, or should and should not, do. Our societal conception of what police should be is far from clear. It is an issue of such immediacy that it has seldom been systematically questioned or analyzed. Before we go on to suggest concrete programs for the improvement of law enforcement, we must have clear and positive ideas of what improvement in law enforcement would mean. If we do not, our efforts will be confined to reacting to crises as they arise, and we will be incapable of action that is coherent and constructive. Worse, we may begin to push police in increasingly dangerous directions.

6

Crime and the Police

CRIME AND THE POLICE are big issues in the United States today and properly so, since most Americans are increasingly afraid, often with good reason. Yet most Americans subscribe unthinkingly to at least three important myths in this area.

Myth number one is that police devote the preponderance of their time and resources to combating serious crime. The second myth is that there is a fairly fixed, definable, and measurable thing called crime. The third is that good police work can somehow lower crime rates regardless of what other institutions do. Without seeking to oversimplify complex issues, I believe that if people understood the facts about these propositions, our national discussion of law enforcement might bear a greater relation to reality.

Police departments are relatively modern inventions. It was not until urbanization was well on its way—less than a hundred and fifty years ago—that the Boston Police Department became the country's first formal police agency. Police departments are descended from night watches that in turn evolved from the British constabulary system of law enforcement around 1700. As cities grew, night watches were unable to deal with the crime that grew up as a result of urban crowding. But the Boston Police Department itself was created in the aftermath of the Panic of 1837, during which a militia brought in to restore order used unnecessary force and injured many citizens. Boston recognized the need for a police force that would be capable of handling further disorders with a minimum of force.

In a way, then, police departments were born in situations of stress which molded them according to the times. It is significant that police departments' first historical role was one of order maintenance rather than strict law enforcement, as serious crimes were handled not by the night watch but by private agents who were armed with warrants from magistrates and collected fees for arresting offenders. As time went on, however, rising crime forced a change in emphasis. The public conception of the police role shifted from order maintenance to crime control and police became regulated by a fixed set of societal ideals embodied in a code of laws.

But the notion of enforcing all of the laws in all segments of society proved impossible in the beginning. Early recruitment standards were so low that even police with a conception of fairness in enforcing the law found it was applicable only to those areas whose crimes they were capable of handling. And these were the areas of the lower middle and lower economic classes. In turn, local political pressures rendered police departments incapable of providing fair and equal law enforcement systematically even to the areas of their effective jurisdiction. But the concept of their essential obligation to a determined political system, with its underlying moral and ethical dynamics, remained. Consequently, the notion of a policeman as a fighter of crime—as a "law enforcer"—became a cover for a whole set of duties, some of them unrelated to law enforcement, which fell to police departments in a series of historical accidents.

The image of the policeman as a crime fighter is so pervasive that

142

the role of contemporary police cannot be understood without an examination of crime itself and the way in which police attempt to handle it.

Crime can be broadly divided into four categories: consensual crime, street crime, organized crime, and white-collar crime. These are intimately related, and some other important areas of crime, such as corruption of public officials and violations of housing ordinances, are not exhaustively explained by them. For our purposes, however, these categories will be more than adequate.

Many people have difficulty in seeing how a consensual crime—a crime to which the "victim" consents—can be a crime at all. Yet police spend much of their "law enforcement" energies attempting to combat them or pretending to attempt to combat them.

Since the failure of Prohibition, it has been a maxim of American justice that you cannot enforce laws that are abhorrent to a significant proportion of the population. Prohibition seems to have shown that enforcing certain kinds of laws places police in improper roles. Today, laws that attempt to regulate an individual's behavior when it has no effect on others or when its effect on others is more or less incidental tend to be unenforceable. Furthermore, since such laws fight against desires deeply ingrained in our culture and perhaps in human nature itself, enforcing them generally does more harm than it does good. Such laws appear to represent an illegitimate incursion of the state into areas that should be left to individual discretion.

In most areas police have not had to enforce Prohibition for decades. But they have had to enforce laws against other consensual crimes, and although the negative effects of their attempts have not been as spectacular as they were during Prohibition, for individual departments they have been very nearly as pervasive. Perhaps the most striking example of this phenomenon has been gambling.

Attempts to stop gambling have proved as ineffectual and as counterproductive as attempts to stop drinking. In the face of an enormous and seemingly ineradicable public appetite for gambling, anti-gambling laws have proven unenforceable, and this has led of necessity to selective enforcement. The corner dice game in a poverty area is broken up and its participants arrested, while the high-stakes poker game in the suburbs goes on week after week without so much as a whisper from law-enforcement officials. Police drive small independent gamblers out of business while protecting syndicated operations and allowing them to consolidate.

In addition to being unenforceable, gambling laws have contributed centrally to the continued vitality of organized crime, which has traditionally dealt in services demanded by the public which are deemed immoral and therefore made illegal. While gambling is only a part of the activities of criminal syndicates, it has long provided them with their most stable sources of income and with capital to take over legitimate business—and, recently, to operate higher levels of white-collar crime. Since Prohibition, gambling has provided most of organized crime's day-to-day operating revenues in the form of broad-based, tax-free income.

Police cannot win with gambling laws as they are now written. If they attempt to enforce them, they bring the moral sanctions of one segment of society—which is rarely willing to take responsibility for them—to bear on another segment of society which resents them. Their credibility and their self-respect suffer. If they do not attempt to enforce them, they are criminalized to a degree themselves, and they indirectly contribute to the whole cycle of crime to which gambling revenues contribute. Since Prohibition, gambling has taken over as the number-one corruptor of police. It is a short step from realizing that gambling laws are unenforceable to accepting money not to enforce them. Although the recent Knapp Commission findings in New York have made it clear that the corrupting influences in police are myriad, once more gambling has emerged as the most pervasive and widespread corruptor of police.

The public at present is unwilling to support the enforcement of gambling laws. Under these conditions the public should not condemn police to this impossible and degrading task. Those who cry that police must be respected should press for the removal of laws that put police in positions in which they cannot act respectably. Only then will the police have the time and effectiveness to treat serious crimes. To this end, gambling should be legalized in this country.

The legalization of gambling might well strike a blow to organized crime from which it could never recover. In order to make legalization effective in this respect, however, the state must provide the same gambling services that organized crime does: daily wagering, small bets, complete convenience and immediate payoffs. Unless it does, it will find that the mere fact that its enterprise is legal will not cause bettors to prefer it.

Our present ideas of individual rights, backed up to a great extent by the Constitution, seem to uphold the notion that society should not attempt to legislate morality. In principle it would seem then that consensual crimes should not be crimes at all. But from a theoretical point of view, it must be admitted that our laws exist to regulate or eliminate behavior that we consider "immoral." Laws against murder, for example, proceed from positive assumptions that human life is inherently valuable and must, except in extraordinary and specifically limited situations, be valued above all else. This is fundamentally a moral assumption. So in a sense all laws legislate morality to one degree or another, and we are faced not with two distinct classes of behavior but with a continuum.

In practical terms this makes the question of consensual crime very difficult. Perhaps, however, distinguishing between a consensual crime in general and a *victimless crime,* a type of consensual crime, will help here.

A consensual crime can still be a crime with a victim—as con games that depend on the greed of the victims show. The question then becomes the meaning of victimization. Prohibition was not enacted by people who felt that they were legislating against a "victimless" crime. It was enacted by people who felt that purveyors of alcohol victimized those to whom it was sold, robbing them of their dignity, their self-control, and often of their lives, for the sake of financial profit, and that those who drank in turn victimized their families and associates by depriving them of meaningful companionship and sometimes of physical support, becoming in the end a burden on society.

Many likewise feel that gambling cannot be said to be victimless. There are compulsive gamblers just as there are alcoholics, and in their cases their "habits" can drive them and their families into desperate straits faster than alcoholism. Gamblers can be seen as corruptors, robbing families of their savings and degrading their "victims" as easily as can liquor dealers.

In sorting out these problems, however, we must remember that it is difficult to see what freedom means if it does not mean to some extent the freedom to err and that to ask police to try to make people perfect may well be to ask for the formation of a police state.

There is not an absolute difference between victimless crimes and crimes with victims, but once more a subtle continuum, calling for involved and delicate decisions.

In the same way, difficulty in enforcing a law does not necessarily indicate that it is invalid. The public may be unaware of what is needed to enforce a law that it considers vital, or unwilling to pay the price for such enforcement. Nevertheless, a law's unenforceability may place police in an illegitimate role. It may indicate that the law is out of phase with the true will of the majority and that the law should be examined and brought up before the people and their representatives for review. Since it takes the cooperation of more than a simple majority of the population for police to be able to enforce a law, legislators should keep from passing laws that are inessential simply to make capital, as has happened so often. Police need fewer laws and simpler ones, not more and more complex ones.

In discussing two kinds of consensual activity—gambling and drinking—I have suggested that they are similar and that laws against them place police in an improper role because they attempt to legislate morality and therefore tend to be unenforceable and to cause more harm than they do good.

In regard to drugs, it would seem that marijuana is in much the same situation as alcohol. Demand for it is extremely widespread. It is easily and unobtrusively grown. There is as yet no convincing medical evidence to prove that marijuana is more addictive or more dangerous than commodities such as alcohol or cigarettes. As a result, the laws against marijuana have proved to be effectively unenforceable, and they place police in an improper and untenable position. In fact, insistence on enforcement of the marijuana laws seems to condemn police to negligence with regard to laws against more dangerous drugs.

When we turn to the question of these more dangerous drugs, the distinction between victimless crimes and crimes with victims becomes central.

Narcotics addiction is a consensual crime. The laws against possession and distribution of heroin have thus far proven to be beyond the capability of police to enforce. This is especially true at the street level. In view of the fact that in many cities well over 50 percent of all street crime is perpetrated by a relatively few heroin addicts, it seems that the costs both to addicts and to society of the laws against heroin addiction may be greater than the benefits.

Addiction, while a consensual crime, cannot be said to be victimless. Present evidence tends to show that the effects of the drug itself are so devastating that it can be looked upon as a poison.

The present unenforceability of heroin laws seems to be not the result of the nature of the crime but of the unwillingness of the public to face the problem squarely. While I do not credit radical theories that the government wishes to foster heroin use in order to keep minorities divided and repressed, it is impossible to deny that politicians have been insensitive to the dimensions of the heroin problem.

POLICE IN TROUBLE

If heroin use is condemned by the vast majority of Americans, and in fact by a vast majority of those who live in the communities where it flourishes, then why are laws against it unenforceable?

The enforcement of laws against the heroin traffic is a national and international problem, and local police cannot in their present state handle such problems. They can rarely handle even the most basic local law-enforcement challenges. The Federal Bureau of Narcotics and Dangerous Drugs alone probably could not stem the flow of heroin. As devastating a problem as heroin represents, it is confined on the whole to big cities and as such is not itself a national issue. And the political power of crime machines and of organized crime does a great deal to ensure that government action with regard to heroin will be fragmented and ineffectual.

There are important differences between heroin and marijuana, for instance, that indicate that heroin laws are in principle enforceable. In contrast with marijuana, the heroin trade requires a highly sophisticated process from the growing of poppies to the refinement of opium derivatives into heroin to the importation of the finished product into this country. This renders it vulnerable in a way that marijuana is not, since crime organizations cannot conceal their operations as completely. There are simply too many people involved for complete secrecy to be practical. This means that discipline must be maintained either through payoffs or by coercion, creating the possibility of weak links, of informers, and of carelessness, even in the most highly secretive and sophisticated dealings. Given this inherent vulnerability, the heroin trade can probably be ended without turning America into a police state.

Solving the problem of drug addiction cannot, however, be looked upon as basically a law-enforcement problem. The criminalization of heroin addicts and the crimes they commit now represent a societal danger that rivals the use of the drug itself, and heroin addiction as a sociological and medical problem cannot be dealt with by police. We must press science to develop solutions to the problem of addictive drugs which are in themselves medically sound and morally acceptable—which free people from heroin addiction without creating undesirable side effects or unnecessary loss of freedom. In the meantime, however, since our present procedures, by assuming that punishment is the answer to addiction, only strengthen the cycle of crime and alienation, we must search for alternatives.

The question of drugs takes on a new dimension of ambiguity when we consider "consciousness-expanding" substances. LSD may be only the precursor to a great number of these and may in the future be looked upon as relatively mild. It may be true, as some people claim, that these drugs, particularly the so-called psychedelic drugs, open new and untapped areas of the mind. But many of them may be highly dangerous as well. The government's vain attempts, in the face of independent scientific research, to prove the harmfulness of marijuana have eroded many people's confidence in the objectivity of its experiments. In delicate situations where legislating morality may be at stake, the government—while maintaining its right to hold newly discovered drugs guilty until proved innocent—must be careful not to publicize facts that will later be disproved and must clearly define the difference between legislating morality and protecting its citizens from the substances that may cause them irreparable damage. If government experiments are not objective, in the years ahead its factual claims will be ignored. The most vital weapon in the fight against drug abuse—the truth about the effects of drugs—will be lost, and police will be forced to attempt to compensate for government negligence.

Clearly the entire problem of consensual crime has fundamental and far-reaching implications for the police role, which encompass considerations of individual rights and liberties and the citizen's relationship to his government—all of which police must monitor in some sense. But in precisely what sense? And to what extent? Until very recent years police have been expected to lurk in train stations attempting to prevent or detect homosexual rendezvous. They have been expected to peek into windows in attempts to catch consenting adults in acts of "lascivious carriage." To good cops,

149

such assignments are meaningless and degrading. To bad ones, they are a license to harass those whose conceptions of what is moral are different from theirs. In both cases, the effects of these assignments have been detrimental to police, and it is difficult to see how they have profited communities. It is a condition of the policeman's job to work in such gray areas. The law is constantly changing, community values are constantly changing, and even notions concerning the most fundamental of human rights and obligations are slowly changing. In the midst of the flux created by these changes, the professional policeman can function. He must function. But he cannot function if he is expected to enforce laws such as those against gambling and marijuana—unenforceable attempts to legislate individual morality.

If enforcing laws against victimless crime puts police in impossible and often illegitimate roles and degrades and corrupts them, this fact has been obscured by the public's notion that victimless crime does not consume much police time. Recent law-and-order rhetoric concerning a far more emotional issue has obscured the fact that it does. That issue is "crime in the streets." It is a real one and a serious one.

Among its many findings, the Katzenbach Commission reported that numerous Americans felt that the incidence of street crime had substantively altered the most basic conditions of their existence. Cities and towns are almost threats by their very existence, and paranoia is looked upon as healthy, as the only way to survive.

But the issue of street crime, while it is exploited for political purposes, is seldom analyzed calmly and rationally. Intimately connected to consensual crimes in some ways and to organized crime in others, street crime in all its ramifications is virtually an unknown quantity. Its extent, its causes, and effective techniques for its prevention remain a mystery.

Perhaps most fundamental to an analysis of street crime is an analysis of exactly what it is. Is a fist fight street crime? Are vandalism, gang warfare, or juvenile crime included? Often this depends on where these incidents occur. If a group of carousing convention-eers blocks traffic while crossing a street, it is not likely to be re-garded as street crime. But substitute a group of high-spirited ghetto youths or a group of hippies, and the complexion of the case changes.

But there are more fundamental ways to question our assumptions about street crime. They have to do with the way we measure it, which reflects our attitudes toward crime. The truth of the matter is that no one knows its full extent. Although statistics compiled by local police departments and eventually by the F.B.I. are offered to the public as hard, objective data on the broad range of criminal activity in the United States, the statistics are so manipulated, and often so narrow in scope, that they give an idea of the extent of crime which has little to do with reality and which often indicate trends that are the reverse of the true situation.

The F.B.I. crime index is taken by Americans to be the most authoritative source regarding the extent of crime. When the F.B.I. says crime is up, people believe it. When the F.B.I. says crime is down, they believe that too.

The F.B.I. makes use of only seven crimes, its so-called Part I offenses, in projecting to the public a picture of the extent of crime in America: homicide, rape, robbery, car theft, burglary, aggra-vated assault, and larceny of property valued at over fifty dollars. The fact that these could all be broadly categorized as "street crimes" leads Americans to believe that street crime is the most pervasive and serious of our problems. But these offenses represent only a minute portion of the reported crime in a given year. In ad-dition to those incidents—undoubtedly the vast majority—that go unreported, and therefore are not reflected at all in the index, there are entire spheres of criminal activity which are not considered. These include offenses that may involve millions of dollars or that may profoundly affect the quality of life for millions of people.

The statistics that go into the F.B.I. index are often so manipu-lated as to be meaningless. The F.B.I. is totally dependent upon local police departments for crime statistics. But on the local level, the manipulation of crime statistics has become so widespread that as a rule their significance is reversed. If a city reports a high crime rate, it is because the police department has insisted upon full and honest reporting of all crimes and of proper categorization of crimes. Thus a police department that is honest about statistics will have a far higher crime rate than one that is not. In addition, in a city with a police department that is trusted and respected by its citizens, people will be more willing to report crimes and to cooperate with police because they believe that something may be gained. In cities with incompetent departments, people feel that reporting crimes only takes up time and causes trouble, and they do not bother with it. It is virtually axiomatic that if a city reports a dramatic increase in the crime rate, it is a function not of reality but of reporting. During my first year as chief of the New Haven Police Department, we insisted on accurate reporting, and crime was "up" 150 percent.

Crime statistics go through many levels of manipulation from the patrolman to the statistician of the police department. The most basic level of manipulation occurs when police simply discourage people from reporting crimes that they see little chance of solving. On a slightly higher level, the definition of a crime itself can provide an opportunity for manipulation.

Police effectiveness is measured not in terms of arrest or of convictions but of "clearances." A clearance means in effect that a crime has been "solved." The premium in police departments is on obtaining clearances for index crimes. Crimes that are not reflected in the F.B.I. index enter into virtually no statistical picture of crime in general and therefore are insignificant. Here the technique of manipulation to obtain high clearance rates is relatively simple. A policeman will define a crime as more serious if he has made an arrest or expects to and less serious if he does not. Is purse-snatching a robbery included in the index, or is it the less-serious offense, theft from person, not counted in the index? If the purse-snatcher is caught, it is a robbery. If not, it is a theft. Is a person involved in a fight guilty of aggravated assault? Or is his crime breach of the peace? If he is caught, it will be aggravated assault. If not, it will be breach of the peace, if anything.

This technique works both ways. If a person has committed a crime that would legitimately be categorized as breach of the peace and is arrested, he will be charged with aggravated assault. The charge will automatically be reduced when the case reaches court, but the arrest—and the clearance—will remain under the aggravated-assault category and will be forwarded to the F.B.I. as such.

The valuation of property is another area in which crime statistics are commonly manipulated. For a theft to be an index crime the value of goods stolen must be greater than $50. If an arrest is made in connection with a case, the property involved climbs in value. If not, its value falls. This often leads to strange contradictions. In unsolved cases complainants often want high property valuations to refer to their insurance companies, while police want low ones so that they will not be saddled with unsolved index crimes. The solution to this dilemma is not as difficult as one might imagine. Often, police departments keep "two sets of books." This practice is so pervasive that one member of the New Haven Police Department actually suggested we computerize two separate sets of property valuation statistics, one for the F.B.I. and one for the insurance industry.

There is yet another level of manipulation of crime in clearance statistics. At this level, incentives to produce high clearance rates often directly pervert justice. A suspect who is arrested for one crime and who is clearly guilty will come under great pressure to admit to having committed other crimes. Police and prosecutors can make it to his advantage to do so, whether he has committed them or not. For if he admits to no other crimes, they will press for maximum penalties in the case for which he is guilty. If, on the other hand, he cooperates and confesses to having committed dozens of others, they will lower their demands for sentencing, or reduce the charges against him. Literally thousands of defendants are prompted by this process to plead guilty to tremendous lists of offenses which they never committed. By this technique, police and prosecutors simply wipe away tremendous numbers of unsolved cases which otherwise would remain so forever.

As if this technique of manipulation were not sufficient, F.B.I. guidelines allow police departments to claim "exceptional clearances." Under this procedure, they can claim to have solved crimes to which no one has admitted. Suppose police have arrested a burglar who entered a house through an unlocked back door, who stole a few highly portable items of great value, and who left no clues. Police are free, through the exceptional clearance technique, to claim to have solved all the crimes they can find which even vaguely fit this method of operation.

Since the F.B.I. index depends completely upon these dubious statistics as the Bureau receives them, it is an index of nothing.

But beyond the fact that the F.B.I. index is meaningless with regard to the crimes it treats, it is invalid and misleading because of the crimes that it does not treat. These include not only "Part II offenses"—all the myriad breaches of peace and simple assaults, petty thefts, and vandalism that consume so much of a police department's time—but also narcotics violations, organized criminal activities such as gambling and shylocking and extortion, and white-collar crime activities such as fraud.

Taking all of these things into consideration, it is plain that the general effect of the F.B.I. crime index, which focuses upon street crimes and ignores other large classes of crime, gives the public a deceptive picture of criminal activity in the country as a whole and is positively harmful in fostering the notion that the "real" crimes that are committed are essentially those of the lower and lower middle classes.

Statistics if accurately and properly compiled can be of enormous value to the police. But police who are so defensive that they must manipulate such statistics to improve their image, and so poor that they must turn the same statistics around and manipulate them differently to try to cause panic and gain approval for higher budgets, are unlikely to be able to generate accurate and meaningful statistics at all.

Street crime can be reduced, and our streets can be made safe again, only when we insist on knowing its full extent and nature. And it can be eliminated only by police departments that are not sent on fool's errands combating victimless crimes. In many ways, although police have a great number of other legitimate duties, street crime, its prevention and prosecution, must and should remain central to the police role. People must be safe to walk the streets. They must be confident that they are safe in their homes. They must know that police consider it a primary duty to restore the most basic characteristics of civilization to our cities once again. On this issue, there can be no "permissiveness," no "soft on crime" philosophy. True criminals must be apprehended and effectively prosecuted. Those who are victimized by criminals—including those who are fighting to make their crime-ridden ghettos livable—can no longer accept clichés like "law and order" from politicians who refuse to support police with the programs and the money they need to combat crime. Cheap rhetoric about law and order means little to the citizen who is mugged or robbed at gunpoint. It means nothing to the cop who looks around him and sees that his ability to fight crime has not been increased one iota since "law and order" politicians came to power.

In order to be successful in eliminating street crime and in making our cities safe once more, we must try to determine the true nature of street crime, its causes and the methods by which it can be prevented.

Nobody knows for certain what causes street crime. Many feel that people will be criminals if they can get away with it, that street crime is simply a result of police failure in dealing with the realities of human nature. Others feel that street crime is the result of a vast complex of societal ills—a lack of jobs, poor housing, urban crowding, poor education, lack of recreational facilities, and a general rebelliousness that is the product of deep-seated political division.

POLICE IN TROUBLE

A realistic and hard-hitting attack on street crime must recognize the truth in both of these positions. There are people who will fall into lives of crime simply because they believe that it is an easier and faster way to make money than the pursuit of an honest occupation. On these people, police action can be effective both in deterring them and in removing them from the streets. There are others who are driven to crime out of poverty, out of a need for narcotics, or because criminal activity is part of a larger pattern of social estrangement into which they have fallen. On these—probably the vast majority of those who commit street crimes—police acknowledge that they have little effect.

Street crime is largely the activity of alienated young men—a relatively small proportion of the criminal population, usually derived from the urban poor, with histories of employment problems, narcotics use, and with backgrounds of exposure to racial or ethnic discrimination. They have not had the support of a responsive educational system, or of positive community or peer groups, and have often succumbed to a pattern of crime as teenagers. Because of the inadequacies of the criminal justice system and the absence of successful rehabilitation, these people spend their lives going in and out of jails, and 80 percent of all street crimes are committed by people who have been previously convicted of crimes. This means that rehabilitation could and should be one of our most powerful crime-fighting weapons. The politicians who are really "soft on crime" are those who sacrifice the lives of prison guards and prisoners in situations like Attica to defend the ideas that punishment can prevent or deter all crime and that subjecting prisoners to absurd or inhuman conditions will make them less likely to be criminals when they get out.

Any successful attack on street crime must include improved techniques of apprehension and deterrence. Although we do not know the preventive value of police patrol precisely, we do know that patrol is effective only in areas where police officers are actually present and that it is usually easy for offenders to avoid police.

Crime and the Police

In addition there are certain crimes, such as assaults and murders —usually called crimes of passion—in which emotions are aroused to such an extent that the relative proximity of police officers has no deterrent effect.

There have been relatively few innovations in patrol techniques over the past few decades. During this time, as police have been faced with a bewildering proliferation of responsibilities, available man hours in police departments have steadily declined, and in many large departments preventive patrol is virtually nonexistent. In the Oakland, California, department some years ago a survey revealed that only 2 percent of police patrol hours was actually being spent on preventive patrol. The rest of the time was spent responding to complaints and attending to administrative functions. Sometimes this kind of inadequacy is caused by a lack of resources, and sometimes it is caused by managerial and administrative inefficiency. Whatever its causes, its effects on police service are devastating.

It is ironic that police are most effective in apprehending the criminals they are least capable of deterring. Murderers are the prime example. The "clearance rate" for murder is high—up to 80 percent, if the statistics are to be believed. (Murder statistics are generally more accurate than other statistics, although murders are classed as accidental, suicidal or natural deaths more frequently than we would like to believe.) Murder is often a "crime of passion," and, along with rape and serious assault, it is usually perpetrated by people known to the victims. Usually the evidence is more or less clear, and motives are easily established. But even if there was a cop on every corner, it is difficult to see how most such crimes could be deterred or prevented.

In solving other kinds of street crime, however, the police in many cities are so ineffective that it is almost as if they did not exist. The public seldom understands why police fail to solve even a significant minority of crimes of stealth like burglaries or crimes of violence like muggings. It is so widely believed that modern scientific techniques such as fingerprinting and microscopic analysis are univer-

157

sally used and unerringly effective that except for those who are familiar with the state of the police art, people still believe that "crime doesn't pay." Partly because no television show or movie is allowed to portray a crime that goes unpunished, the public conception of police efficiency is completely erroneous.

A patrolman who responds to a report that a burglary has been committed does not arrive with half a dozen detectives who search the house for fingerprints, who comb every inch of it looking for threads from the burglar's clothing, or who make casts of footprints from the ground outside of windows. He arrives alone or with a fellow officer. If the victim wishes or insists, he writes out a report. Then he leaves. If detectives follow up the case, they more or less duplicate the patrolman's function; they make their own reports, then leave. Even if fingerprints are taken, the most that detectives can do unless they have a single suspect or a number of suspects whose fingerprints are on file somewhere is to compare latent prints with those from other burglary scenes and attempt to establish a pattern, and this approach is seldom fruitful.

But even to talk of fingerprints and other scientific crime-detection techniques is misleading. Detectives inevitably make use of informants in attempting to solve important cases. But informants are rarely useful in court, and knowing who committed a crime is not evidence. Even if there is evidence, including witnesses, if a suspect in a minor crime has fled the jurisdiction, the chances are that if he is ever apprehended the case will be too stale to prosecute successfully anyhow. Since detective divisions also have other duties, such as enforcing gambling laws, and since legwork (including neighborhood checks and records checks with other police departments) is so time-consuming, meaningful follow-up investigation on street crime beyond the informant level is virtually nonexistent. And since patrolmen must break off their attention to cases as soon as emergencies are over, reports have been taken, and crime scenes have been protected, their follow-up role is equally nonexistent.

Any approach to the detection and prevention of street crime must focus on the criminal justice system as a whole. Even if police could catch every perpetrator of a crime within their city, they would be relatively powerless to prevent crime. The courts are so slow and so inefficient in dispensing justice that effective prosecution is a rarity.

When a criminal suspect is arrested, he is arraigned and bail is set. If he can make bail, he is out on the streets immediately—but he may not be tried for six months or a year. During this time he may commit numerous other crimes. Even if he is eventually convicted, it may well be on a lesser charge that has nothing to do with the crime he has committed. In addition, the time lag between the commission of his crime and his prosecution has been so long that the meaning of the conviction is lost—particularly since he may have committed many crimes in the meantime.

The solution to this problem is not preventive detention. Preventive detention is a violation of a defendant's Constitutional rights. As such it is likely to alienate him further and drive him more deeply into criminal behavior. In addition, preventive detention exposes a suspect to the corroding influences of incarceration which, as it does nothing to rehabilitate him (and in principle should not, since he has not been convicted of a crime), is counter-productive.

Neither is the solution to attempt to eliminate or limit the Constitutional rights of defendants by other legalistic gimmicks. This approach can only hurt us all.

The solution is to provide speedy trials as required by the United States Constitution. It should be clear that this provision is not only vital to the protection of the rights of the accused; it is also vital to the protection of the rights of honest citizens who are victimized. If a suspect is innocent, he has the right to be proven innocent immediately. If he is guilty, society has the right to require that he be convicted with equal immediacy. These things can be accomplished only when we eliminate the plea-bargaining process from the back rooms of our courthouses and display it to the public, where it can be observed and where we can assure that the guilty do not escape without correction. In addition, there must be full-time prosecutors whose loyalty is to the cause of justice rather than to their private practice and whose professional credentials place them above political influence. Full-time defense attorneys must be provided for defendants who cannot afford private counsel. Courts must remain in session more often and for longer hours. And the selection process for judges and prosecutors must be removed from the political spoils system. Only with such reforms will the court system be able to function in a manner that will restore respect for the courts and for the law.

Any significant strategy for dealing with violent street crime must upgrade our juvenile justice system. From their enlightened origins several decades ago, the juvenile courts and detention facilities have deteriorated to the point where they promote rather than combat juvenile delinquency. If the juvenile delinquent is to be helped, improved services must be made available and effectively coordinated. Full-time psychiatrists and psychologists must be provided. Social and medical agencies should be funded at a level that would permit them to expand both their staffs and the hours that they work. Police departments must be encouraged to staff their youth divisions with case workers as well as police officers. Unless the police, juvenile courts, and correction facilities can offer the teen-age offender meaningful alternatives to the street or reformatory, he is likely to continue and escalate his criminal career. While it may seem farfetched to say that the most important step we can take toward eliminating street crime is to treat juvenile delinquents with justice and with humanity, a simple look at the facts of street crime proves that this approach is absolutely vital. A vast majority of serious criminal offenders begin their careers as juvenile delinquents. This nation is in the dark ages as far as criminal corrections are concerned. While countries like West Germany are preparing long-range plans to phase out prisons in favor of alternative methods of rehabilitating prisoners, we continue to maintain crime factories which we call correctional institutions. We take men whose needs are for personal support and a feeling of identity, for meaningful jobs and psychological assistance, and lock them up in depersonalized environments where their identity is shattered, where they have nothing to do, and no psychological support. This is bad enough for older men; it is hideous for juveniles. By this approach we foster the very street crime we supposedly seek to eliminate.

Street crime is a vital concern—but it cannot be considered in a vacuum. The dynamics of city politics ensure that it is intimately related to consensual crime and organized crime and indirectly to white-collar crime.

Organized crime provides narcotics that drive alienated young men to commit burglaries and robberies.

Organized crime must be eliminated from our public life. It can be done. Although organized crime directly involves perhaps no more than a few thousand individuals on its highest levels, it employs hundreds of thousands of people on its lower levels, and its corrupting and coercive power reaches from the streets of our cities into the halls of Congress.

There are many kinds of crime that are conspiratorial. Many of these have not been called organized crime. They include car-theft rings, smuggling operations, hijacking rings, and organizations that deal in stolen goods. It is largely irrelevant whether these organizations are syndicated or not. They still commit the same amount of crime. At times they may gain a certain amount of political power. But when we speak of organized crime, we usually mean the syndicated variety.

Syndicates operate in cities throughout the country. No one knows the true extent of their involvement or their power. They pervade so many levels of society and government, they corrupt so many people and multiply crime in so many ways, that their effect is virtually that of a cancer in a city's system.

Organized crime, where it exists, is too widespread an activity to be carried on without some measure of protection from the criminal justice system and from the government. If this is its strength, it is also its vulnerability. Ensuring its security by bribes and payoffs in some cases, and by violence and coercion in others, the syndicates are enmeshed in a tangle of political and criminal connections that cannot be unraveled from the bottom; it must be attacked from the top. Many local police departments are rendered powerless by syndicate influence, or they themselves become implicated in the tangle through corruption. It is only when they see forces coming to their assistance that are as powerful as organized crime that they are able or willing to make a true contribution to eliminating it. The strike forces have been effective in getting to the source of power in several cities.

Organized crime is a pervasive force that paralyzes police in cities and in fact often corrupts them. White-collar crime is like a huge umbrella above their heads which they know about but which they are powerless to touch. The policeman is likely to have so accepted societal ideas of his limitations that he seldom wonders why he is never called upon to enforce laws against such crimes as embezzlement, tax fraud, price fixing, consumer fraud, anti-trust violations, and insurance fraud—to name only a few of the activities of criminals who happen to be businessmen, lawyers, doctors, or politicians. He knows that white-collar crime is an accepted part of American life; that, to paraphrase Woody Guthrie, there are those who steal with a gun and those who steal with a fountain pen and that in some mysterious way the latter, although their illegal activities bring them far more money than the total proceeds for all other kinds of crimes put together, are very seldom detected or prosecuted. He knows further that when they are, the punishments meted out to them are often little more than a slap on the wrist.

The policeman feels this inconsistency acutely. Others in society also see it. The poor know when they have been bilked out of what little money they have, when their landlords are violating housing regulations, and when price-fixing conspiracies in their neighborhood force them to pay more for consumer commodities than others do. And lower-middle-class people know that behind the scenes of

Crime and the Police

American economics and politics people are stealing huge sums of money with impunity. The corrosive effects and the widespread insidious nature of white-collar crime prove to all that criminal activity as such is not solely the result of societal deprivation but that different levels of society foster different varieties of crime.

The extent and definition of white-collar crime is even more indeterminate than that of street crime, victimless crime, or organized crime. Banks that catch employees embezzling money wish above all to protect their reputations. They are likely to handle such matters internally. On other levels, white-collar crime may not be considered crime at all. If a businessman gets away with activities that are illegal, he is a "good businessman." If he does not, he simply gives the money back and tries again. In 1961 when two of the nation's largest producers of electrical goods were found guilty of a massive price-fixing conspiracy that had bilked municipalities of millions of dollars, two-thirds of their fine was adjudged by the Internal Revenue Service to be deductible from their corporate taxes as "legitimate business expenses." It is this kind of high-level concession to massive criminal activity which undermines the moral fiber of the nation, which makes its most prestigious and powerful forces subject to profound suspicion, and which in the end contributes to an aura of lawlessness that makes it extremely difficult for police to function.

For some reason, the public is especially willing to accept that political figures will become rich by virtue of the fact that they hold office. If a politician happens to be a lawyer, his private practice will boom because clients realize that a "good lawyer" is not necessarily one who is intelligent and conscientious but one who has the political influence necessary to sway decisions on such crucial matters as zoning, licensing of businesses, and awarding of contracts. Whoever he is, a politician has inside information which enables him or his associates to capitalize on governmental decisions. Often politicians have an interest in corporations that do business with the government. These connections, which are carefully hidden and rarely discovered, enable them to make vast sums because of their

163

political influence. If they are discovered, they are discovered for the wrong reasons. A Supreme Court nominee's conflicts of interest are publicized only when his political opponents find it expedient to do so.

So accepted is illegal or unethical activity in high places that even when it is uncovered, unless it is of great political significance, it is often ignored. For instance, an Administration that was elected to office largely on the basis of its supposedly strong stand for "law and order" does not seem to have taken the threat or the possibility of white-collar crime within the very Justice Department that is supposed to provide Americans with law and order seriously. In the late summer of 1971 it was learned that Will Wilson, Assistant Attorney General of the United States in charge of the Justice Department's Criminal Division, and the man therefore directly responsible for federal criminal prosecution throughout the country, had been involved in a holding company that was accused of stock fraud. The revelation hardly caused a ripple, in spite of its implications for the entire criminal justice system. For the Attorney General not to have temporarily suspended Wilson pending a full investigation seems to indicate the existence of a double standard which ignores the interconnectedness of all crime and chooses to concentrate only rhetorically upon emotional political issues in attempting to obtain "law and order." In the end, further disclosures prompted Wilson to resign.

Measured in dollars, white-collar crime is by far the most serious crime problem existing in America today. It has been so long ignored as a criminal problem, and has become so rampant, that any competent and professional investigation into any of its many realms immediately uncovers startling and disquieting evidence of its existence.

If Americans realized the extent to which every expenditure that they make, from taxes to consumer purchases, is liable to be increased by the crimes of white-collar offenders, they would recognize at once that if law and order is to mean anything, it must mean full,

Crime and the Police

fair, and effective enforcement of the law on all levels of society. This can be done. White-collar crime is perhaps more subject to deterrence than other varieties of crime, since it is seldom undertaken out of dire economic necessity and since those involved in it fear a loss of prestige and reputation if they are caught. Until police are selected, trained, educated, and equipped to deal forcefully with white-collar crime, police action will continue to be selective and therefore intrinsically unfair, the moral fiber of our nation will continue to deteriorate, and the entire interconnected realm of crime will never be meaningfully attacked.

It is obvious that basic institutional changes are needed in order to adjust the police role to meet society's needs. Police must be freed from the necessity of enforcing laws against victimless crime; they must be given the technical assistance, support, and training which allows them to fight street crime effectively, and at the same time must be assured that society is doing what it can to eliminate the causes of street crime; they must be given outside support in order to fight the regional and national problems of organized crime and municipal corruption; and they must be professionalized to the extent that they can deal effectively with white-collar crime.

7

Professional Police
and
Democratic Control

THE FIRST STEP toward making substantive changes in the police role is to realize that fighting crime is not a full definition of it. The term "law enforcement officer" when applied to policemen is itself somewhat misleading. Policemen are only one part of the criminal justice system which is responsible for law enforcement, and since it is the courts that "give the law its force" by determining guilt or innocence and meting out punishment, the policeman's job can be seen as only a prelude to law enforcement.

But if the policeman is only a small part of law enforcement, law enforcement in turn is only a small part of the policeman's job. The vast majority of the patrolman's time and energy is spent not in law enforcement but in "order maintenance," in which the law is only one of many tools he possesses. It may be contended that the police role should be limited strictly to one of treating crime and that societal order is none of his business. But these contentions do not account for the fact that at least in the patrol function, the policeman finds that his essential role is never to initiate investigations but to respond to complaints. He does not seek incidents out; they confront him. And in dealing with them, one of his prime functions is to determine whether in fact a crime has been committed. Often when a policeman is called, he finds that none has, or that if it has, there is no one willing to sign a complaint and therefore he is powerless to "enforce the law." But this does not mean that he has no function in such a situation. He is faced with the situation, and it may be potentially explosive or violent. More often than not, he must deal with people who demand that something be done but who are unwilling to resort to criminal sanctions; in other cases an arrest may be totally inappropriate. In these situations, the patrolman has to deal not with crime but with people. That is his stock-in-trade.

Dealing with people is obviously the main problem in some order maintenance functions such as attending to barking dogs or traffic obstructions. It is equally important in law-enforcement situations. The patrolman who receives a call to respond to a robbery in progress thinks not of crime prevention or control, but of how he will handle a potentially deadly situation involving people. His job is not to enter judgment, since he does not know the facts before he arrives, but to bring the parties involved under control, to ensure the safety of victims and innocent bystanders, and to apprehend a suspect regardless of how he reacts. The patrolman must instantly determine whether a crime has been committed and if so, what kind of crime, but this knowledge will be only one element of his total assessment. Once he has acted, and once the crisis has been resolved, although he may well have to spend long hours in court, he has finished the most fundamental portion of his task.

If we grant—as we must, considering that eight out of ten calls a patrolman answers will be of a "social service" variety—that order maintenance is a valid function and that police discretion cannot be eliminated, the question arises as to what variety of order the policeman must maintain. Although earlier analysis has shown that police can sometimes deal effectively with street crime, they have not been able to meet the challenge of more sophisticated kinds of criminal activity.

The price that ghetto residents pay for police protection seldom seems worth it—especially considering its ineffectiveness—when the police functionally become their enemies. The institutional situation of police has left their departments too weak to resist the warping influences of power and money from which their very existence as public agencies should in principle have separated them. Therefore police must be on the lookout first of all to maintain the rights and the privileges of the working classes and of the poor. To do this, however, police must be independent of the power of the rich and the politically well connected and subject to an independent ethic which builds upon their obligation to all the citizens of a city and strengthens it.

Police in America, and those who would help them, face a dramatic dilemma: how to eliminate illegitimate political and criminal interference in police departments and yet strengthen democratic controls on police.

This is not a new problem. Every city that has discovered its police department to be corrupt or unmanageable in the past has had to face it. Most have changed the department's relation to government by placing the chief of police under the control of another agency or an independent board, or by removing control of local police to the state level. Because there have been bad police chiefs and bad police-department administrations, it has been assumed that the answer to police problems is to build fences around chiefs and departments that would limit their authority and, in effect, keep them from being bad. Kansas City, Missouri, St. Louis, Boston, and Baltimore all have had control of their local departments removed to the state level in the wake of major scandals. But the limitations of such tactics were made evident, at least in the Boston case, by the fact that corruption there flourished more abundantly than ever with the real power of the department's administration so far away.

169

Eventually, in the wake of another scandal, control of the department was returned to the local level.

Because these efforts are essentially directed toward building systems that will make people perfect, they do not attack the most fundamental problems of police in a meaningful way. Creating new boards and superagencies to keep police—and especially police administrators—in line does not attack the problem. In fact, they usually do more harm than they do good because they tend to remove the decision-making procedure from the public, which is the only effective check on illegitimate interference in police departments in the long run. But the individual or group that is placed above the chief in authority is seldom elected; they are usually appointed. And since they do not owe their positions directly to the electorate, they are more likely to be responsive to the structure of the party that appointed them than to the voters. When independent boards are placed above chiefs, they function as multiheaded chiefs hidden in the shadows, blurring the lines of responsibility in police departments. If something goes wrong, who is responsible? If the board or agency really controls the police department—or if anyone else does—it is still the chief who is fired. This may be unfortunate for the chief, but it is disastrous for the public, because firing a chief does no good; it does not get at the heart of the problem, at the people who really control the police department.

This syndrome may be present even if there is no board or other agency that controls the chief. If promotions within the police department can be controlled from outside, if the behavior of policemen can be influenced, if there is a whole set of hidden political forces with which the police chief must deal, then, once more, he is rendered relatively meaningless in terms of improving his department.

The only direct control that an electorate has over a police department is through the mayor to whom the police chief is responsible. The electorate can, if it disapproves of the way a police department is run, demand that the mayor fire the police chief and replace him, and they can make it clear that if he does not, he will not be reelected. But if firing the chief does not change the fundamental orientation of the department, the mayor, like the chief, is powerless to reform. And if this is so, what power do the people have?

If the democratic electorate is to be the final authority for the way in which police departments are run, then the system of police accountability should be open to public scrutiny. The public should be able to see clearly who is responsible for police policies and procedures and should have some assurance that, if they do not like the police service they are getting, the removal of the person responsible will lead to swift and decisive reform.

This means a system in which the police chief runs the police department and is responsible to the mayor for carrying out programs and policies that the mayor—openly and publicly—directs him to follow. It also means that the police chief should have the power to make promotions on professional grounds without political interference.

In order to assure that the police chief is not vulnerable to every behind-the-scenes power play that takes place in city politics, he should be protected by a term appointment during which he cannot be removed for political reasons. But he should not have tenure that would permanently insulate him from public recall. In most instances, term appointments that do not directly coincide with the terms of mayors seem to work best, as in New York, where the commissioner's term is five years and the mayor's four.

That this kind of streamlined system can work was clearly shown by the F.B.I., which is an extreme example. The F.B.I. as it was taken over by J. Edgar Hoover was a corrupt, inefficient organization that was a national scandal. Hoover succeeded in building it into a highly professional organization with a reputation for integrity beyond question. This was done without benefit of Civil Service or any other regulatory apparatus. Hiring and promotions were handled strictly on the basis of effectiveness as evaluated by an

171

agent's superiors, and the chain of command was tight from top to bottom. Although some of Mr. Hoover's recent personnel decisions may be doubtful, the administrative structure of the F.B.I. would indicate that its orientation could be changed much more rapidly than that of most local police departments.

While there is in a broad sense a dilemma involved in eliminating illegitimate interference in police departments while retaining and strengthening democratic controls, on a practical level it is something of a false dilemma. The police department that is corrupt or that has turned into a political weapon does not need to be burdened with complicated new boards that diffuse accountability, that too often serve as newer, more subtle, and more permanent vehicles for the kind of interference they are supposed to prevent. Nor does it need to be run from the state level.

It needs, first of all, a mayor who will not claim in public to have a "hands-off" policy with regard to a department for which he is supposed to be responsible, while he uses it behind the scenes for his own political advantage. What a police department needs above all is openness. It needs exposure of the hidden influences upon it. It needs a mayor who admits that as the people's elected representative he must take responsibility for the over-all policy and direction of the department. Such a mayor should appoint a fully professional chief who has the power to control the inner workings of his department while following the broad policy guidelines of the mayor—or while disagreeing publicly and openly with them if he believes they involve a violation of professional ethics or practice.

A police department also needs a press that can and will hold a chief directly responsible for deficiencies within his department— for corruption or brutality—and a public that can evaluate the press to make sure that it is objective and fair and not itself a weapon of any political party.

Many fear that large, bureaucratized police departments have reached totally inhuman proportions. They seem so remote from the human values of everyday situations and so attuned to the realities of power on high political levels that individual citizens cannot exert any influence on them. There is a pervasive fear that police departments have outgrown the communities with which they deal and that they have become immune to criticism; that they have gained the power to enforce majority will upon minorities in such a way as to deprive them of their rights and their dignity.

These fears have validity. Police exist to enforce the law, not the will of the majority. They must resist pressures to go beyond the law—or to bend the law, or to enforce the law selectively, or to order their priorities in illegitimate ways—in order to make people conform to dominant patterns of behavior or thought. They must be sensitive to human problems and to the peculiarities of communities as well, especially in order-maintenance situations. This means that the nature of communities, and especially of minority communities, must be central to the way in which police departments are run.

The suggested solution to large, unresponsive police departments is often community control of police. While it is true that there are problems with oversized departments that have become bureaucratized, insensitive, and discriminatory, and while control should be diffused in many larger cities, community control involves serious problems that make it suspect as a panacea for police inadequacy.

A community is taken to be a group of people with agreed-upon values, a more or less homogeneous group which is entitled to have police maintain the kind of order it desires. A community is thought to be in need of protection from larger governmental units which are taken to be hostile. Those in favor of community control typically believe that intimate contact between people and police will lead police to understand an area's special needs and increase the capacity of policemen to understand ambiguous human problems. In this way, police will be more responsive and less authoritarian.

But this suggestion, while it is undoubtedly the result of human-oriented values, seems to be a concealed repetition of the kind of programmatic tinkering that has proven ineffective in the past. It

173

assumes that by changing the organizational chart of city government, the people who run police departments can be changed or made to act in better ways. This may be true in specific instances, but it is not necessarily true in all cases.

Beyond the initial shallowness of the community-control approach there are more profound reasons for suspecting it. First, in any situation it will turn out that the "community" as a group with similar values is extremely difficult to define. If the object of community control is to ensure minority rights, then what is to keep the majority of a given community from using the police to oppress its own minority? If community lines are drawn ethnically or racially, what is likely to happen to the few blacks who end up being policed by the Polish-American police, or the few Polish-Americans who are left in the black neighborhood?

The problem of majority will and minority rights cannot be solved by changing the basic unit of police service—unless we are willing to make those units so small that every person is his own majority, with his own police force.

The very absurdity of this idea leads to another difficulty with community control of police: It threatens to divide cities into closed communities, enclaves that stultify social mobility and grow increasingly defensive, that polarize people and set communities against each other even more radically than they are at present.

Suppose one police force operates under a policy that allows police to shoot fleeing felons, and a neighboring one allows such use of force only when the suspect is firmly believed not to be a juvenile. A thirteen-year-old youth from the second community goes into the first and is caught in the act of burglarizing a house of a substantial amount of money. He flees, and a policeman shoots and kills him.

The second community, however enraged it may be, has absolutely no recourse. The police are not theirs and not responsible in any way to them. The policeman's action was legal. They cannot demand the policeman's removal, or the chief's.

Professional Police and Democratic Control

Suppose that one community decides it does not want police to enforce laws against gambling or against drugs other than heroin and cocaine. People who want to gamble or use drugs from a community that does enforce these laws flood in. Parents who find that their teen-agers can buy LSD and mescaline openly in the streets in another community become enraged. But there is nothing they can do unless they choose to send their own police across boundary lines and infringe on another community's domain.

Already there are problems like this with police service. Already police in well-to-do areas stretch loitering and breach-of-the-peace laws to keep "undesirables" out. Already police use their power in some places to block open-housing law enforcement, or to try to preserve segregation.

Community control of police seems to mean systematized unevenness in the quality of police service. The unevenness we now have within jurisdictions is remediable at least in principle. Under community control, it would not be. Community control of police seems to mean institutionalized selective enforcement of the law. That is a problem now, but in principle it need not be. Under community control, it is difficult to see how it could be avoided.

If minority groups and poor people think they can profit from selective law enforcement and from unevenness of police service, they would seem to be ignoring a mass of historical evidence to the contrary.

Although large cities should probably decentralize their police departments in order to increase their responsiveness to communities, certain services such as training, record keeping, crime laboratories, and other support services should remain centralized to retain efficiency, as should the determination of fundamental policies. But in the majority of cities, decentralization is probably not to be desired.

The only way to improve police service to the point where it will be fair and equal in law enforcement and sensitive to community values in order maintenance is to concentrate on the peo-

175

ple who must do the job. This entails "professionalism," and it is highly controversial. Whether it has merely been misunderstood by its critics or whether it is intrinsically capable of abuse is a question to be considered seriously. If police are professionalized, what kind of values will they be likely to pursue? Obviously, this depends a great deal on what we mean by professionalism. But whatever we mean by it, unless it leads to some drastic change in the way police relate to the rest of society, it is highly suspect.

Some people have maintained that America has been saved from evolving into a police state in recent years only by police inefficiency and impotence. While it would be ludicrous to maintain that police incompetence is the only way to preserve our freedom—in the face of overwhelming evidence that it tends rather to destroy it—it would be foolhardy to strengthen an institution if we sincerely believed it to be out of phase with the mood of the nation and with the requirements of justice. The answer, of course, must be to change its direction *and* to strengthen it. It may be, as I will contend in advocating a special variety of professionalism, that one cannot be done without the other.

Professionalism for police is only desirable if it can be proved that the perspectives and prejudices of many contemporary policemen are not a necessary part of the police role as such; that they are in fact accidents of the peculiar way in which police have come to function in America; and that professionalism will tend to change these peculiarities and widen these perspectives.

The policeman's *task*, as it is now performed, is by definition the kind of work that is performed in our society by professionals.

James Q. Wilson, former director of the Joint Center for Urban Studies of M.I.T. and Harvard University, writes:

> Occupations whose members exercise, as do the police, wide discretion alone and with respect to matters of the greatest importance are typically "professions"—the medical profession, for example. The right to handle emergency situations, to be privy to "guilty information," and to make decisions involving questions

Professional Police and Democratic Control

of life and death or honor and dishonor is usually, as with a doctor or a priest, conferred by an organized profession. The profession certifies that the member has acquired by education certain information, and by apprenticeship certain arts and skills, that render him competent to perform these functions and that he is willing to subject himself to the code of ethics and sense of duty of his colleagues (or, in the case of a priest, to the laws and punishments of God). Failure to perform his duties properly will, if detected, be dealt with by professional sanctions—primarily, loss of respect. Members of professions tend to govern themselves through collegial bodies, to restrict the authority of their nominal superiors, to take seriously the reputation among fellow professionals, and to encourage some of their kind to devote themselves to adding systematically to the knowledge of the profession through writing and research. The police are not in any of these senses professionals. They acquire most of their knowledge and skill on the job, not in separate academies; they are emphatically subject to the authority of their superiors; they have no serious professional society, only a union-like bargaining agent; and they do not produce, in systematic written form, new knowledge about their craft.

In sum, the order maintenance function of the patrolman defines his role and that role, which is unlike that of any other occupation, can be described as one in which *subprofessionals, working alone, exercise wide discretion in matters of utmost importance (life and death, honor and dishonor) in an environment that is apprehensive and perhaps hostile* [italics added].*

From this analysis, it should be clear that although the heart of the policeman's task is analogous in some ways to that of a doctor or a lawyer or a teacher—although he must diagnose some of the problems that relate to these technical fields, and although there are other fields, notably the handling of violent situations, that are

* James Q. Wilson, *Varieties of Police Behavior: The Management of Law and Order in Eight Communities* (New York: Atheneum Publishers, 1970), pp. 29–30. Wilson cites Michael Banton, *The Policeman in the Community* (New York: Basic Books, Inc., 1965), pp. 105–110, as the source for this analysis of the professional role.

by definition his province alone—he is selected and trained not as a professional but as a semi-skilled laborer.

There are two possible solutions to this disparity. One is to narrow the police role to the point where it can be performed by a semi-skilled laborer. The other is to professionalize police to the point where they can handle their jobs as they are presently constituted.

In a sense, both of these things must be done. A policeman is emphatically not a doctor or a lawyer, and if his first aid is the last medical help an injured child receives, or if his determination of a legal situation remains as final, it is more society's fault than his. This cannot be tolerated. In addition, there are certain enforcement roles—such as those connected with victimless crime—which should be eliminated. If they are the business of anyone, they are the business of the clergy. But as the policeman's role is narrowed in these ways, it should be widened in others. The policeman should be made capable of handling white-collar crime, at least on the diagnostic and initial investigative levels. To do this, he must have advanced education and training. More important, he must be able to deal with people, and in this area he must gain professional expertise.

Professionalism in its final state is largely an attitude or a state of mind. But it cannot be arrived at by police through simple and cheap "image making" any more than it can be arrived at in medicine by putting on a white coat, or in teaching by standing up in front of a classroom and making marks on a blackboard. To some degree, although the mistakes of other professions must be avoided, it must be arrived at by giving police work some of the characteristics of those professions.

The very mention of police professionalism evokes sinister images in the minds of many people. They see visions of militaristic, super-efficient, semi-thoughtless automatons marching in lock step to a set of "police values" that are independent of democratic controls and backed up by tear gas and guns.

Professional Police and Democratic Control

But this is by no means the implication of the meaning of professionalism *per se*. Police already have the tear gas and guns, and some are semi-thoughtless and ready to march in lock step. The problem is to stem this trend. No professional group does or can consider itself outside the law to the extent that certain policemen and certain police departments do today. In fact, the strictures of professions typically arise because it is realized that the minimal standards of the law as they apply to the profession in question are inadequate. This may be a necessary function of the latitude of freedom that the law must allow to individuals. But it can also be disastrous—as quackery is in the medical profession and as performances like those at Kent State and Jackson State are in law enforcement. In order to take up the slack left by the law and to provide their professions with a credibility that the public will accept, professions form organizations around the relatively technical knowledge involved in their disciplines. By means of these organizations, members can be kept in line by other members even when they cannot legally prosecute them. This is the case with doctors who administer narcotics when they may not be indicated, or with lawyers who invent practices that are patently unethical but not demonstrably illegal. All this is certainly not to say that the American Medical Association or the American Bar Association always or even usually takes desirable stands on substantive issues. They, like all organizations, tend to become static and self-protective with time. But it is to say that the *notion* of such organizations add a much needed dimension to the accountability of the professions involved and raises debate within them to an ideological level which takes for granted certain minimum standards of competence and honesty.

But the disciplinary functions of professionalism are not its most important aspects. A profession, as Wilson points out, typically encourages some of its number to engage in systematic research. While there is no reason to pretend that police work can or should be made as scientific as the medical profession, it is plain that police

179

have very little notion of exactly what they are about and how efficient they are at it. Police must relate to constantly changing realities of society, economics, politics, law, ethics, and so on *ad infinitum*. They must realize their obligation to define their position and watch its evolution with care and reflection. Some aspects of police work can be quantified and examined. Such performance variables as response time are among them. Others, such as the crime rate with which police must deal, are difficult even in principle. And still others, perhaps in the long run the most important, such as the meaning of the individual in society and the definition of human nature, will probably never be capable of quantification. The point is that none of them has been broached as questions within police circles in meaningful ways, and there is not even a basis at present for research which can be systematically disseminated.

In addition to research organizations, professions are characterized by highly developed notions of service. A professional as such takes pride in his accomplishments not in making money or in acquiring power or in dominating people, but in contributing to the quality of life. This can be expressed in terms of increasing the fundamental freedoms of society's members: freedom from disease, physical or mental, from social deprivations, from ignorance, or from crime and injustice. Unlike the unskilled laborer or the wealthy capitalist, the professional would seem entitled to believe that without his services the condition of life for other people would be measurably different. In addition to this feeling of indispensability, the professional is also typically well aware, because of his extensive training and education, that he does not work in a vacuum and that he is indebted to others whose dedication to certain ideals has made his own success possible.

The key factor that militates against police professionalism on a systematic basis is the pseudo-military command structure of the police department. This structure is largely unnecessary to police work. It breeds a notion of supervision that is inappropriate to the patrolman's discretion and forces police departments to perpetrate monstrous fictions about the very role of the patrolman itself. If chiefs of police were called directors, if captains were called supervisors, and if titles were changed on down the line to the point where patrolmen were called generalists and detectives investigative specialists, little would be substantively changed, but a far more accurate picture of the discretionary patterns of the police department might emerge. For in fact, as has been pointed out again and again, it is the patrolman who exercises individual discretion in situations involving life and death, honor and dishonor. His superiors may set policy and hold him to its guidelines, but they cannot tell him what to do every day or even every week. A military unit always works as a unit and must be coordinated. Some city services, such as fire protection, can legitimately be organized in this way. But police work individually and must be dispersed. At present, most patrolmen exercise discretion with a lack of policy and leadership, on the basis of their own street sense. Because of the frustrations of their jobs and their limited education and training, they often do so according to inappropriate prejudices. Although a temporary solution might be to place them under closer supervision and to spell out policy in order to contain behavior, in the long run, as the patrolman changes and becomes more able to handle his discretion effectively, the supervisor's role must change. He must supply the patrolman with positive support for professional conduct and with the resources that he needs to do his job. He must become more involved in how the patrolman is used and in high-level policy decisions and planning and less concerned with knowing where every cop is every minute.

The militaristic concept of police work probably was a natural result of the period during which police departments were formed. Possibly because they were expected to take the place of militias in putting down civil disturbances when they arose, and possibly because recruitment standards were virtually nonexistent and policemen therefore *had* to be overseen in a military manner, the police

181

department was organized along the lines of a body capable of acting *against* large, identifiable groups of hostile people. From the beginning, the individual "private" was hardly conceived of as a professional.

As the years have progressed, the organization of police departments, if it ever was appropriate to their function, has become increasingly invalid. But the aura of danger, of violence, and in fact of "war" has persevered—centered largely around the fact that a policeman wears a gun. Even though the majority of policemen never fire their guns in the line of duty, and even though they are not subject to arbitrary military discipline when they do, the military mystique still lingers. For this reason, professionalism in police circles has seldom meant professionalizing the patrolman in the manner I have been suggesting. More often it has meant professionalizing them as if they were in fact military operatives. Police departments have given attention to equipment rather than to personnel and have in fact treated personnel much as one might treat equipment. If anyone is to be a professional in a police department, it is considered to be the chief.

The only professional organization in police work today is the International Association of Chiefs of Police, which is international primarily in name. It consists of chiefs of police from the United States, with a few from Canadian and South American departments. I.A.C.P. serves a useful function for police chiefs, and it is the only group attempting at present to further police professionalism. It is the only organization that has brought any intellectual effort to bear on police problems, and Quinn Tamm, its director, has not been afraid to disagree with such agencies as the F.B.I. over fundamentally philosophical issues.

But the I.A.C.P. is largely limited in its capabilities by its constituency. I.A.C.P.'s membership, each member possessing an equal voice, includes nearly every police chief in the United States, regardless of the size of his department or the complexity of his problems. Consequently, the vast majority of its efforts go toward conducting management studies in police departments which center around matters of technique and equipment. The I.A.C.P. journal, *The Police Chief*, fulfills the current demand for information about equipment far more effectively than it promotes broader discussions concerning institutional change and personnel.

But more important, the I.A.C.P. tends to reinforce the notion that if a department has a professional chief, he can implement professionalism in his department from the top down. *The Police Chief* calls itself "The professional voice of law enforcement." This implies that only police chiefs need to be professional. Attention is thus diverted from the patrolman.

The patrolman is the one who needs a professional organization. He is the person upon whom professionalization must focus. Pretending that improvement in police departments can take place from the top down is like pretending that if a school has a good principal, its teachers will automatically be effective. Because the patrol function is the basis of all police operations, all of the most profound questions concerning the police role and police professionalism come to concrete expression in his day-to-day work. One of the most central of these is: What are the policeman's fundamental obligations, and how should they be discharged? Without a clear view on this subject, police professionalism is directionless and may tend to become reactionary by default.

The conception of a policeman as one whose primary duty is to fight crime and whose job is "law enforcement" has so pervaded our notions of the police role that it largely determines how we will answer these questions. Almost anyone who is asked would be likely to say that a policeman's fundamental obligation, and perhaps his only obligation, is to the law.

On the face of it, this is unarguable. In order to function, society must be governed by laws. Police are but one element of our elaborate system of justice. The people as a whole are supposed to be able to enact laws, to make sure that the laws correspond to the Constitution, to change the Constitution if it proves inadequate, and to enforce legitimate laws under procedures provided for in a complex criminal justice system. It would seem that a policeman as citizen has as good an opportunity to change the laws through the proper channels as anyone else and that as a policeman his sole duty is to enforce them as they are written.

But aside from the fact that policemen cannot possibly enforce all laws at all times and thus are forced to choose when and when not to make arrests in specific situations, a little reflection will cast doubt on the assumption that the policeman's obligation to the law is absolute.

Suppose, for example, that a policeman works in a section of a large city which is predominantly inhabited by homosexuals. Behavior that would seriously disrupt most other communities is accepted in such areas, and in many ways it is the norm. There may be laws against it. Is the policeman's role to enforce laws against homosexuality there? Or does he have a certain obligation to the community's wishes and to its values?

Or suppose that the policeman works in an urban ghetto. Is he obliged to enforce there all the laws passed by legislatures dominated by middle and upper-class representatives, regardless of whether or not they correspond accurately to the wishes of the overwhelming majority of the community? Must he do this at the price of alienating and possibly destroying the community?

Or suppose that the policeman works near a college community whose liberal attitudes lead it to tolerate behavior—be it sexual, obscene speech, or even trespassing—that would not be tolerated in other parts of the city. Is his role to use the law to enforce the moral views of society in this environment?

In the light of such instances, it might be contended that the policeman's primary obligation is to the community in which he serves—to preserve its stability, to keep the kind of order it values, and to be responsive to its wishes and needs, rather than to some abstract notion of the law as absolute. Certainly this is the thrust of much contemporary criticism of many of our social institutions, and the impetus behind demands for community controls of police, of schools, and of other agencies. And, despite the limitations of complete community control of police, certainly in many instances it is well founded. On this view, the strict enforcement of law becomes secondary to the policeman's central obligation to the community.

As it turns out, the question of the policeman's fundamental obligation seldom arises. When it does, it is only because people disapprove of his conduct and accuse him of disrespect for the law, or of insensitivity to the community, or of callousness to basic human values. This is to say that they manipulate these three categories, or others, in order to condemn him.

The policeman cannot be programmed to act appropriately in all situations any more than anyone else can. In turn it should be obvious that what is important in the long run is not the "program." What is important is the person—his ability to choose between the values at stake in a given situation in a sensitive and enlightened manner. Police discretion cannot and should not be eliminated. Police must be aware of their profound obligation to the law, to the community in which they work, and to fundamental human values. They must be made directly responsible to broadly based democratic controls, and they must be isolated from illegitimate influence.

Many people would be tempted to say that if a policeman's conscience and his own values so conflict with those of society that he cannot enforce laws that he believes to be evil, or societal and community standards which he feels to be unjust, he has no right to be a policeman. It is here that the question of the policeman's role comes full circle. To assert that he has no right to remain a policeman is to say that police departments must be made up of those who are willing to act like automatons in response to the dictates of enacted laws (which have been shown repeatedly to have no necessary relation to justice) or to the most powerful elements of a given community (which certainly have no demonstrable monopoly on justice either). It is to close police departments to the point where they contain only the more reactionary elements of society.

But to say that such a policeman does have a right to remain on the force, aside from raising serious questions about what he is going to do, seems to be to say that there is no valid police role in society—that a policeman has obligations no different from those of anyone else. If this is true, what is it that sets him apart, that gives him the authority to wear a badge and carry a gun, to make arrests and to mediate in disputes?

Although questions of fundamental police obligation do not arise this starkly during the day-to-day operations of a department, they are always operative behind the scenes. For instance, many blacks will not work on police forces because they plainly see that they cannot enforce the laws, the community standards, and the background assumptions of the powers that run those departments. Police tacitly accept this situation, because they believe that dissenting blacks would render their operations nonfunctional. Does the true police role require the sacrifice of openness and susceptibility to change?

The possibility of fundamental change is raised dramatically and concretely in demonstrations, protests, disruptive actions, and in revolutionary violence. Typically police have responded that they are not, in situations when they must handle these incidents, trying to repress dissent, or to stifle change, but that they are merely trying to minimize violence. In view of this claim, what is to be made of the fact that in situations like Attica, violence seems to have been maximized for the sake of abstract notions of propriety or narrow legalistic prerogatives?

Unlike the situation at Kent State, in which (as nearly as we can determine) a number of National Guardsmen acting on their own either panicked or acted in anger, the decision to invade the Attica prison with guns blazing was made by a State Corrections Commissioner, with the full knowledge, approval, and, seemingly, encouragement of the Governor of the state, who was immediately

186

congratulated publicly by the President of the United States for his decision. The issue seems to have been a fundamental one. Should those functioning in a police role act in such a manner as they believed would immediately put an end to prison revolt and all violent acts of dissension? Or should they act in such a way as to preserve human life as the most fundamental value involved in the situation? At bottom, the issue comes down to this: In situations in which the most basic authority of the state is challenged, what is the police role? Is it to preserve that authority and the right of the state to protect its power? Or the right of a government to perpetuate itself? Or is it to act as mediators who have an obligation to a value even more fundamental than the right of the state to protect itself?

This question can be brought into focus around a concept that was introduced earlier in connection with the handling of demonstrations: the police as referees. Traditionally, when the government or the structure of a nation has seemed in danger, police have considered it their role to be willing to die and kill to preserve it. In effect, as politically related crime rises to the proportions of warfare, they have considered it their duty to enforce laws more strictly than ever. Should police in such situations attempt solely to minimize violence and allow the chips to fall where they may as long as human life is preserved?

For this as for many similarly basic questions, there seems to be no answer that will fit all situations. The situations themselves determine what values are at stake, and there is no way to foresee what they will be. What we can say at this point is that if a balance is to be maintained between these elements, this has not been accomplished with American police in recent years and that there is a clear need to move in the direction of valuing human life if that balance is to be obtained. And if we move in that direction, in the direction of making police referees—increasingly as political frictions increase—then the whole conception of the role of police in America, and indirectly of the legitimate use of force in societies in general, will change, and with it will change police behavior, training, education, and attitude. For if the police become so tied to a society as it exists that they are placed in the position of defending it in principle, no matter what it does, we may find them ready and willing to defend a dictator.

Once more, there is no answer to this question apart from the values of specific situations. And once more, it is vital to attempt decisions like this before the situations arise. In the end, such contradictions are the boundaries of our speculations. They are both the end and the beginning of our efforts to define the police role.

If police are to move generally in the direction of professionalism, if they are to see themselves as mediators and not antagonists in all disputes, from domestic arguments to crises of political dissent, police departments must be altered radically. As they now function, it may be accurate to say that only their inefficiency and weakness insulates us from the excesses of police departments that may be used as weapons, or from individual policemen whose discretion cannot ultimately be controlled by authoritarian means. But this attitude admits defeat. It means that crime in America, from the street crime which so threatens us day and night to the organized crime which corrupts and corrodes our public life, to the white-collar crime which robs us of millions of dollars and destroys our moral fiber, will become more powerful and widespread. And this in turn means that police will be further manipulated, that they will be more frustrated, that they will be increasingly dangerous, and that eventually our society will be in danger of becoming crime-dominated and so controlled by networks of illegitimate power that no progress and no change of any kind will be possible.

Before this happens, we must make our criminal justice system work. This means making the courts and prosecutors fair and effective. It means making rehabilitation a reality rather than a myth. It means providing broad societal support for the changes that are necessary to root out the causes of crime and eliminate them wherever possible. For police, it means a commitment to restructuring and reform of local departments on a scale that is far greater than anything we have yet conceived. It means reforming and restructuring them until they can cope with the problems of crime and the problems of human beings in a way that is now completely beyond their capacity.

8

Rebuilding Our
Police Departments

THE LOCAL POLICE DEPARTMENT must continue to be the nation's basic police agency.

This statement contains nearly all that should be preserved of our present wisdom about police departments and how they are run. For in order to ensure that Americans have the proper balance of police protection and protection from the police, the police department as an institution must literally be turned upside down. Americans are not safe from criminals when the agencies that are supposed to protect them are internally stagnated and externally stymied. Nor are they safe from police departments that have gradually become islands of hostility and resentment in chaotic seas of cultural and political upheaval.

Nearly all serious students of police problems today recognize that the crisis in law enforcement can be characterized in one word: people. Police departments operate with the wrong people, under-

191

educated and poorly trained. Until this situation is rectified, there can be no hope of improving American law enforcement.

The restructuring of police service must begin by making the last first. This means making the patrolman, who is at present looked upon as a clerk and an errand boy with the intelligence and sophistication of a professional wrestler, into a thoroughly educated, highly sensitive professional with competence equal to that of a skilled teacher or social worker.

The patrolman in today's police department exists for the sake of his superiors and for the politicians who control them. If he has any ambition, it is to get out of patrol and into the departmental hierarchy, or into the detective division. But the patrolman should not exist for the department; the department should exist for the patrolman. In the overwhelming majority of cases it is the patrolman who responds to the bewildering variety of calls that pour into police switchboards. It is the patrolman who interacts with the public, who cruises the streets around the clock, and who makes decisions—whether they usually involve life and death or not—that have profound effects on his community. There is no way to eliminate a patrolman's discretion. He *must* work alone, or with one other patrolman at most, and he must handle chaotic situations. The solution is to make the patrolman a person who is capable of handling the discretion and responsibility that is intrinsic to his job.

All of a police department's services should be oriented toward support for the patrolman. The investigative services of the detective division, the supervisory assistance of the department's hierarchy, and such technical services as communications should be structured to ensure that the patrolman will be capable of doing a first-rate job.

This means that he cannot work in a vacuum. It means that once he has succeeded in controlling a chaotic situation and in diagnosing its fundamental elements, his efforts will be followed up immediately, effectively, and in depth. This should apply whether the incident is a homicide or a domestic dispute.

Rebuilding Our Police Departments

If the incident is a serious crime, the patrolman should know that the newest and most scientific methods will be brought to bear immediately and that the case will be followed up in a coordinated manner from the local to the state and national levels if necessary until it is solved. At present, the patrolman responding to an armed-robbery call sees a carbon copy of a thousand hopeless situations he has seen in the past. When he arrives, he does what he has been programmed to do: He protects the crime scene, he interviews people to try to find witnesses, and he waits for the detectives to arrive and take over, at which point he will move on to the next impossible situation. He knows if there are fingerprints, clues, or obvious leads at the scene, even if he has taken the trouble to piece them together and brief the detectives, his efforts will have been wasted. And should any of the elements he has pointed out prove crucial in the final solution of the case, he knows that detectives or his superior officers will get the credit anyhow.

If the incident is a domestic dispute, the patrolman should know that there are places that he—or the disputant—can turn to with an equally meaningful follow-up effort. Social agencies of the government or the community, employers, legal help—all should be capable of supporting the patrolman's original diagnostic observations with action that will ensure that he will not have to return again and again, night after night, to the same hostile and dangerous scene, until someone is jailed or seriously hurt.

To get the kind of person that police departments need, they must move on several fronts at once. Police departments must become active, rather than passive, recruiters. They must set higher standards for entering recruits so that the public gets better people for the increased salaries it is being asked to fund. They must offer comprehensive educational programs with wide latitudes and strong incentives. They must support bold innovations in training that prepare police for the jobs they really have to perform.

Police departments as they now exist make no effort to broaden their recruitment bases. They are threatened by people of intelli-

193

gence; they are threatened by people of divergent views; they are suspicious, to say the least, of minority groups. This trend must be reversed. It is becoming increasingly difficult for police recruiters to brave the hostilities of large segments of the population in search of qualified men. But that is all the more reason that they must make the effort. A good police recruiter will not sit at a desk waiting for local politicians to bring their nephews and their neighbor's children to him. He will go out into the community in search of talented people and convince them that in fact there is a meaningful future in police work.

Once the recruitment base of a department has been broadened so that it represents not the special province of any ethnic minority or political power group, the process of selection begins. With regard to the patrolman, this selection must be rigorous. In my opinion, initial selection should ultimately be based upon three criteria: intelligence, psychological balance and sensitivity, and education.

There should be no room in a police department—at least not among the ranks of patrolmen—for recruits who do not meet certain standards of intelligence. Although intelligence in itself is difficult to measure, especially for cultural groups whose values may be different from those of the people who make up the standard IQ tests, and although we may not even be sure exactly what intelligence is, we cannot ignore it. The solution to this problem is not to discount the validity of objective testing. It is for police departments—perhaps more than for any other agencies or institutions—to press for the development of tests that are capable of searching out intelligence regardless of cultural differences or of educational deprivation. To continue to place people of mediocre intelligence in police departments as patrolmen is to ensure that police will at best be inefficient and ill-managed.*

* The ambiguities of the value of objective testing with regard especially to minority groups are somewhat ironically demonstrated by the fact that in 1970 while there was a lawsuit in Oakland by minority groups to require more ob-

Rebuilding Our Police Departments

At present, testing for psychological fitness and sensitivity is even more difficult than testing for intelligence. It has proven almost completely impossible for police departments to screen out recruits who want to be policemen because they are eager to impress their own values on society by force, or who are interested solely in proving their "manhood" to themselves or to others. Police departments must press for the development of such tests. But in the meantime, they must make sure that recruiters and trainers are fully aware of this problem and that they agree that such motivations are completely incompatible with police work. They should attempt to develop their own methods of identifying such people and to disseminate the results of their experiments to other departments if they seem to be successful.

It has been suggested that the educational requirements for entry into police departments be extremely high. At a time when half of the nation's college-age population is attending college, it would seem logical to require that police patrolmen have at minimum a college education. However, as police departments are presently structured such an expectation is unrealistic and may in fact not be desirable. Eventually police departments should be able to require that advancement to the rank of full patrolman be contingent upon a college education, or at least upon a meaningful exposure to a broad-based higher education. But this implies the existence of ranks in a police department below that of full patrolman. And it should also imply a responsibility on the part of police departments to ensure that qualified people in those lower ranks can get a college education and advance accordingly. This means that police departments must place a high premium on college education. It means that they must make available financial support and prolonged leaves of absence to policemen who want to go to college—to the

---

jective testing for admissions to police departments as a way of eliminating administrative bias, there was a simultaneous suit in Washington, D.C., by minority groups to increase administrative discretion and decrease the weight of objective tests because of their cultural bias.

college of their choice, in order to pursue any field of study which is related to police work, no matter how remotely. In this respect, police departments should clearly separate education from training and should understand that it is only by getting out of the "closed fraternity" and gaining independent knowledge and varying perspectives that cops will be able to become fully professional and to serve their communities fairly. Programs such as the one currently financed on a very small scale by the Law Enforcement Assistance Administration (L.E.A.A.), which grants loans to policemen for educational purposes which are forgivable at the rate of 25 percent for every year of subsequent police service, should be made practically universal. Police departments may fear that such a procedure would lead men to take advantage of education provided by police departments, to put in four years of service, and then to get out. But if police work were truly a profession, this fear would have less validity than it now does. And it is only by offering such incentives that police departments can ever hope to attract large numbers of recruits of potentially professional caliber.

If police departments are to be drastically upgraded in this manner, and if patrolmen are to become a department's most important professionals, many people now in police work may have to be left behind. Those who have lost their enthusiasm, their ambition, their honesty, or their dedication will be among them, as will those who simply do not have the basic intelligence to meet new police standards.

However, in this process, we must realize our monumental obligation to those who have stayed in police work, who have "kept the faith," while working at impossible jobs under absurd conditions. For whatever effort is made to get a new kind of person into police work, double that effort must be made to give the people already in it opportunities to readjust, to hold their own, and to advance. In some cases this may mean offering policemen such basic remedial education as reading and writing, and it may mean persistent efforts to follow these basic necessities through with continued support all the way up through higher education. Despite the cost and care implied in such efforts, they must be made, because many policemen now on the job have had little more educational opportunity, or opportunity for personal growth, than have many of the criminals with whom they deal day in and day out.

Nothing would be more unfair—and more foolish—than to write off the cops who are now at work. If anyone has an opportunity to gain from the upgrading of police service, those who have perhaps suffered most consistently from its present abominable state should be first. For dedicated and honest police who have been stuck in the "closed fraternity" for years to stand by while their newly vitalized departments take off into a new era without them would be monumentally cruel. It would also produce in them a justifiable bitterness that could render police departments nonfunctional for years.

A police department that has attained a broad recruitment base, rigorous standards of selection, and offers attractive incentives for higher education has made a vital—an indispensable—leap toward progress. But progress has not yet been made. The next step, the step without which these people will not even be given a chance to help turn police departments upside down, is meaningful training.

The first place to start the revitalization of a police department is in its training program. A local administration can do a great deal in training for a price which is relatively small in comparison with its total expenditures. Training cannot be education. In fact, in some ways it is antithetical to education. Education by its very nature raises profound questions about police and their role in society. Training attempts to orient the recruit toward the job he will actually have to perform. As such, its first responsibility is to allow the recruit to know who he is as a policeman and how he will handle complex and often dangerous situations under pressure. Although any good training program will give attention to basic skills such as first aid and the use of firearms, it should be made plain that the knowledge of these skills is incidental to the central function of policemen.

197

POLICE IN TROUBLE

Sophisticated police training is in its infancy. Traditional training has been so totally sterile that virtually no meaningful experimentation has gone on outside of a few isolated departments, and the results of these experiments have not been disseminated.

The first task of the police trainer is to break down the recruit's preconceptions about police work. At present, many police recruits come from the military. A substantial number have been military policemen. Whatever their previous occupation, however, they invariably enter with the notion that they will immediately be issued two-way wrist radios and sent out to match wits against sophisticated criminals. They see themselves—in the words of one training lecturer—as new recruits in the army of law enforcement enlisted in the war against crime. Somehow they have forgotten the policemen that they have actually seen—directing traffic, arresting drunks, and performing other mundane duties. While in future years a patrolman as such should not direct traffic and probably should not arrest drunks, he will always mediate in brawls and disputes and in general, control situations in which it is not at all clear who is right and who is wrong.

New Haven's Training Director, John Heaphy, developed a training program which made extensive use of innovations and experiments designed to break down the trainees' stereotype of police work and to allow the cops to see the realities of the police role. He began training programs with a full week of laboratory training —which has similarities to sensitivity training and encounter-group experience—in order to uncover these stereotypes. In role-playing and in other situations recruits had the opportunity to act and react in situations analogous to those they would have to face on the job. The function of such techniques is not to remake a personality but to readjust the values to reality and to attempt if at all possible to show trainers which recruits will and which will not prove to be suited to police work.

Along with such self-revelatory procedures, training must of course impart vital information. The key word is "vital." Police trainers have been so taken in by mass-media portrayals of the police role, and so enmeshed in the twisted workings of police departments as they now exist, that police training has come to consist almost solely of irrelevant and badly presented information structured around a set of carefully preserved fictions. The policeman does need to know about criminal law, but he does not need it fed to him in a monotonous stream from a lectern. He needs it taught in such a way that the provisions of it which he will have to use day in and day out have become a part of him before he leaves the police academy. One of the most promising developments in this field is programmed learning. Programmed texts which the police recruit can work through at his own pace, and which virtually assure that once he has worked through them he has mastered their informational content, have proven to be an efficient, economic, and dynamic method of teaching such subjects. There may be better methods, but they have not yet been tried or discovered. The point is that police departments should be hungry for the very latest innovations in educational theory and should be made capable of experimenting with them and adapting them to their own uses as a vital part of the testing and research on these methods. Police departments can ill afford to lag half a century or a century behind in these fields.

In addition to getting to know himself and getting to know the basic information that he will need to do his job, the patrolman must be made aware first during his training, and constantly thereafter, of the subtleties of the human relations which he is asked so frequently to deal with. There is no way for a policeman who has been in a department for twenty years to know what is going on in the minds of juveniles or of college students or of members of ethnic groups who differ significantly from him. Human-relations training should attempt to make trainees aware of these things. One of the most effective ways for the police trainer to do this is to bring in the people, sit down the trainees, and have them talk to each other. New Haven's trainer brought in groups of semidelinquent teen-agers for discussions and confrontations with police recruits. They were his "experts" when it came to training police to deal with juveniles. When it came to discussing civil liberties, he brought in groups of college students for similar discussions and confrontations. When a policeman is chasing a juvenile through a darkened housing project, or when he is facing a hostile demonstration of college students, it is too late to try to get him to understand. Unless he has come to grips with these people as human beings his reactions are likely to be inhuman.

Police training should contain elements of experience which allow the recruit to see the relevance—or irrelevance—of what he is learning as he goes along. Of New Haven's twenty-week training program, several weeks were dedicated to observation of police work. Five to seven weeks into the training program, New Haven's recruits were sent into the field for two weeks of observation with carefully chosen experienced patrolmen. In many departments—and New Haven was no exception—the selection of these "model patrolmen" is one of the trainer's most difficult tasks. First, they must be the department's most competent patrolmen. Second, they themselves must be extensively trained.

Once more, toward the end of the training program, recruits were sent out into the field—this time to operate patrol cars and to handle situations themselves under the close supervision of trusted patrolmen. These sessions, perhaps more than any laboratory training or group discussion or proclamation by the trainers, serve to show them exactly what a policeman really does.

Among the informational needs of a policeman are knowledge of departmental rules and policies, of motor-vehicle laws, of first aid, of firearms, of procedure for handling disturbances, etc. Concealed in such vague terms as "departmental policy" are vital issues. Simply telling a trainee that he must not see the mayor without the police chief's authorization is not enough. The recruit must be made to understand the extent to which he is responsible through the proper channels to the democratically determined will of the people, and on the other hand the extent to which he as a professional must scrupulously hold himself above partisanship and favoritism. In addition to understanding abstractly the reasoning behind such policies, the recruit must be aware of the structures by which they are enforced. To some degree he must be aware that they will be enforced by departmental sanctions. But in a larger sense he must be aware that there are certain practices that do constitute accepted and legitimate professional conduct and others that should be completely below his capacity as a professional. Just as effective recruitment is futile if a department has not been radically reformed, training is not effective if recruitment has not succeeded in providing the department with people of high ideals and good instincts.

In the final phase of his training program for the New Haven Police Department, John Heaphy put his trainees through an exceptionally complex and arduous series of role-playing situations designed to test every aspect of a policeman's self-knowledge, his knowledge of his trade, and his sensitivity to the subtleties of human interaction. Heaphy went so far as to bring in professional actors to act out complex dramas with patrolmen, ranging from domestic disputes to situations involving serious breaches of the criminal law. If in these situations trainees—as they often did—misquoted the simplest statutes, or took actions that would have been likely to precipitate violence, or refrained from intervening in potentially deadly situations, they made their mistakes in the laboratory and not in the field. It is one thing to make a mistake on a test. It is another thing to make a mistake in a palpably real situation and to see before one's eyes the kinds of tragedy that can result. It is one thing to chew on a pencil, to whisper for a friend to help with an answer, and in the end perhaps to put down a combination of words that is right or at least nearly right. It is another thing to have to act in a split second and to have to live with the results of that action.

Since police training is still in its infancy, the foregoing descriptions and suggestions are tentative. It is important to note in terms of traditional police training that what has been omitted is as sig-

201

nificant as what has been included. Little if any emphasis should be given at present to such subjects as the investigation—at least in detective style—of such crimes as homicide and bank robbery with which the patrolman does not need to be concerned. Although the F.B.I. has for years dominated the training of local police departments, it knows virtually nothing about the day-to-day problems that occur on the local scene. In most regions the F.B.I. provides a systematic lecture service which is available to local police departments. This service consists of a number of carefully marked filing cabinets and a number of F.B.I. agents or ex-agents who make use of them. A local police department will request an F.B.I. lecture—for instance, on juvenile delinquency. The F.B.I. assigns someone to give the lecture, who goes to the filing cabinet and pulls out, under the letter J, a prepared lecture on the topic. At the time he delivers it, he may have read it or he may not have. At any rate, he has certainly never handled juveniles himself, and even if the lecture should have any applicability to the local police department, he will be unable to answer questions. Obviously this canned approach by an agency concerned solely with national law-enforcement problems and with serious crime is completely sterile in all but the areas of the F.B.I.'s particular jurisdiction and competence. The New Haven Police Department in the end reduced the role of the F.B.I. to one lecture—concerned with the federal jurisdiction.

One area in which the F.B.I. *can* be helpful is in the area of technical training and sophisticated investigative techniques. The F.B.I. runs a police training academy to which local departments send perhaps one or two officers at a time. Although the academy cannot be a substitute for local police-department training, there are other functions of the academy which are valid. These are, once more, scientific and technical areas in which the F.B.I. excels. In training, however, the domination by default of the F.B.I. over the local police department must cease, and local police departments must be given the incentive and the capability to do for themselves those things which they should do and which the F.B.I. should not do.

Although most larger cities would probably have most effective training if they simply concentrated upon the problems that needed attention, using advanced and innovative training methods and moving beyond the F.B.I., many smaller departments cannot afford to put together first-rate training programs on their own. In dealing with this problem, as with in-service management training, detective training, and other more sophisticated forms of training, a regional approach seems most effective. Departments in certain areas would be well advised to pool their resources and establish regional training centers.

If the patrolman, once he is properly recruited, selected, educated, and trained, is to be the primary professional within the structure of the police department and the person toward whom all department services are directed and upon whom the success of the department rests, he must not be asked to perform essentially mechanical functions that waste his time and talent. As it now stands, the patrolman is the lowest rank in most police departments, and the man in the squad car is forced to direct traffic, give out parking tickets, spend endless hours doing clerical work, and is rendered generally ineffective. It does not take a patrolman to do these things, and assuming they are truly the responsibility of the police department, they should be done by people who are in effect "subpatrolmen" and who do not have to meet the requirements of training and education of the patrolman.

While the subpatrolman could merely be a person who performs tasks like writing tickets, to think of his or her role totally in that context would be a mistake. A recognizable career ladder should be built in the police department as a whole, and it should especially be built around the position of patrolman. The subpatrolman position could represent the first step in that career ladder. For young men or women without the means of educating themselves, this position could be used as a way of giving them an income, of introducing them to police work, and, if they were interested, making the educational opportunities of the department open to them. The subpatrolman might in some cases be a meter maid without advancement ambitions, or he might be an investigative aide with the responsibility for doing much of the mechanical and time-consuming leg work and records checks for the detective division.

In areas of cities where crime is so highly concentrated that foot patrol can be effective, this function can be performed by subpatrolmen. Armed with radios and supported by highly mobile professional patrolmen in squad cars, these "night watchmen" should serve as a neighborhood's eyes and ears. They could be taken directly from the neighborhoods they served. There is no need for such a person to be a sworn officer, there is no need for him to be highly educated or trained, and therefore no need for him to be highly paid. Such people could be college students, people seeking part-time work, etc. They should be employed primarily during high crime hours as deterrents. They should be unarmed.

It might be suggested that these people, unarmed, would be highly vulnerable to attack. Such patrols, however, already exist in many cities on a private basis. Businesses and industries use night watchmen. Block associations hire private guards who are more vulnerable than subpatrolmen would be because they do not have police radios. Now only the rich and the organized can afford such luxuries. They should be made available to the poor as well, and such people could be taken from the communities involved. Once more, if they proved capable of advancing to become patrolmen, every effort should be made to ensure that they could do so. This would expose new people to police departments, open new possibilities for community responsiveness. Upward mobility for these people should be swift and meaningful.

The creation of such a subpatrol force would in effect create an unarmed parapolice force that might, if successful, show the way toward disarming both criminals and the police. It might provide a meaningful experiment in the direction of the English model. It would tend to decrease the criminal's need to carry weapons and help to destroy the military notions of police work which are so pervasive. Whatever role the subpatrolman performs, he should be observed closely and evaluated thoroughly in his performance in such a way that will allow the department to know quickly whether it wants to invest in him the substantial effort necessary to make a professional patrolman.

In addition to the position of subpatrolman, which provides a kind of a floor for the patrolman's activities and a steppingstone into the promotion to patrolman, there should be ample room for advancement and pay increases within the ranks of those who perform the patrol function. Some departments have experimented with the notion of a "master patrolman," which attempts to give the successful patrolman advancement avenues that allow him to stay on the street. It is my feeling that there should be several gradations of patrolman and that promotion within those gradations should be contingent upon the department's evaluation of the patrolman's field performance. While Civil Service should be retained in some form, as a security factor and as the regulator of promotions from rank to rank, advancement within the patrol rank might well be outside Civil Service. There should in the end be room for a first-rate patrolman to earn as much as or more than his immediate superiors if he is good at his job and if it is worthwhile to the department to keep him in it.

But what could a patrolman possibly do to be worth $15,000 or $20,000 a year? Right now, nothing; but there must be a radical revision of the entire concept of what a patrolman does and who he is. The patrolman should be capable of handling, at least on an emergency and diagnostic level, any situation relating to crime or disturbance of any variety within his city. Although it is humorous now to imagine a business which suspected embezzlement calling a patrolman, it should not be so in the future. Patrolmen should be capable of handling white-collar crime, they should be capable of penetrating organized crime, and they should still be capable of providing effective and meaningful service in such areas as juvenile problems, domestic disputes, and street crime.

The patrolman's job as it is now structured is a young man's job. This must continue to be true to some extent, but hopefully as the policeman becomes more sophisticated, the possibility of having to wrestle a drunken husband down three flights of stairs or of having to break up a barroom brawl will diminish. Nevertheless, police departments should be prepared to accept a much higher rate of turnover than they do now, which would mean a higher percentage of young men in the department at a given time. As it is now virtually impossible for a patrolman to remain in his job for twenty-five years and retain any kind of enthusiasm or effectiveness, it would seem that strong incentives—such as the educational incentive mentioned previously—should be offered to induce large numbers of young men to become policemen, who could then—after having met the educational, psychological, intelligence, and training requirements —be observed on the job and eventually be marked for advancement either within or outside the patrolman's position or oriented toward career routes outside police service. This means that people who are interested in police work for other reasons besides steady employment and attractive pension benefits will be drawn in.

There is no reason why everyone working in a police department should be a sworn officer. Sworn officers are simply too expensive and too valuable to perform many of the routine and largely clerical functions which now take up so much of their time. A patrolman should not be a secretary; he should have one, or he should have access to one.

If police departments are truly to be opened up, civilians should be placed in many positions that do not by their nature require a sworn officer.

Many civilian positions that could be filled by men could also be filled by women, as could many sworn positions as well. Women should not be used in positions in which physical strength is essential, but women are obviously capable of performing many detective functions as well as certain patrol functions, and certainly of occupying administrative and policy-making positions up to and including the position of chief of police.

In the use of civilians, local police departments would do well to follow the example of the F.B.I., which uses civilians for laboratory work, as fingerprint experts, as planners and technical advisers, and in many other capacities. There is no reason for a police photographer to be a sworn officer—in fact, there is every reason for him not to be. Besides the fact that his training and expertise are wasted, he is unlikely to take good pictures.

In addition to performing clerical and support functions, civilians should be used in crucial policy-making positions. Especially in such areas as administration, planning, and legal counseling, civilians can bring in diverging viewpoints and particular expertise that police officers are unlikely to have. The gains in openness and efficiency that result from the use of civilians can be spectacular. In departments that fear civilian influence and that maintain the rigid boundaries of the closed fraternity, it is almost a necessity that policemen be promoted to do things that they cannot do and that many important tasks are seldom even attempted.

But a police department should not be allowed to become an internally divided agency in which civilians and sworn officers are constantly at odds. Provisions should be made for civilians to become sworn officers if they wish to. On the other hand, the road should be open for sworn personnel to acquire the kinds of in-service training and academic education necessary to fill positions that at present would logically be filled by civilians. While there is no reason to assume that someone who has attained the rank of captain in a police department today has management and administrative capabilities, there is also no reason to assume that he cannot gain them with training and education.

Perhaps the central element in the efforts of any agency to upgrade its personnel is its system of rewards and promotions.

POLICE IN TROUBLE

At present promotions are so slow in police departments that informal reward systems—rewards outside the purview of Civil Service—are more important. These rewards, such as transfers to squad cars, to a detective division, or to soft inside assignments, nearly always encourage the wrong kind of behavior, or behavior that has little or nothing to do with the fundamental police function. When they are not given on the basis of political interference or favoritism, they are given for performance in atypical situations. The result is often reward or promotion by accident. It is never the policeman who cools a potentially violent or dangerous situation, who is sensitive to human needs and human problems, or who exercises his discretion with professional restraint, who receives commendations or special promotions. It is always the cop who, arriving at the scene of a fire, manages to rescue a building's occupants, or a cop who, coming upon the scene of a robbery in progress, manages to shoot a fleeing suspect. Although there is nothing wrong with rewarding bravery above and beyond the call of duty, it is far more important to reward consistent and effective performance in situations that recur day in and day out. Often a policeman, by handling a situation badly in the first place, precipitates a crisis that could otherwise have been avoided and after resolving it with his night stick or his gun, receives a commendation or a transfer. And as always, the only routes upward in police departments lead away from patrol. Even if such rewards and commendations were given for the right reasons, they would tend to take the best and most professional people out of the very areas in which they are most important.

With regard to actual promotions in rank, Civil Service is more often than not self-defeating. This does not mean that Civil Service should be eliminated. As a mechanism for avoiding illegitimate political interference, it should be made more objective and strengthened. This means more objectivity and relevance in written testing and more direct departmental evaluation in determining efficiency ratings. Police departments should press for the development of tests that suit their needs. Hiring outside testing firms to devise

Rebuilding Our Police Departments

and administer such tests is an important step—as long as those firms can be made aware of what they are really supposed to be testing for. In the long run the police profession itself should devote considerable energy and attention to these tests while realizing the limitations of tests, which cannot by their nature determine such factors as honesty or courage—or efficiency.

Determining a patrolman's efficiency is something that only his superiors can do. Police departments should regularize this practice. Evaluation on this model gives ranking officers the opportunity to review findings with regard to specific patrolmen. It also gives top administrators the opportunity to evaluate the way the department supervisors themselves evaluate patrolmen and to encourage rewarding the right kinds of behavior. It builds a chain of accountability around an evaluation process that is open and direct and which is subject to numerous checks and balances. A police chief who suspects that a supervisor is giving high evaluations to patrolmen for political reasons can eliminate such procedures, and a supervisor who sees a police chief manipulating efficiency ratings for political reasons at least has written evidence and factual information with which to counter such manipulations.

It is only within the context of meaningful rewards and promotions that true leadership can take place. Leadership is meaningless if the patrolman is no more than an automaton incapable of independent judgments. But most important, positive leadership is impossible if supervisors cannot reward good conduct. At present, the "Gamewell Box" model of supervision—which attempts to eliminate the policeman's discretion or to use it against him in a purely negative manner—is the only way supervisors can attempt to control their men. If, however, promotions are given for the right reasons and supervisors have a direct voice in determining who will be promoted, a supervisor can be looked on not as a punitive figure but as someone who is capable of supporting and rewarding the policeman.

This is not to say that the supervisor should support the policeman no matter what he does. Undeniably, one reason for close supervision is to eliminate the present situation—in which, too often, *nobody* is responsible for improper police behavior—and to substitute it with a situation in which *everybody* in a police department's hierarchy is responsible. This means that discipline for improper actions must be as firm and as swift as rewards for proper ones. But if police departments begin to operate with the right people, gradually a supervisor's role should shift from an authoritarian one to an interactive one. A supervisor responding to a complaint upon which patrolmen are working should be able to analyze the situation in broad terms, to discuss it with the patrolmen from administrative and policy viewpoints, with the aim of improving the department's ability to support the patrolman in all situations. The supervisor should be able to suggest systematic changes when the need for them becomes obvious in view of his experience, in addition to making sure that patrolmen are properly deployed, and drawing their attention to potential areas of sensitivity or complication. He should assure that patrolmen's time is used to best advantage and that patrolmen are assigned to tasks on the basis of their talents and abilities. Supervisors, in conjunction with patrolmen, should be capable of coordinating investigations, of drawing upon resources within and outside the police department, and of setting priorities for police action.

Insofar as possible, police departments should have clear and unambiguous written policies which, going beyond the statutory limitations upon police, codify practices and procedures that promote good behavior and define the meaning of professional police behavior in broad terms. A policeman who operates in a vacuum of policy is vulnerable to criticism and discipline which is arbitrary and after the fact; he is without true support. In addition, the police administrator who fails to clarify policy with regard to such vital problems as the use of deadly force, what does and does not constitute corruption, and the limits of legitimate political influence is hard put to justify disciplinary action in concrete and unambiguous terms.

A department which operates with the right people at the "bottom" and supports them with meaningful leadership and policy has gone a long way toward turning itself upside down and in becoming capable of providing its community with responsible and responsive police service. Professional patrolmen who are performing valid functions and who have leadership and incentive have been given the proper context in which to work. Within this context, their real responsibilities can be increased and broadened.

In a restructured department a patrolman would often handle criminal cases from start to finish. The patrolman arriving at a crime scene, if he is truly professional, will be capable of handling it and diagnosing its elements himself. If, for instance, he responds to a robbery complaint, he should be the one to determine whether detectives are needed. He should initially determine what avenues of investigation the detectives will follow, and it should be part of his job to assemble all pertinent information and to make sure that it is properly followed through by detectives. The case should be his case. He should be kept informed of new developments in it. In comparison with the patrolman's job, the detective's job is highly specialized and, at least with regard to most street crime, more routine. Detectives should continue to initiate their own investigations into areas of organized crime and should branch out into other areas. In cases which they initiate, they should of course present evidence in court and claim credit for arrests which are theirs.

The relationship between the detective division and the patrol division of the police department should be a working partnership between equals. The patrolman's anticrime role is to maintain a highly visible patrol and to attempt to prevent crimes. But the patrolman should not be the only one on the streets. In most police departments, patrolmen drive cars and detectives sit in the

211

detective bureau doing clerical work or following up investigations. Needless to say, a detective should no more do clerical work than should a patrolman, and detectives should be provided with investigative assistance as well as secretarial help. Thus freed from the mundane duties of their specialty, detectives should be used for inconspicuous patrol. Driving unmarked cars and in plainclothes, they can often observe criminal activity that high-visibility patrols cannot. In addition, if they are assigned to regular patrol when they are not following up other cases, detectives can be immediately available to assist patrolmen in investigations and to carry on prolonged and intensive investigations for which special training has prepared them. One of the specific findings of the Katzenbach Commission was that rapid response tremendously increases the possibility of solving cases. Rapid response does not ensure that a fleeing suspect will be apprehended, but it ensures that witnesses will not have disappeared, that their memories will remain fresh, that they will be able to give more accurate descriptions and detailed accounts. It also ensures that crime scenes will remain undisturbed and that evidence will be intact.

But detectives are only one variety of support that the patrolman should be able to call on. In addition, police departments should have full-time lawyers available to help in training and to assist patrolmen in preparation of warrants and other legal papers. Lawyers could be used not only in police headquarters to assist in the preparation of cases for court but also in the field. A patrolman faced with a legally ambiguous situation should have immediate access to a lawyer who could clarify the rights of disputants in various cases, or help determine whether probable cause for an arrest is present. It would even seem advisable to have lawyers patrolling with detectives so that they could reach patrolmen quickly. If a patrolman does a preliminary investigation in a white-collar crime case and determines that further investigation is warranted, the police department should also have an accountant he can call in.

In addition to providing accessibility to specialists like lawyers and accountants, patrolmen should be supported in a number of other, more mechanical ways. Patrol beat plans should not be devised, as they are now in most places, by a combination of guesswork, instinct, and apparent need. In this and in a number of other areas, computers, if properly used, can prove invaluable. They can store, analyze, and feed back data about where and when different kinds of crimes occur. This can assure that the deployment of preventive patrol is used to optimum efficiency. But this is not the only use for computers. A patrolman on his way to investigate a domestic dispute should not have to walk into a situation with no background knowledge if the disputants have been involved with police before. Computers could be used to feed out data on previous police encounters.

A particularly effective method of improving response time and police efficiency would be the use of "car locaters," which, by flashing the positions of all cars in service onto a map of a city, could tell dispatchers at a glance which car was closest to an incident and which cars were available for assistance. Such a system, which might use radio-sensitive receivers on telephone poles throughout the city and which would detect the presence of passing police cars, exists and could be provided to cities the size of New Haven for a cost of approximately $200,000.

Before such innovations are made, however, police departments must be provided with the basic equipment necessary to save police time and to improve police working conditions. A police department, for instance, which is forced to drive cars for hundreds of thousands of miles with inadequate maintenance facilities loses a great deal of time through breakdowns.

Policemen spend far too much time writing out reports. In New Haven, a survey showed that this time accounted for 21 percent of the patrolman's working hours. In order to cut down on this waste, New Haven instituted a system whereby patrolmen making reports went to a police call box after the incident in question and called headquarters. They were connected to a dictating machine, which took their reports in a fraction of the time it would have taken to write them up. The reports were then transcribed by secretaries, and the amount of time spent in report writing was reduced to 5 percent. This meant a substantial increase in real police man hours at a cost far below what would have been required to hire additional patrolmen.

Mechanical aids, however, are of no use unless the personnel using them are competent. For example, many cities which have installed complex computer systems have found that the data supplied to them are so inaccurate and ambiguous that their mountains of computer print-out are of little value except as curiosities. A computer system attempting to establish patterns of MO's (modi operandi) can be fouled up by a cop who characterizes an MO poorly or inadequately. Consequently, before making any large-scale investment in computers, a police department should have in mind precisely what it needs to know—precisely what questions it wishes the computer to answer—and must make sure that it has personnel capable of feeding accurate and unambiguous information to programmers. To fail to do this is to put the cart before the horse and to invite tremendous waste with little hope of gain. In addition, computer data banks should be restricted to hard data about criminal activity; information concerning political activities must be summarily excluded.

In addition to the use of computers, there are many other techniques which local departments or groups of local departments should attempt to develop. These include the use of photographic equipment, fingerprint equipment, drug testing devices, and microscopic analysis capability. Few departments have been able to develop scientific and technical capabilities on their own. Once a police department is capable of using these techniques by virtue of its professional personnel, it should make every effort to utilize them, both to increase effectiveness in apprehending criminals and in deterring crime and to save invaluable police man hours.

In conjunction with these efforts other policies should be experimented with. For instance, it is difficult to see why a person who is apprehended for a breach of peace or other misdemeanor should be arrested, thrown in a police wagon, and taken downtown. It would make more sense to issue citations like traffic tickets in these situations instead of taking the accused persons into custody. As long as the policeman can determine that the person involved is not dangerous, he should not have to make him go through the process of incarceration, with all the inconvenience and complications it involves. In most cases such a procedure would involve a change in state statutes, and this is one area in which lawmakers could be of assistance to policemen.

Since on the whole a good policeman's instinct is to avoid making an arrest in ambiguous situations like domestic disputes, it has been widely suggested that alternatives to arrest be explored. In New Haven there was considerable public pressure for police to refrain from making arrests in emotional situations, but to take the disputants instead to a community center or social agency for a "cooling-off period." This seems to be worth experimenting with. However, it could become a license for abuse of police power, since police would be able to detain people without actually arresting them. The question as to whether such a cooling-off period would be mandatory or optional is largely an academic one, since a policeman could always threaten those who did not want to "cool off" with arrest. This kind of procedure might allow policemen to detain citizens unlawfully for whatever reasons they chose. Suppose, for example, that a policeman wanted to question someone about his political connections. He could seize upon any small altercation in which the individual was involved as a pretext for detention and interrogation.

Alternatives to arrest are especially needed in cases where the basic problem is medical or psychological rather than criminal. Alcoholics are perhaps the prime example here. Every town has incurable alcoholics, and every police department is forced, for lack of any other approach to the problem, to lock up the same alcoholics for the same reasons time after time. This represents not only an immense waste of police, court, and corrections time but also a meaningless and degrading experience for those who are arrested. Police should be able to refer alcoholics to governmental agencies with some confidence that a sustained effort will be made to help them. As has been discussed elsewhere, a parallel effort should be made with those who are addicted to hard narcotics.

To say that these things should be done is to say that many police problems are community problems and that in addition to breaking down the closed fraternity by introducing civilians into it, police should introduce themselves to the community. This means being frank about the police department's problems. Police chiefs should be honest and candid about what their departments can and cannot accomplish. No longer should they pretend, as the public wants them to pretend, that police are capable of handling everything from barking dogs to the narcotics traffic and organized crime. If police chiefs and their men are being asked to do the impossible, they should say so.

There is no reason that a police department should not open all but the most necessarily secret of its intelligence operations to the public. Civilians should be encouraged to observe police operations, to ride in patrol cars, and to invite police officers to talk to them, not about the ancient stereotypes of police work and about the clichés that surround the profession but about the policeman's real role, his true problems, and what he attempts to do about them.

But the openness of the police department cannot be confined to an informal level. Every local police department should have an effective formal policy, and an internal investigative agency, for civilian complaints about police. The existence of such an agency to "police the police" should be publicized, and it should be easily accessible to the public. Police departments should have standard civilian complaint forms, and all policemen should be required to carry them and to produce them on demand to civilians.

Once a complainant has filled out such a form—which may in

itself act as a deterrent to those who want to criticize police irresponsibly but who find that when it comes to lodging a complaint they are not quite sure of themselves—he should be assured of prompt action from the police department and a full disclosure of the investigation's findings. During this process, the rights of the policemen must be scrupulously protected. In New Haven, the officer involved had a right to be present if a complainant was to make a statement about his case, and the complainant had a right to be present when the policeman made a statement.

If such internal investigations are conducted fairly and effectively, police can police themselves. In a truly professional organization this would not be a problem. Policemen may initially be hostile to the idea of certain members of the profession investigating others, but when they see that people trained in the techniques of investigation and therefore singularly qualified to do it act as swiftly to exonerate policemen unfairly charged as they do to expose policemen who have violated departmental policy or exceeded the bounds of professional behavior, they tend to accept them.

In principle it would seem desirable to have civilians participate in such investigations—and preferably civilians from outside the police department. Civilian police review boards are an emotional matter. They need not be, since most civilian review boards have proved to be more sympathetic to individual cops than good police administrators would have been in many cases. If legal and democratic controls on police are working properly, and if the public demands a department that is open and responsive, civilian review boards, which too often merely proliferate bureaucracy and are open to political manipulations themselves, are unnecessary. The problems of police departments originate deep in their historical and political foundations, and to mislead the public by pretending that review boards reacting piecemeal can solve their problems and meaningfully influence police behavior is too often to divert attention from the real problems at hand. In some situations police departments are so out of control that civilian review boards are necessary, but in such situations the ultimate solution cannot be civilian review boards but revitalized political leadership that is willing to make fundamental institutional change. For civilian review boards are not an effective solution even to the limited type of brutality or corruption problem that they attempt to deal with. When police departments are bad, the roots of their problems are far deeper than any civilian review board can penetrate.

Openness within police departments should not be a one-way street. While police must admit to their limitations and attempt to bring civilians into their ranks as department members and into their operations as observers, they must make it clear that communities, cities, states, and the federal government have obligations to attack social problems that become police problems through neglect. In many cases it is true that a police department takes action only after society—governments, welfare institutions, schools, churches, parents, friends, and a host of other institutions—has failed. Too often police departments become an accelerating factor in the cycle of failure.

If police realize that the overwhelming percentage of street crime in their city is being committed by people from broken families, with poverty-level incomes, in areas where housing and education and basic public services are inadequate, and in which the use of drugs thrives, they must insist that society respond meaningfully to these problems. If they do not, they will find themselves battling for decades against the products of the same crime factories. If they realize that the victims of street crime are likewise predominantly from these areas and that these are citizens whom it is their job to protect, they will realize that their task is doubly important.

While it is the policeman's task, perhaps above all else, to maintain the notion of individual responsibility, individual integrity, and freedom within society—and to maintain, as a professional, his own individual responsibility for his actions—it is also his task to examine the underlying causes of crime. In this connection, the policeman must have a double message for his community, and especially for its middle- and upper-class members. With regard to street crime, he must make it clear that, given the underlying causes of such crime, there is a serious question concerning the ultimate responsibility for it.

But he must not, in talking about street crime, pretend that it is the only kind of crime that exists. He must make it clear, not only in words but by investigations and arrests, that he is aware of the white-collar crime problem and that its invulnerability, which has in the past provided one of the prime rationales for police corruption itself, is at an end. Police must make it clear that while the attention of the public is focused on street criminals who steal ten dollars or a hundred dollars at a time and on the pervasive threat of violence that accompanies street crime, businessmen, lawyers, doctors, politicians, and others are stealing thousands, hundreds of thousands, or even millions of dollars with impunity.

If police do not have the capacity to investigate white-collar crime, they must make it clear that they will not be used by one segment of society against another or forced into patterns of selective and discriminatory law enforcement. They must demand that *someone* enforce the laws on all levels of society and that the far more inexcusable crimes of the rich create reactions equally as profound as the scandals created by the violence of the brutalized poor. For while the policeman's task is primarily to deter and neutralize violence, and above all to protect human life wherever it is threatened, it is also his task to show how crimes of property on a high level contribute both to poverty and to a lack of moral character on all levels of society and help to perpetuate the endless cycles of street crime against which he must battle every day.

Police departments should steadfastly resist expansions of their roles into such areas as school discipline. Although policemen must respond to emergencies in schools and investigate criminal behavior there, police action is no substitute for basic reforms in our educational system. The police should be the first to say that if education must be carried on with a policeman in every classroom, it is not worth the price. Policemen cannot enforce insensitive and obsolete methods of education any more than they can enforce laws against gambling and marijuana, or any more than they can enforce poverty and discrimination. Here as in so many other areas, the police role is not to enforce the views of an individual school administrator, or even of a school board or a state legislature, on substantial segments of the population or on the students themselves. Policemen and police administrators must make it clear that it is not their job to enforce the status quo or to stifle change by force. When they are asked to do so, they must object as professionals and as public servants within the channels provided by government.

If a police department is willing to open itself up in these ways, it should receive support from the community, which will no longer make it necessary to protect the ineffectual, corrupt, and brutal individual within its ranks because of the internal needs of the closed fraternity. It is this kind of relationship with the community which comprises true "community relations."

Many police departments in recent years, realizing that large segments of the population are hostile to them, have instituted "community relations" units. This was in fact a recommendation of the Katzenbach Commission—and one that seems to have been put into practice in such a way as to defeat its purpose. Any department composed of frustrated cops who may have become reactionary and even brutal can find within its ranks half a dozen or so policemen who are presentable enough to residents of hostile areas that they can try to do gently what their fellows would do less gently. Too often, however, community-relations squads represent no change in the police department as an institution or in the attitudes of the people in it. If this is true, the community-relations unit becomes a public-relations gimmick that misleads the public. It may be a slick temporary answer to community pressures, but it is more than likely to turn into a fraud. A community-relations unit makes a department no more responsible and no more responsive than it was before. Invariably it is an ornament that distracts attention from a bewildering variety of institutional ills. Often in troubled situations a department's community-relations unit is given a short period to try to "cool it." If this does not work, the department reverts to its old ways, and people's heads get cracked. A community that is hostile to police will be increasingly and not decreasingly embittered when on one night a community-relations squad is trying to convince them that the police department is a good thing and the next night the "real cops" beat a narcotics addict within an inch of his life or arrest someone on trumped-up charges.

For some departments, the "tactical squad" is the functional opposite of the community-relations squad. A "tactical squad" is essentially a violence squad whose function is to operate saturation patrols in certain areas or to respond to disturbances with shows of force.

Community-relations units and tactical squads are both admissions of the failure of police professionalism. The creation of a community-relations squad says that a police department cannot relate to a community through decent and fair responses to that community's problems as a whole and that it must create a gimmick to gloss over its deficiencies. The tactical squad says that a department is incapable of handling potentially violent situations in nonviolent manners and that a single patrolman or a few patrolmen conventionally trained and armed are simply incapable of preventing or controlling significant crime or disturbances. While the community-relations squad as it now functions is usually a distortion of a fundamentally good impulse, tactical squads point toward a militaristic elitism—a kind of shock-troop emphasis—which could lead police departments toward a model even more inappropriate, and in the end more dangerous, than the Dick Tracy crime-fighter image they now promote.

A police department's community-relations program should be directed toward assuring that patrolmen are capable of relating to individual members of the community in just and humane ways. Police departments need not seek to publicize their successes; they should seek to analyze their failures and make the public aware of the deep-seated reasons for them. This cannot be done, however, without significant community support and without removing police departments from the patronage system.

A large part of police community-relations work should be concerned with taking the criticisms of citizens seriously and using concerned citizens groups as wedges to open up police departments. Dealing forthrightly with such groups can sort out those who are sincerely interested in helping police from those who are concerned to make headlines for themselves, or to protect special interests. For instance, just before May Day in New Haven, a group called the Medical Committee on Human Rights came to request access to police detention facilities over the weekend to make sure that those arrested would not be beaten or mistreated. I welcomed them —but I was curious to know where they had been for years when ordinary prisoners had suffered inhuman conditions in obscurity. As I suspected, although the group was quite outspoken over May Day, once the crisis had passed, I saw no more of them.

Police should not wait for such groups to form spontaneously around crisis issues. Departments located in or near college towns, or with access to colleges or universities, should induce academic groups to study law enforcement and criminal justice and to use their considerable prestige and moral leverage for reform. A police chief—or a professional patrolman—should be so on top of his situation, and he should have such good liaison with groups and institutions that may be able to help him, that he can assist their efforts and ask meaningful questions of them. He should keep in mind that the task of such research groups should not be to advertise what is good in a police department. This should be taken for granted, as a starting point. They should try to determine what is wrong—and having so commissioned them, police should expect and welcome criticisms and not be defensive about them.

Again, however, openness should not be a one-way street. A police chief who realizes that his department is being asked to treat problems which are not in principle police problems should challenge the community to meet its obligations. Police problems are intimately related to community problems, to difficulties with individual laws, and to broad social and political dilemmas in general. If, for instance, a policeman's community has a serious narcotics problem and no significant rehabilitation programs under way, the policeman should not pretend that arresting addicts will stem the tide of drug-related crime. He should insist that he is powerless unless rehabilitation is effective and that the dynamics which lead to addiction and perpetuate it are simply not related to traditional notions of punishment by detention.

If, as is usually true, the courts in a policeman's city do not function meaningfully, if people arrested by police are not tried for months or years and commit numerous other crimes while out on bail (or who languish in jails because they cannot make bail), police must insist that speedy trials be provided. This must be done as much to protect the state's right to effective punishment of offenders as to protect the defendant's right to fair judicial proceedings.

Since as much as 80 percent of all crime is committed by recidivists, police must speak out more strongly for rehabilitation than for any other single criminal justice reform. At present something like 5 percent of the up to $8,500 a year which is needed to keep a man in prison is spent for rehabilitation, and even that money is most often misspent. Since statistics suggest that effective rehabilitation could diminish crime by as much as one half, police should point out the simple economic fact that increased expenditures for rehabilitation could save society fantastic amounts of money in police service, courts, prosecutors, and in fact prisons themselves. But this realization should be only the beginning of the recognition that to ignore rehabilitation is to ignore sensitivity and human compassion as well.

If police insist that their communities and society in general must concentrate on rehabilitation, they must insist upon effective rehabilitation of juveniles first of all. Police now know when they pick up a boy for shoplifting that there is nothing that can be done, no matter how they do their job, to keep him from turning eventually to purse-snatching, burglary, or armed robbery. There is excellent evidence to indicate that juveniles *can* be effectively rehabilitated.

Police juvenile divisions should be staffed with men of great patience who have specifically requested such duty because they can communicate with juveniles. Such men should be backed up by case workers with social-work backgrounds or strong community ties which give them an understanding of the child's environment so they can talk to him in a language that he can understand. The New Haven Juvenile Bureau experimented with neighborhod centers to which juveniles could be brought for conferences with case workers and parents. Although such "outposts" of the police department in poverty areas met with hostility that made the experiment difficult, there was a feeling that with persistence—and with the right people—perhaps it could in the long run be effective.

One thing is certain: Police chiefs, and other police officers down to the rank of patrolman, must make it clear to their communities that present ways of handling juveniles tend to criminalize them without giving them the kind of attention that might keep them from recidivism. At present one of two things usually happens to a juvenile offender: If his offense is not considered serious, he is simply "marked bad" (in Connecticut, by means of a "referral" to juvenile court) and thrown back into the situation he came from. In more severe cases, he may be put in a reform school where he learns all the lessons that a veritable "school for crime" can teach him.

It cannot be stressed enough that the crime preventive role of police is extremely difficult to evaluate but that one area in which concrete progress can be made is in the treatment of juveniles by juvenile courts and correction systems.

Public opinion can contribute most significantly to the improvement of police departments by removing illegitimate political interference from them. Citizens must be aware of municipal corruption which tends to invade police departments and must insist that high public officials, and especially the press, be energetic in rooting out corruption and exposing its workings. In the end, of course, only institutional changes can succeed in limiting the extent to which such corruption influences police departments—institutional changes which change policemen into the kind of people who are above such corruption and interference.

One of the most important ways in which a department can increase its efficiency and the quality of its service is to cooperate with other departments and to move toward regionalization. This is the only way in which small and medium-sized departments will be able to gain the resources for proper support services like training, and for effective elimination of complex crime problems.

There are many things that a local department can do to promote regionalization. It can start with a regional pooling of personnel who are working on similar or related crime problems. It would allow coordination of their efforts and make sure, for example, that the elimination of organized crime from one jurisdiction does not simply mean their removal to another. Regionalization should reach the point where groups of departments cooperate on patrol patterns, on sharing records and data, on constructing laboratories and other technical facilities, and in installing common communications systems. In the end, training could often be conducted on a regional basis with a considerable gain in efficiency and a broadening of the kinds of training that are available. Regionalized training should begin in such specialized areas as management, investigative techniques, and crime detection which small local departments cannot afford to develop and finance for themselves.

Regionalization is perhaps the ultimate step in the attempts of a professional police department to meet the responsibilities of the law-enforcement profession as it applies to them. But there are many things that regionalization cannot accomplish. There are

225

national problems that escape regional and even state jurisdictions. And there are problems within cities themselves that are caused by interference of corrupt political officials and organized criminals which police departments by definition cannot handle. In addition, although police departments can take dramatic and meaningful steps to break their present pattern of failure, they do not have—and cities as a whole do not have—either the financial resources or the research capabilities for carrying police professionalism through to its completion. For this task, and for others, there is only one entity that is capable of providing the kind of concerted effort needed to rejuvenate local police departments. This is the federal government.

9
The Future
and the Federal Role

THE FEDERAL GOVERNMENT must enter the field of law enforcement dramatically and decisively to support efforts to ensure police effectiveness, police professionalism, and police responsibility. There are dangers in federal involvement in local law enforcement, but they can be avoided, and they must be. Forty thousand different police agencies—an average of eight hundred per state—now comprise a helplessly fragmented jungle whose complexity alone makes accountability almost impossible and whose lack of coordination and cooperation virtually assures that the nation's largest crime problems will never be subjected to meaningful attack.

Americans have a healthy skepticism concerning centralized power. Unfortunately, this skepticism is often not sustained or consistent enough to keep illegitimate power from becoming concentrated and working its will behind the scenes of American politics. It is only institutionalized enough to keep legitimately established power from attaining the ability to deal with illegitimate power.

POLICE IN TROUBLE

A hard-hitting approach by the federal government to the problems of law enforcement does not mean the creation of a national police force. Local and regionalized departments must continue to be independent of federal control and responsible to their constituencies. There is no reason to believe that federal intervention in absolutely crucial areas would necessarily lead to concentrations of power any more dangerous than subterranean concentrations of power that have already been built up. In fact there is reason to believe that certain areas of crime cannot be treated at all without limited consolidations of power.

Although Congress can provide proposals for changes in the criminal justice system, and although its leadership and funding is essential to the improvement of police service, it cannot lead the way in saving American law enforcement. And although the Supreme Court can and should attempt to clarify the meaning of the police role in terms of the United States Constitution, neither can it substantially change the conditions under which police operate. Any initiative for reform of law enforcement which is to be effective must come from the executive branch of the federal government, which must act immediately to initiate truly profound changes in the criminal justice system. Only the administrative branch is capable of designing and implementing the kind of coordinated long-range plans that are needed.

Perhaps the most fundamental element of any Administration's approach to the criminal justice problem is an intangible one: the moral tone and quality of idealism which it brings as its first approach to the problem. Across the vacuum of leadership in law enforcement, strong positive signals must be sent out that promise institutional change in the long run and that promise approval of and rewards for sensitivity, imaginative initiative, and respect for human rights and dignity immediately. If the tone of an Administration's approach to "law and order" tends to isolate police from the rest of society, to make them defensive and in fact self-righteous, and in effect to make the President of the United States and his advisers seem to be members of "the closed fraternity," there can be no hope of progress. Unless the individual policeman's best instincts are appealed to, he will end up identifying with and attempting to justify his police department as it now exists and will reject out of hand any attempts at reform or innovation.

Since the mid-sixties, Administrations have taken two different approaches toward the law-enforcement problem. One I will call the legalistic approach and the other the institutional approach.

Although the legalistic approach to the improvement of law enforcement was evident in the mid-1960's, within Administration circles the institutional approach prevailed. The establishment of the Katzenbach Commission, and the substance of its report, brought an emphasis on reform of the institutions and agencies of the criminal justice system. Although the Omnibus Crime Control and Safe Streets Act of 1968 contained such provisions as increased use of wiretapping, and although it authorized the use of federal funds for such hardware as guns and tear gas, these provisions were not part of the Administration's intention and were certainly not recommendations of the Katzenbach Commission report which led to the original drafting of the legislation. The heart of the Omnibus Crime Control Act was internal police-department reform, improvement of police operations technique, and upgrading of police personnel. The inclusion of such gimmicks as wiretapping and increased hardware and the attempt to circumvent landmark Supreme Court decisions were largely the work of Senate conservatives.

The undercurrents of the legalistic approach which surfaced briefly in portions of the anti-crime bill became the dominating force with the advent of the Nixon Administration. Its assumptions are that police institutions are fundamentally sound and that "law and order" depends upon an end to permissiveness, which can be obtained by adopting new legal rules. Since 1968 these assumptions have been the underlying impetus for our federal approach to law enforcement. Thus although law and order had become a major political issue in President Nixon's successful 1968 campaign, by the third year of his tenure attention to institutional reforms in police work had withered away to nothing. In place of this, legislative measures such as preventive detention, no-knock laws, and expanded wiretapping prerogatives were enacted supposedly in order to "take the handcuffs off police." Other legalistic measures which would have gone further in the same vein were proposed or studied. Among them were proposals for the abandonment of unanimous-decision requirements in jury trials, the abridgement of appeal rights in certain cases, and even a study which looked into the feasibility of repealing the Fifth Amendment to the Constitution of the United States.

Along with substantive legislation and legislative proposals, executive "signals" of a certain variety fall into this category, as do administrative decisions, especially within the Justice Department. The Justice Department's selection of cases for federal prosecution is another area in which this noninstitutional approach to law-enforcement problems manifests itself. The decision not to empanel a grand jury at Kent State is one example. The Justice Department's advocation of illegal mass arrests in protest demonstration situations, as seen in Washington, is another. And the appointment or attempted appointment of lackluster and sometimes suspect judges to the Supreme Court because of their political acceptability is yet another.

These legalistic gimmicks have been used by an Administration which claims to favor a return of power from the federal government to the state and local governments. By refusing to institute basic changes that would allow police to be both professional and responsive to the needs of their community, however, they have tended to perpetuate the present condition of law enforcement. As a result, the position of the present Administration might be deemed, on the level of reality if not of rhetoric, to be soft on crime because it is soft on the shortcomings of our current system of criminal justice.

The Future and the Federal Role

Thus the widely advertised pretensions to cut back the power and authority of the federal government have in fact led to an increased dependence of police upon those politicians who are willing to "support them," no matter what form that support might take. And they have led in this manner to a *de facto* increase of power for national politicians who seek to play off police against the rest of the population in emotion-charged ways which they believe will win them elections.

The legalistic approach is not appropriate as a response to the national crisis of law enforcement. Most of what the Nixon Administration has done in the area of criminal justice has been at the expense of the hard-won civil liberties of Americans. Institutional change, not legal gimmickry, is needed if police departments are to become once again the protectors of liberty rather than the enemies of liberty and if they are to stop moving in the direction of becoming the personal armies of partisan politicians and party bosses. The leadership vacuum in law enforcement must be filled rather than exploited if law enforcement is to be saved.

Institutional change on the part of the federal government should take two basic directions. On the one hand, the federal government must support local police departments in their efforts to upgrade their personnel and to handle every problem that they should properly deal with. On the other, the federal government must realize its duty to remove responsibilities from the shoulders of local police departments that they cannot handle even in principle. In addition to these two basic directions, there is a further dimension to federal support: Although the creation of a professional police organization as such is not intrinsically a responsibility of the federal government, and in fact although such an organization should ultimately be oriented toward resistance to great concentrations of federal power, at present the federal government is the only entity capable of initiating such an organization. The federal government should move in this direction as well.

Federal support for the internal improvement and increased effectiveness of local police departments should itself take two forms. The first should be the provision of technical assistance that can be used by departments as they now exist. The second should be the provision of financial incentive and professional leadership for internal reform and reordering of police departments.

The first area should be the responsibility of the Federal Bureau of Investigation. The F.B.I. must be transformed from an isolated to a responsive resource for local police departments. This means that it should structure its technical facilities in such a manner that it can be more useful to them. Except in the most delicate situations, the F.B.I. should be willing to disseminate to local police departments investigative information that it has gathered from other local departments and leads that it gathers on its own. There is no excuse for a local police department holding an investigation of an organized-crime case to be denied access to F.B.I. data about it. The only way in which departments have traditionally received information from the F.B.I. is through informal channels based on personal cooperation between police detectives and F.B.I. agents.

While the F.B.I. should make its own investigations more accessible to police departments, it should at the same time encourage large city departments, and regionalized groups of smaller departments, to gain the technical skills of scientific criminal investigations that it has long had. Local departments have traditionally been discouraged from gaining any degree of sophistication in these techniques because of the widespread feeling that the F.B.I. could supply them with all they needed in this field. As a result, the F.B.I. has gained a reputation as the nation's elite crime-fighting force, and most technical expertise in these areas has been confined to a federal agency and a few large police departments. The F.B.I. should send teams of experts out to consult with local departments and to advise on how crime laboratories, computer systems, and other technical aids could best be used for handling serious crime. Such techniques as microscopic analysis of blood types, of various artifacts at crime scenes, such procedures as clear, accurate, and complete photographic coverage of crime scenes, and such techniques as computerization of physical descriptions should cease to be myths and become realities.

The F.B.I. should be encouraged to provide supportive resources for local police departments. Such a development would mean a true diffusion of centralized power in an area where such a diffusion would be useful. Scotland Yard performs similar services in England, and there seems to be no reason why the F.B.I. could not be so styled in this country.

In addition to support for the technical needs for local departments, however, the federal department must prod local departments to restructure themselves drastically. The institutional changes foreseen by the Omnibus Crime Control Act were to be administered by the Law Enforcement Assistance Administration. Unfortunately, L.E.A.A. has become—and increasingly so under the Nixon Administration—a viaduct for the dissipation of federal funds into local political boondoggles. Its effect has been not to help local police departments but to create fifty separate state bureaucracies which channel money into local police departments that have proven through the years to be unworkable. L.E.A.A. money has been primarily spent for such devices as tanks and radio voice scramblers, despite the fact that the most pressing need in police circles is for better trained and educated personnel. Since it has been forced to make block grants to states, L.E.A.A. has not been able to exercise control over the way the money is spent, and consequently it has been unable to spur drastic police reform.

L.E.A.A. should be given the power to develop sets of standards toward which local departments would have to move in order to obtain federal funds. These standards should include training, in which field L.E.A.A. should take the lead in developing and approving training curricula for local departments which are suited to their needs. L.E.A.A. should in addition conduct experiments with methods of teaching police and should press for the adoption of new techniques such as programmed learning, psychodrama, and other innovations in training. It should also fund ongoing research programs both within local police departments and within educational institutions to investigate new training and educational methods as they are developed in other fields and to determine their applicability to police training. Research on these subjects should go on to attempt to evolve new techniques especially suited to police work. Above all, successful programs should be widely disseminated and used to shape criteria for evaluating new program applications. There is no reason whatsoever for the federal government to continue to fund police training programs—or any other police programs—which merely perpetuate the stagnation of a closed fraternity on a grander scale.

In the field of education, the L.E.A.A. program, called the Law Enforcement Education Program (L.E.E.P.), has been a disaster. It also has operated by giving grants to colleges and universities which, with one or two exceptions, have turned out to be second or third rate. These schools have seized upon federal monies and used them to develop police science programs which segregate police trainees from the rest of the academic community and foist off shallow and imaginative uneducation on them. Such courses as "police psychology" and "police sociology," which are typically developed for police science programs, are nearly always watered-down versions of the disciplines that they claim to represent. As such, they insult the intelligence of those police officers who might profit from them, and for those who probably would not they are a waste of time suffered only because they are necessary to career advancement or because they are free. Police science programs, in the words of L.E.A.A.'s former director, Charles Rogovin, usually represent training more than they do liberal education. This expensive "training" handicaps the student, who, because he cannot use it for anything but police work, tends to be locked into a police department as completely as ever, and it therefore handicaps the department by allowing it to continue to be complacent and to stagnate.

234

The Future and the Federal Role

If the development of police science courses is to continue in spite of intrinsic difficulties, programs must be subjected to some kind of national evaluation standard. Charles B. Saunders, Jr., has suggested that this be done by establishing a national board for accreditation of law-enforcement degree programs.* This is a sound suggestion if police science programs are to continue to be developed. In the end, what matters is not whether they continue to be developed or whether substitutes for them are found but that some system be used to break police out of the "closed fraternity" syndrome. And this must be done, in my opinion, by a combination of liberal education, which allows police to see society from the perspective of a broad overview, and concrete training at the local police-department level.

The British have reacted to the challenge of police leadership by creating a special police college at Bramshill. According to Herman Goldstein, of the University of Wisconsin, "approximately one-half of the course offering" at Bramshill is in liberal studies. The balance relates to police functioning. Considerable emphasis is given to instruction in history, political science and economics in an effort to provide the students with a better understanding of their country's political and social institutions. International problems and current world events come in for special attention. Goldstein notes, "There is not, in this country, any effort to provide as broad an educational program for supervisory officers and to provide a sound foundation for understanding the police role in democracy." † Since this country has a widespread system of public higher education which is not available in Britain, it would seem logical that we make use of the existing institutions of higher learning in order to give police recruits and officers, as well as super-

* Charles B. Saunders, Jr., *Upgrading the American Police: Education and Training for Better Law Enforcement* (Washington, D.C.: Brookings Institution, 1970), p. 156.

† Herman Goldstein, "Report to the Ford Foundation on European Police Departments" (unpublished, 1966), unpaged.

visory personnel, liberal educations. It may be, however, that such institutions as the Southern Police Institute, which for many years has led the way in meaningful police education, also have a valid role in this area.

However it is done, the practice of giving block grants to institutions should be stopped. Grants should be made to individual policemen to attend institutions of their choice. On the whole, liberal education and police training should be separated—especially in view of the fact that first-rate colleges and universities rightly refuse to set up curricula that represent primarily technical training. Since this distinction has provided the justification for the elimination of R.O.T.C. programs at such universities as Yale, it seems unlikely that this trend will be reversed. Only if policemen are able to attend the highest quality institutions will the public get what it is paying for in terms of police education—and only then will police be subjected to viewpoints that will stimulate their thinking. Existing programs defeat the entire objective of a liberal education for a policeman, which is to open his mind to areas which he would not otherwise have encountered and precisely to give him a perspective on his job which is *not* simply a traditional "police perspective."

One way in which L.E.A.A. could stimulate educational advancements within police departments would be radically to expand its program of forgivable loans to policemen for educational purposes. These loans should be made available to individual policemen to allow them to attend any accredited institution rather than to the institutions themselves. Such an expanded loan program could be used to give packages of grants and loans to virtually any qualified person interested in making a commitment to police work and could be used as well to offer full scholarships to those who proved exceptionally qualified.

L.E.A.A. should also concern itself with recruitment and selection policies of local departments. By assisting in education and training, L.E.A.A. could provide departments with the resources they need to be able to demand higher standards in these fields.

The Future and the Federal Role

L.E.A.A. should fund research for the development of objective tests that are free of cultural bias and that, in addition to testing intelligence, would more specifically determine whether an individual was suited to become a professional police officer. L.E.A.A. should offer funding incentives in the form of subsidies to police departments to upgrade their selection criteria and make their recruiting procedures more aggressive. At the same time L.E.A.A. should try to learn from local departments the successes and failures of their approaches to these problems and to disseminate information among all departments as to which have proved most effective. These allocations should be contingent upon the department's meeting concrete requirements such as ethnic and racial balance and meaningful promotion procedures.

L.E.A.A. should also assist local departments in the development of uniform sets of policy standards. Although state laws on such matters as hot pursuit may differ, there is no reason why the law-enforcement profession cannot voluntarily come to agreement on such standards which exceed the minimal requirements of the law. At least L.E.A.A. should suggest sets of standards and disseminate the results of their adoption by individual departments along with evaluations of their success. These standards would especially be applicable to procedures in crowd- and riot-control situations, and all police forces and potential police forces such as the National Guard should be made aware of them. In addition, L.E.A.A. should attempt to devise standardized procedures for governmental agencies to adhere to in emergency situations when law-enforcement and military units act jointly. Thus when crises come, there will be no question as to who is accountable and who is responsible in a crisis situation. This may mean the recommendation of changes in such policies by state legislatures. As police become more professional, they should become increasingly able to assume the responsibility for such operations and to use outside forces as extensions of police departments in crisis situations rather than dealing with them as independent military forces. L.E.A.A. should also

237

make grants to institutions, or it should set up its own research staff, in order to study the effects—social as well as legal—of all such policy determinations.

Originally L.E.A.A. was supposed to do many of these things. But partially because of the changing emphasis of approaches to "law and order," it has become increasingly removed from the area of institutional and systematic change and threatens to become irrelevant to true police professionalization. It has tended to concern itself more and more with mundane matters such as equipment and mechanical procedure, and even in these areas it has not done a great deal to improve a major flaw that besets even the most innovative police departments: a lack of meaningful evaluation.

An extreme example of the thoughtless funding of poorly conceived projects arose in Connecticut while I was serving on the state planning board. The state had long operated a training academy that provided rudimentary training to recruits from smaller police departments. The New Britain Police Department sought and obtained funds to provide the same very basic instruction to experienced officers as in-service training. Nobody cared enough or looked far enough to identify the absurdity of what was going on.

An immediate and relatively inexpensive step that L.E.A.A. could take in this direction would be a national registry of all experimental innovations within police departments. If this information were in turn sent out to larger departments or regionalized groups of departments, they could at least coordinate their efforts and gain by each other's experiences. In a field that is so stagnant that the only real innovations in patrol technique in the last hundred years have been the adoption of the automobile (and this was accepted only reluctantly) and the use of radio dispatching, duplication of experimentation can no longer be tolerated. Police departments must be bold and even daring in experimenting with techniques that allow them to relate to the human beings in their community and allow them to operate efficiently. But without evaluation, and without dissemination of information, experiments are meaningless.

Regionalization is another area in which L.E.A.A. initiative is desperately needed. For smaller and medium-sized departments, regionalization of some services is vital to adequate police service. At present, regionalization is little more than a dream. Most local law-enforcement agencies are so beset by political interference and interagency jealousy that they have no desire and no capability to attempt it. In the New Haven area a regional crime squad that pooled the resources and jurisdictions of a number of area police departments was successful in investigating specific and highly significant cases to an extent that for its limited resources was spectacular, but the regional crime squad consisted only of a number of officers from various jurisdictions operating together as an isolated unit. Regionalization must go far beyond this. It must involve common records systems, common patrol organizations, and even redrawing or dissolving certain jurisdictional limitations. An average of eight hundred police agencies per state is absurd. The duplication of effort, the inefficiency, and the wide disparity of goals and aims, initiatives, and standards which they represent must be done away with. There is no reason for a five- or six-man police department in a suburban town to send officers into the field with absolutely no training (not an uncommon occurrence) while nearby cities have complex training facilities. L.E.A.A. could once more use the promise of federal funds to promote regionalization. This could be done in a manner analogous to that which prompted the consolidation of school districts. L.E.A.A. could make its policy not to give grants to departments that were below a certain minimum size or that contained a certain minimum area or population within its jurisdiction.

But the efforts of L.E.A.A. and the federal government should attempt to open law enforcement in yet another manner. One of the most important recommendations of the Katzenbach Commission was that a national system of pension credits be established in order to allow lateral entry between police departments. At present, if a lieutenant in one police department realizes that the way to advancement in that department is blocked, or if he realizes that his experience and his talents are not being properly used, or if he simply wishes to make a jump to another department where the challenges are greater and the problems more complex (or, on the other hand, if he finds that the pace of a particular department is too fast for him and he wants to move to a less-demanding department), wherever he goes he will have to start out again as a patrolman. He will lose his pension benefits, and he may even have to go through training once more. Needless to say, the effects of the impossibility of lateral entry are devastating to the police profession. As with so many other deficiencies, this one certainly would not be tolerated in any other profession. Imagine a high-school teacher or a college professor forced to spend his entire professional life in one institution, no matter how agonizingly clear it became to him that he was not helping the institution and the institution was not helping him. Much of the stagnation of the "closed fraternity" would be dispelled if policemen could gain the broadening of experience and the interchange of information that would result from their ability to change from department to department. This fact has been realized in England, where, as Herman Goldstein has pointed out, "A positive value is attached to transfer between and amongst forces as a means of broadening a man's experience. Indeed, the Home Office is likely to recommend against appointment of an officer as Chief Constable if he has not served in more than one jurisdiction." There is no excuse for American police departments to continue to be closed enclaves that trap policemen and cannot or will not let them go.

With proper Congressional and Presidential support, institutional change in police departments could be rapidly under way. This change is essential to the internal development of police departments if they are to professionalize and move into the twentieth century. But beyond institutional help for internal development, the federal government must support local police in another and equally essential way: It must provide major assistance and assume prime responsibility for enforcement of laws that are patently beyond local enforcement capability. This should be done only in limited areas, but where it is applicable it should be done forcefully and immediately. At present there are two such areas: The first is narcotics, and the second is organized crime and corruption.

The problem of narcotics and dangerous drugs is a national and international one. Local police departments that find heroin, cocaine, and other dangerous and addictive drugs flowing into their cities at an incredible rate cannot possibly be expected to solve the drug problem by gathering up shipments as they come in piecemeal or by attempting to sweep drugs from the streets. It cannot be said often enough, however, that the federal role concerning narcotics cannot be limited to enforcement. It should be a three-pronged attack.

First of all, the federal government should make a massive commitment to mounting a medical response for narcotics addiction. Such a program should encourage research into the causes, cures, and rehabilitation of narcotics addiction. Although a medical approach will not solve the problems that influence an addict to retreat into a life of addiction, it will be a powerful tool for helping him at least to deal with those problems without having to look every day for his "fix" and for helping the literally millions of people whom he and other addicts rob and terrorize. The potential to solve this problem at the moment lies dormant in the nation's medical centers. Only the federal government has the resources to fund and coordinate the attempts necessary to bring this potential to fruition.

Second, until a medical cure for narcotics addiction is found, the federal government must support with greater intensity the experimental programs of drug rehabilitation. While Methadone maintenance cannot be a final solution, and while it has its dangers and disadvantages, we must take the word of addicts who have chosen it that it does represent a temporary source of hope for hard-core addicts who themselves do not want—and whose society cannot afford—to return to the streets in a life of perpetual crime and violence. In addition to Methadone maintenance, such programs as Synanon and Daytop Village must also be supported and expanded. There is every reason to believe that addiction to hard narcotics is increasing and spreading every day, and if we are truly interested in saving those who have found their way into a life of addiction, we must proliferate treatment centers as fast as drug use itself proliferates. These efforts are the best that we have, and there is absolutely no excuse for addicts to continue to steal every day to support their habit while they are waiting to get into such programs.

But we cannot simply give up on the enforcement of laws—especially those against heroin—at the risk of turning the entire country into one massive drug rehabilitation center. The third federal effort should be toward stopping the flow of addictive drugs into this country. While realizing that law-enforcement efforts mean little unless those deprived of heroin and other addictive drugs are at the same time medically cured, psychologically assisted, and economically and socially readjusted to society, the federal government must make an immediate and dramatic effort to shut down the heavily concentrated entry of heroin into the United States at the Port of New York. If federal law-enforcement agencies could find the manpower for Project Intercept—if they could seal off an entire border and subject thousands of tourists and working people to hours of delay in an effort to stop the flow of marijuana into this country—surely they should be able to saturate the Port of New York and other major ports with law-enforcement officers efficient enough—and honest enough—to reduce the flow of heroin into this country drastically. In fact, if the federal government could create an entire police force overnight to deal with a delicate, dangerous, and highly complex problem like airline skyjackings, it should be able to create a similar task force to fight those who continue to profit in the heroin traffic. To mount such federal efforts on a secondary problem that concerns a large and wealthy industry while neglecting the heroin problem is of such gross negligence in the ordering of priorities that it cannot help arousing public suspicion of a deeply rooted cynicism in the highest levels of government.

The heroin problem, and the problem of dangerous drugs in general—which, as Ramsey Clark, among others, has pointed out, is bound to include an incredible proliferation of synthetic drugs that may be far more dangerous than anything we have yet experienced—is so acute and so pressing that any effort toward a solution of it which is channeled through existing separate agencies is bound to be inefficient. The federal government should, therefore, create a single agency to coordinate and direct all of the various drug-related programs now scattered throughout the federal bureaucracy, from research and rehabilitation to law enforcement. This agency should bring together the efforts of all other agencies now involved in the problem: several units of the Justice Department, especially the Bureau of Narcotics and Dangerous Drugs, and various agencies of the Department of Health, Education and Welfare, the Internal Revenue Service, and the U.S. Customs Service. It should be responsible for clarifying and carrying out a coherent national policy with regard to narcotics. It should set priorities for enforcement, and it should disseminate funds for research and rehabilitation. It should make certain, for instance, that when the flow of heroin is drastically cut, there will be facilities available to receive addicts who are deprived of the drug. Otherwise, the price of the drug will simply be forced up, and crime rates will soar. Such an agency should have access to the most sophisticated and professional enforcement systems and personnel available; nothing less will suffice if it is to take meaningful action against the leading source of crime in our cities and save the people who have fallen victim to it.

POLICE IN TROUBLE

The second area into which the federal government must move to relieve local police departments of responsibilities they cannot handle is connected to the first. It is equally pressing and even more pervasive. In this area—the area of organized crime and governmental corruption—the federal government should likewise create a powerful agency to deal with the problem. The implication of creating such an agency is emphatically *not* that police are by nature too corrupt and too ineffective to police themselves. The implication of creating such an agency is that police departments that are so surrounded by organized crime and corruption on all levels, and that are rendered powerless by their lack of professionalism and by the other elements of the criminal justice system with which they must deal, cannot in principle begin to attack the problem. This agency should not write off local police departments; it should be their salvation. It would have functions analogous to those of the federal organized-crime strike forces. Given the present political orientation of the Justice Department, however, it may be that it should be removed from that department and put under the direction of an independent board—on the model of the various federal regulatory agencies—which would appoint a director with responsibility for its investigative and administrative operations.

Such an agency should be independent enough that it would not act as a Republican tool rooting out corruption in Democratic cities, or as a Democratic weapon rooting out corruption in Republican cities, but as a truly national organization dedicated to the elimination of organized crime and corruption wherever it occurs. As long as Americans know and accept unethical practices and outright corruption in high places, they must expect that as a direct result they will continue to have a criminal justice system which has little to do with justice, part of which is a system of police service which does everything but serve.

While the federal government is helping to build police professionalism on the local level and while it is relieving local police

244

departments of responsibilities that they cannot in principle handle, it must also foster the creation of a police profession as such. Although the suggestions made here for increased federal involvement in limited areas should be more than countered by a strengthening of local police departments, we must also remember that it is the individual patrolman and his sense of commitment to a concrete ethic of law enforcement that will in the end be our most important deterrent to an undesirable concentration of federal power and to unprofessional police conduct. In some sense, then, the federal government must act to decrease its power at the same time as it acts to increase it in certain areas. The most direct way in which it can do this is to support and encourage the development of a professional police organization for all policemen. This will be a difficult problem, because professional organizations such as the American Medical Association and the American Bar Association take for granted the existence of professionals who themselves create such organizations more or less spontaneously. But with regard to police, no such professionals exist as yet. This means that leadership is needed on many fronts, and it means that a professional organization must be created at the same time as those who enter it are being educated and trained to be professionals. Such an organization should first of all be concerned with developing ethical standards and with providing police with support for behavior that conforms with them. It must give them support that will enable them to transcend illegitimate political interference and become responsible to democratic controls.

The federal government should provide the impetus for beginning such an organization by establishing a commission to get it started. Composed of such people as university presidents, civil-rights leaders, business and professional leaders, and law-enforcement officers, the commission should have a budget sufficient to finance its operations for a specified period of time, after which the organization could be expected to fund its own growth and development. After a few years of funding by the government, at decreasing rates for each year, the organization should—if it provides a meaningful service to policemen who are emerging as the result of increased selection and education—be able to become independent.

At present, police have only their unions to support them, but because unions must so often be in conflict with police administrations, they tend to aggravate the divisions within police departments. It is not inevitable that unions should stand in the way of professionalism in performing their vital and positive role of representing the employment interests of policemen. Their tendency to obstruct police professionalization has grown up only in recent years because police unions must fight incessantly with city governments that are under pressure because of rising costs and decreasing tax bases and therefore tend to cut financial corners wherever they can. If cities received the kind of help they needed to deal with their own overwhelming problems, it would soon be realized that police service is one vital key to the solution of these problems and that police-union negativism is in effect a product of the cities' failures.

A professional police organization should in the long run attempt to supplement, or perhaps in time to supplant, L.E.A.A. in some of its functions. In addition to developing codes of ethics for police, it should require high standards of education, training, integrity, and competence for its members. It should encourage research into police problems. It should publish a regular journal dealing with reflections upon police work and with the results of new experiments in the field. It should lobby for legislation that would have the effect of increasing efficiency and professionalism in the field of law enforcement, and it should pay particular attention to the way in which police relate to the rest of the criminal justice system—to courts and prosecutors and to corrections. Above all, it should condemn unprofessional conduct wherever it occurs and point out ways in which it could be avoided.

Such a professional organization should have existed at the time of the 1968 Democratic convention and of the Kent State and

The Future and the Federal Role

Jackson State incidents, and it should have been capable of bringing in immense weight of qualified opinion in order to show the public that actions such as were taken in these incidents are *not* to be either expected or tolerated. In analyzing such incidents, a professional organization could point with authority to political currents and "signals" which helped to precipitate bad police behavior, as well as to the underlying conditions of the policeman's lot which make it possible in the first place. In addition to its own internal disciplinary actions in incidents like this—which would parallel disbarment in the legal profession—such an organization should make it clear that policemen who break the law should be prosecuted just as anyone else would be. Such a professional organization should assist other groups and organizations who wish to do research on police matters and act as a clearinghouse for such activity. It should ask searching questions about the ultimate role of police in society, and it should scrupulously examine police institutions as they now exist and as they now relate to the political structures of the communities. In doing this, it should compare American police roles and American police procedures with those of police in other countries. It should authoritatively evaluate such initiatives as the English experiment with the legalization of narcotics from a police point of view, in order to provide a channel by which police can participate in such deliberations, which too often exclude them because they are thought to be too incompetent and ignorant to have informed opinions on them. In the long run, it should be able to move the art and science of police work forward on a systematic basis, to provide initiatives for the kinds of radical innovations and experimentations that can be conceived of only by people who are outside the mainstream of political and professional exigency, and to test these innovations objectively and thoroughly within the framework of real police activity.

It is only with the kind of high standards that such an organization could provide that police work can gain the prestige that will inspire men of intelligence and integrity to enter police work, to stay in it, and to raise the quality of their own performance and of police departments in general to the level required by the complex society of the late twentieth century.

The federal government can and must act immediately to fill the leadership vacuum in law enforcement. This means both moral leadership and substantive initiatives for institutional changes. In addition, it means an effort to foster independence in local and regional police departments that will ultimately lead them to greater self-sufficiency.

But if the efforts of local police chiefs acting in this vacuum are meaningless without federal support—at least in the early stages—so are the efforts of the federal government going to be meaningless without a massive public commitment to change on the local level. This means nothing more nor less than a willingness of citizens to make representative democracy work on its most basic levels. It means electing good mayors who will appoint good police chiefs. It means an end to political interference and corruption. Above all, it means people who are willing to "support your local police" by turning police departments upside down and making the police on whom they depend the kind of professionals who can do their jobs well within strictly defined limits of legal and ethical practice.

The maintenance of societal order is an index of the basic state of civilization at any given time. Slick public-relations gimmicks and legalistic ploys, rhetoric, and condemnation are entirely inappropriate to the attempts of a free people to remain secure in their persons and property and to protect the rights of the least of their number as assiduously as the rights of the greatest. Tricks and gimmicks may win elections, but in the process they may lose the nation. The roots of police failure are buried deeply in the failures of society, and every day these roots are deepening and strengthening their hold. If the state of police is not changed, if police continue to be exploited in their weakness, then they may one day turn, and the nightmare of a police state will be upon us. Already large segments of our population—among them those whose protection should be the policeman's most cherished task—instinctively turn their heads in retreat at the sight of a police car. They have come to believe that in the eyes of the police, their very existence is a sin. Others look upon the police as so incompetent, so stupid, and so corrupt that they are no better than the criminals with whom they deal. To them, the police problem is something far beneath them, that is manifested only in the ghettos and poverty areas of this country, and that is beneath their notice. The policeman is not insensitive to these attitudes. They merely compound his frustration and his misery and accelerate the cycle of his degradation, driving him ever more deeply into the "closed fraternity."

Although few of us realize how late it is, it is not too late to save the police. They want to be helped. The policeman who walks his beat in the early-morning hours is out of a job. He feels the same lack of self-respect—however deeply he may hide it—as any man must who feels that he has been born to do something worthwhile and yet has been denied the opportunity. In all professions there will always be the dishonest, the unethical, and the incompetent. But if significant numbers of one profession fit this description, it is an indication that something is dreadfully wrong. This is tragic enough when it happens to a group of people who wear badges and carry guns, who patrol the streets of every city and town and village in the country twenty-four hours a day, seven days a week, three hundred and sixty-five days a year, for decade upon decade; when it happens to a group whose proper functioning is essential to the preservation of the basic elements of civilization, then it is worse than tragedy.

The streets of our cities and towns are hostile places now, where silent cars with dome lights lie scattered like leaves. As you read these words, there are cops sleeping behind the wheels of their cars. There are cops taking bribes, and there are cops beating up junkies and long-hairs.

But there are also cops climbing dim flights of steps, knocking on third-story doors, listening to the screaming and wailing of incessant fights, their palms sweating—hoping that help is on the way,

249

but knocking on the door in the meantime—and wondering whether guns or knives or merely hateful invective is being prepared for their arrival. Right now there are cops trying to find lost children, cops searching through endless files and records trying to find just one clue—cops laughing, cops crying, and cops pounding tables and shouting, and wondering when . . .

The "when" must be now. It cannot wait. The stakes are too high, and the time is too short. There is work to be done. It is hard work, but the road is clear. It is complex, but the needs are pressing. There are people who can do it. There are people in Congress. There are people in city halls. There are people in grade schools and high schools who never would dream of being policemen. And above all, there are people in dim, shabby police stations, sipping stale coffee, listening to the din from the lock-ups, wasting time as though all of time were a waste, waiting to be policemen.

Index

Index

Index

257

Index